Peacekeeping and the United Nations

STEPHEN M. HILL and SHAHIN P. MALIK
Security Studies Research Programme
University of Birmingham

Series Editor
STUART CROFT
Security Studies Research Programme

Dartmouth

Aldershot • Brookfield USA • Singapore • Sydney

Published by
Dartmouth Publishing Company Limited
Gower House
Croft Road
Aldershot
Hants GU11 3HR
England

Dartmouth Publishing Company
Old Post Road
Brookfield
Vermont 05036
USA

British Library Cataloguing in Publication Data
Peacekeeping and the United Nations. - (Issues in
    international security)
    1.United Nations 2.Security, International 3.International
    organization
    I.Hill, Stephen M. II.Malik, Shahin P.
    327.1'72

Library of Congress Cataloging-in-Publication Data
Hill, Stephen M.
    Peacekeeping and the United Nations / Stephen M. Hill, Shahin P.
Malik.
        p. cm. -- (Issues in international security series)
    Includes index.
    ISBN 1-85521-620-5 (h). -- ISBN 1-85521-613-2 (p)
    1. United Nations--Armed Forces. 2. Security, International.
I. Malik, Shahin P. II. Title. III. Series.
JX1981.P7H55 1996
341.5'84--dc20   96-19228
                                                                CIP

ISBN 1 85521 620 5 (Hbk)
ISBN 1 85521 613 2 (Pbk)
Printed in Great Britain at the University Press, Cambridge

Contents

List of Tables   vii

Glossary   viii

Preface   xi

Introduction   1

Chapter 1   The Primary Responsibility   5

Chapter 2   The Evolution of UN Peacekeeping 1947-
                 1987   25

Chapter 3   The Rebirth of Peacekeeping   59

Chapter 4   The Expansion of Peacekeeping   91

Chapter 5   Crisis in UN Peacekeeping November
                 1992-1993   117

Chapter 6   The Retrenchment of Peacekeeping 1994-
                   1995   155

Conclusion   211

Appendices   217

Index   233

List of Tables

Table 1:   Principles of International Conduct   7

Table 2:   Peacekeeping Operations during the Cold War,
            1945-1987   27

Table 3:   Peacekeeping Operations Established 1988-1991   61

Table 4:   Peacekeeping Operations Established 1992   94

Table 5:   Peacekeeping Operations Established November
            1992-1993   119

Table 6:   Peacekeeping Operations Established 1994   158

Glossary

ANC	Armee Nationale Congolese
ARENA	Alianza Republicana Nacionalista
CDR	Coalition pour la Defense de la Republique
CIAV	International Support and Verification Commission
CIVPOL	Civilian Police
COPAZ	National Commission for the Consolidation of Peace
CPSC	Comprehensive Political Settlement of Cambodia
DMZ	Demilitarized Zone
DPKO	Department of Peacekeeping Operations
EAM	National Liberation Front
ECOSOC	Economic and Social Council
ELAS	National People's Liberation Army
FADM	Forcas Armadas de Defensa de Mocambique
FMLN	Farabundo Marti Front for National Liberation
FRELIMO	Frente da Libetacao de Mozambique
FYROM	Former Yugoslav Republic of Macedonia
GPA	General Peace Agreement
ICJ	International Court of Justice
JNA	Yugoslavian National Army
KKE	Greek Communist Party

MINURSO	United Nations Mission for the Referendum in Western Sahara
MINUSAL	United Nations Mission in El Salvador
MNC	Mouvement Nationale Congolese
MPLA	Movimento Popular de Lieragao de Angola
MRND	National Revolutionary Movement
MSC	Military Staff Committee
NATO	Northern Atlantic Treaty Organization
NGOs	Non-Governmental Organizations
NCP	National Civil Police
NP	National Police
OAS	Organization of American States
OAU	Organization of African Unity
ONUC	United Nations Operation in the Congo
ONUCA	United Nations Observation Mission in Central America
ONUMOZ	United Nations Operation in Mozambique
ONUSAL	United Nations Operation in El Salvador
ONUVEN	United Nations Observer Mission to Verify the Electoral Process in Nicaragua
PDK	Party of Democratic Kampuchea
PLO	Palestine Liberation Organization
POLISARIO	Frente Popular para la Liberacion de Saguia el-Hamra y de Rio
PD	Presidential Directive
RENAMO	Resistancia Nacional Mocambicana
RPF	Rwandese Patriotic Front
RRF	Rapid Reaction Force
RSK	Republic of Serbian Krajina
SGSR	Secretary General's Special Representative
SNC	Supreme National Council
SoC	State of Cambodia
SWAPO	South West African People's Organization
SWAPOL	South West African Police
UNAMIC	United Nations Advance Mission in Cambodia
UNAMIR	United Nations Assistance Mission in Rwanda
UNAVEM	United Nations Angolan Verification Mission
UNCRO	United Nations Confidence Restoration Operation
UNDOF	United Nations Disengagement Observer Force
UNEF	United Nations Emergency Force
UNFICYP	United Nations Force in Cyprus
UNGOMAP	United Nations Good Offices Mission in Afghanistan

UNHCR	United Nations High Commission for Refugees
UNIFIL	United Nations Interim Force in Lebanon
UNIIMOG	United Nations Iran-Iraq Military Observer Group
UNIKOM	United Nations Iraq-Kuwait Observer Mission
UNIPOM	United Nations India Pakistan Observer Mission
UNITA	Uniao Nacional para a Independencia Total de Angola
UNITAF	United Task Force
UNMOs	United Nations Monitors
UNMOGIP	United Nations Military Observer Group in India and Pakistan
UNOGIL	United Nations Observation Group in Lebanon
UNOMUR	United Nations Observer Mission Uganda-Rwanda
UNOSOM	United Nations Operation in Somalia
UNPAs	United Nations Protected Areas
UNPREDEP	United Nations Preventive Deployment Force
UNPROFOR	United Nations Protection Force
UNSAS	United Nations Stand-by Arrangements System
UNSCOB	United Nations Special Commission on the Balkans
UNSCOP	United Nations Special Commission on Palestine
UNSF	United Nations Security Force
UNTAC	United Nations Transitional Authority in Cambodia
UNTAG	United Nations Transitional Assistance Group
UNTEA	United Nations Temporary Executive Authority
UNTSO	United Nations Truce Supervision Organization
UNYOM	United Nations Yemen Observation Mission

Preface

Peacekeeping developed during the Cold War as a response to the needs of the Cold War system. The dangers of nuclear war were deemed to be so great, in circumstances where the superpowers had allies around the world, that it was important to find ways of damping down the dangers of escalation from regional conflicts to global war. Peacekeeping was, therefore, a tool of conflict management, a means of preventing war in one part of the world drawing in the superpowers, and escalating to the brink of nuclear war, as had been the case with the Cuban Missile Crisis. But there was another important element to peacekeeping; and that was the idealistic belief that it was important for the international community to save lives wherever possible. This dual imperative of peacekeeping during the Cold War - realpolitik and humanitarian - always created tensions, with humanitarian concerns always demanding a greater involvement on the part of the international community than the requirements of realpolitik would allow.

With the end of the Cold War, therefore, peacekeeping was initially viewed as being released from this dual imperative. With widespread retrenchment on the part of the superpowers from their engagements around the world, humanitarianism seemed likely to dominate the old demands of realpolitik. This period is dated from 1988 in terms of UN peacekeeping, which is significant in that this was before the revolutions in Eastern Europe and the collapse of the USSR, but was the time when the Soviet Union was withdrawing from Afghanistan. From 1988, the UN took on a range of operations that seemed to prove the point that humanitarianism had triumphed over realpolitik. Within a few years of 1988 22 operations were established, many more than during the whole of the Cold War. And the depth of these operations - overseeing elections, as well as simply standing between opposing forces - led some to argue that the UN had developed a new concept, second generation peacekeeping, which involved not only preventing conflict from reemerging, but the reconstruction of failed states. The UN operations in Namibia, El Salvador and Cambodia indicated an apparent willingness on the part of the international community not only to stop violence in these countries, but also to create democratic and economically viable societies. However, this period of optimism was to be seriously questioned by the humanitarian failures of the international community in Somalia, the former Yugoslavia, and Rwanda. The reemergence of realpolitik, in the guise of national interests narrowly defined had, by the mid-1990s, called into question the very future of peacekeeping in a far more fundamental way than had ever occurred during the Cold War.

This book provides by far the most comprehensive assessment of UN peacekeeping efforts published in the English language. It examines the transition from the limited peacekeeping efforts of the Cold War to the expanded activity of the immediate post-Cold War period, through to the reemergence of the realpolitik theme, and the consequent downturn in the commitment of the international community to peacekeeping by the mid-1990s. As Series Editor, I would like to thank Stephen Hill and Shahin Malik for their efforts in producing this volume. The difficulty in writing such a comprehensive analysis in a limited space while ensuring accessibility should not be underestimated. This book examines every single significant instance of UN peacekeeping, while focusing on the main themes of the rise and fall of international commitment to its practice.

This is the third in the Series *Issues in International Security* published by Dartmouth on behalf of the Security Studies Research Programme at the University of Birmingham. The first in the Series was *European Security: An Introduction to Security Issues in Post-Cold War Europe* (1995), written by Andrew M.Dorman and Adrian Treacher, and the second was *American Security Policy in the 1990s: Beyond Containment* (1996), written by Wyn Q.Bowen and David H.Dunn. The purpose of the Series is to provide a thorough introduction to particular security issues for those coming to the subject for the first time, and to act as a reference volume for more experienced researchers. As such, each book contains a substantial section of appendices which provides access to key documents and speeches and, in this book, assessments of particular issues and operations.

Completion of this book has proved to be a particularly complex task. In part this has been due to the number of UN operations and their complexity, and in part it has been due to the lack of existing introductory books in this area. For these reasons, this book is likely to prove to be particularly useful to students and researchers alike, and the authors should be congratulated for producing such a comprehensive and clear analysis. Thanks are due to Amanda Griffiths and Rob Shaw for their help in the production of this book.

Stuart Croft
Birmingham

Introduction

One of the factors which characterized the end of the Cold War was the propulsion of the United Nations (UN) into an elevated position with regards to maintaining international peace and security. The UN's role during the Gulf War clearly demonstrated that as long as there was a consensus in the Security Council, the Organisation could be successful in maintaining peace. Whereas the Cold War was characterized by superpower competition between two ideologically opposed blocs, consensus and cooperation for a time became associated with the post-Cold War period. This new accord clearly manifested itself in the successful formation of the coalition force opposing Iraq in 1991 and the role that the UN played during the crisis. It appeared that the international community had finally emerged from the conflictual relations which had dominated the past 45 years.

Greater understanding between the superpowers also enabled the UN to dramatically increase the number of peacekeeping operations in the post-Cold War period. As such the UN's impressive role continued as it played a central role in resolving long-standing regional conflicts such as those between Iran and Iraq, Cambodia, overseeing the Soviet withdrawal from Afghanistan, the change of regime in South Africa and its withdrawal from Namibia. The UN established ten new peacekeeping operations by the end of 1991 and this rapid expansion seemed to indicate that the UN would finally be able to fulfil its primary goal - the preservation of peace.

Chapter 1 sets the basis of the book by identifying the primary role of the UN as being the maintenance of international peace and security. Attention then shifts to an account of the main sections and Articles of the UN Charter primarily concerned with maintaining this peace. Related to this are the important roles played by the Security Council and the Secretary General. It is important to realise that peacekeeping does not appear anywhere in the UN Charter. As chapter 1 will demonstrate it was developed during the Cold War in response to the impasse reached in the Security Council, and as an alternative to collective security. Because of the importance accorded to peacekeeping during the Cold War, and the fact that it was the key tool through which the UN attempted to fulfil its primary goal, the chapter ends with a brief evaluation of the concept itself.

The analysis of the evolution of peacekeeping during the Cold War is carried out in chapter 2. Here it will be shown that since peacekeeping remained undefined in the UN Charter various characteristics of the concept were established as the Cold War progressed. Elements of peacekeeping began to be instituted once the basic observer missions were set up soon after World War II. As the chapter will show, the progression of UN peacekeeping during the Cold War was not uniform. Instead, it is argued that the Cold War must be separated into three well-defined periods of differing levels of assertiveness. During the first period, labelled in chapter 2 as *the birth of peacekeeping* (1947-1956), various observer missions formalized basic characteristics of peacekeeping such as monitoring, observing, reporting and persuading. The second *assertive period* (1956-1974) was to see the establishment of the first sizeable peacekeeping forces infinitely more complex in structure and mandate than their predecessors. The final *quiescent period* (1974-1987) saw the UN withdraw dramatically from the pattern it set previously. Chapter 2, therefore, analyses the various peacekeeping operations under each time period by attempting to highlight the contribution that each new operation made to peacekeeping.

The remainder of the book is concerned with the post-Cold War period and this is where the similarity with Cold War UN peacekeeping becomes apparent. Instead of three time frames, however, this book separates the post-Cold War period into four levels of UN activity. These are the *rebirth of peacekeeping,* the *expansion of peacekeeping,* the *crisis in peacekeeping,* and *retrenchment.* During the 'rebirth of peacekeeping' requests for UN assistance for conflict ridden states provided the UN with the opportunity to re-establish peacekeeping after almost a decade of dormancy as manifest in the *quiescent* period. As such, by the end of 1991 the UN had established ten new peacekeeping operations in various parts of the world. After analysing each of the peacekeeping operations established between 1988 and 1991 chapter 3 goes on to discuss some of the successes and problems encountered in various operations.

Chapter 4 explains that after this initial period a further expansion in the UN's role was to take place. During this time it increasingly became clear that peacekeeping was emerging as merely one of a number of conflict resolution tools which the Secretary General (in *An Agenda for Peace*) called preventive diplomacy, peacemaking and post-conflict peace-building. As the chapter will show, the UN was no longer limited to maintaining ceasefires and the goals of peacekeeping had widened to include attempts at reaching long term political solutions.

One of the common themes in both chapter 3 and chapter 4 is the analysis of the various problems encountered by the UN during its post-Cold War operations. It was clear that the growth of peacekeeping was to take place with very little appraisal of how the problems posed by the various operations might affect future, more ambitious, missions. The chapters will show that because of the successes of the operations in the initial period, the UN was to overlook inadequacies in its ability to handle large multi-dimensional peacekeeping operations. It was this crucial oversight which meant that the UN committed itself to larger and more complex peacekeeping operations.

The realisation of the fact that the UN did not have the ability to manage such large operations is highlighted in chapter 5. The failure of the UN to bring peace to Somalia even though force was used was crucial. Chapter 5 begins with indicating that the deaths of American soldiers in Somalia tested the resolve of the US government to the extent that US financial and political support for the UN was reduced. With the US interest in UN peacekeeping diminished it was inevitable that even greater financial and structural problems would beset the Organisation during 1993. *Retrenchment* was, therefore, unavoidable. Chapter 6 will show that the failure of the international community to adequately address the Organisation's problems were to have disastrous consequences in Rwanda, and at the same time leaving the UN looking impotent.

Finally, in the Conclusion the concept of *peacekeeping* is looked at in its overall context. It guides the reader through Cold War development into the post-Cold War period. The analysis accounts for the high expectations amongst the international community that with the end of the Cold War and with greater superpower cooperation the UN would finally bring seemingly intractible conflicts to an end. The use of force in the post-Cold War period created the call for a 'second generation' category of peacekeeping and it appeared that force would increasingly be used to achieve peacekeeping objectives. Yet, as the Conclusion states and the book demonstrates, the establishment of a large number of new and vastly more complex peacekeeping operations meant that the UN overstretched itself to the point where the international community began to withdraw previously optimistic commitments. The UN's relapse into impotency meant that it was no longer possible to argue for the existence of second generation peacekeeping. The Conclusion ends by stating that the UN's sudden retrenchment combined with its dismal financial record means that the future of UN peacekeeping is uncertain.

Chapter 1
The Primary Responsibility

Introduction

The stated purpose of both the League of Nations and of the United Nations was to promote international peace and security. There was a general feeling during the years leading up to the establishment of the UN that the League had not been strong enough to deal effectively with the aggressions first of Japan, then of Italy, and finally of Germany. It was to correct the supposed weaknesses of the League as a system for providing both international security and peace that a new and stronger body had to be created.[1] Declarations in Moscow and subsequently Tehran in 1943 by the Big Four Powers indicated their intention to take concrete steps towards establishing an international organisation. In a joint statement Churchill, Roosevelt and Stalin confirmed their plans by stating that they recognized

> ... the necessity of establishing at the earliest practicable date a general international organisation, based on the principle of sovereign equality of all peace-loving states, and open to membership by all such states, large and small, for the maintenance of international peace and security.[2]

Following this declaration various proposals for a world organisation were discussed at Dumbarton Oaks in late 1944 and at the Yalta Conference in February 1945. The proposals which were to come out of both conferences were adopted as the basis for the 1945 San Francisco Conference on International Organisation. It was at these occasions, however, that it became apparent that there were significant differences of opinion between the major powers.[3] This is an important point since the deepening divisions between the USSR and the West were to have a major impact upon the effectiveness of the Security Council as soon as the UN became operational. Nevertheless, short term compromise on many of the issues made the establishment of the UN possible and, as a result, the San Francisco Conference concluded on 26 June 1945 with the signing of the UN Charter.

However, despite the establishment of the UN, the period after the adoption of the Charter was characterized by superpower competition and lack of cooperation among the Permanent Members. The appearance of the Cold War manifested itself most clearly in the emergence of stalemate within the Security Council. As such, the continuing relevance of the Charter in maintaining international peace and security through a system of collective security, as envisaged by the founders, seemed far from assured. For the UN to have any relevance in the area of peace and security it was necessary for the international community to adopt a new method for keeping peace, which was ultimately to become known as *peacekeeping*.

The purpose of this chapter is to analyse the component parts of the UN system which interact to contribute towards maintaining international peace and security. For the sake of clarity, a two-pronged approach will be taken. First, it is important to see what the UN Charter itself has to say about fulfilling the primary responsibility, that of ensuring peace and security. As the task accorded to the Council is crucial, there is an analysis of the main aspects surrounding its work. Following this, another important component is the Secretary General of the UN and there is, therefore, a brief account of this position. The second purpose of the chapter is to discuss the nature of peacekeeping as this practice has emerged as a substitute to the provisions envisaged in the Charter.

The UN Charter

The Charter is a long and complicated document. However, for the purposes of this book, only the central issues need to be dealt with. In simple terms the UN Charter is a treaty, albeit a special kind of treaty.

Article 103 of the Charter states that 'In the event of a conflict between the obligations of the Members of the United Nations under the present Charter and their obligations under any other international agreement, their obligations under the present Charter shall prevail'.[4] This clearly places the Charter in a preeminent position over and above any other international obligation. In theory, therefore, the Charter has priority over future treaties in the same way that a national constitution has over ordinary law.

The primary goal of the UN, as stated in Article 1 Paragraph 1, is the maintenance of international peace and security. In order to fulfil this goal the Articles in the Charter established various objectives, procedures and organs within the United Nations' system. To begin with the Members themselves agreed to abide by the following Principles of International Conduct when signing the Charter.[5] (See Table 1.)

TABLE 1: Principles of International Conduct

The Organisation and its Members, in pursuit of the Purposes stated in Article 1, shall act in accordance with the following Principles.

1. The Organisation is based on the principle of the sovereign equality of all its Members.
2. All its Members, in order to ensure to all of them the rights and benefits resulting from membership, shall fulfil in good faith the obligations assumed by them in accordance with the present Charter.
3. All Members shall settle their international disputes by peaceful means in such a manner that international peace and security, and justice, are not endangered.
4. All Members shall refrain in their international relations from the threat or use of force against the territorial integrity or political independence of any state, or in any other manner inconsistent with the Purposes of the United Nations.
5. All Members shall give the United Nations every assistance in any action it takes in accordance with the present Charter, and shall refrain from giving assistance to any state against which the United Nations is taking preventive or enforcement action.
6. The Organisation shall ensure that states which are not Members of the United Nations act in accordance with these Principles so far as may be necessary for the maintenance of international peace and security.
7. Nothing contained in the present Charter shall authorize the United Nations to intervene in matters which are essentially

> within the domestic jurisdiction of any state or shall require the
> Members to submit such matters to settlement under the present
> Charter.

Taken from: Article 2, *United Nations Charter,* 26 June 1945.

The Charter then goes on to deal with other issues including membership; major organs; the pacific settlement of disputes; action with respect to the peace, breaches of the peace, and acts of aggression; regional arrangements; international economic and social cooperation; the Economic and Social Council; non self-governing territories; the international trusteeship system; the Trusteeship Council; the International Court of Justice; the Secretariat; miscellaneous provisions; and finally, transitional security arrangements, amendments to the Charter and ratification.

As the main objective here is to analyse the UN's primary purpose of maintaining international peace and security, reference to Chapters VI and VII is of particular importance (see Appendix 1 and 2) as the provisions in these Chapters refer to international situations which are serious enough to endanger international peace and security. As set down in the two Chapters, the Charter advocates the establishment of two complementary mechanisms for maintaining international peace. First, nations wanting to join the UN had to accept, through signing the Charter, the high standards of international behaviour contained in the document and outlined above (Table 1). In addition, Chapter VI itself says something on what acceptable conduct should be. Article 33 states:

> The parties to any dispute, the continuance of which is likely to
> endanger the maintenance of international peace and security, shall,
> first of all, seek a solution by negotiation, enquiry, mediation,
> conciliation, arbitration, judicial settlement, resort to regional
> agencies, or other peaceful means of their own choice.[6]

The essential difference between the two Chapters is that whereas Chapter VI empowered the relevant organs - the General Assembly and the Security Council - to deal with potential breaches, Chapter VII allowed the Security Council alone to deal with actual breaches of the peace.

As such, the second mechanism, enshrined as Chapter VII, stands in direct contrast to the provisions outlined in Chapter VI. This included the creation of a set of tools which could be used to deal with states that had actually failed to honour their obligations, particularly not to use force. The Charter recommended that the collective strength of all the members should be used to punish belligerents. The main requirement of such a collective security system is that the members would have to give up a significant portion of their freedom to act independently. The extent of action permitted would be limited to the right of self-defence until the central body, in this case the Security Council, assumed responsibility.[7] Chapter VII, therefore, is that portion of the Charter which is devoted to the centralisation of the UN's coercive powers. Under this the Security Council was provided with unprecedented power to take military and/or economic measures against a belligerent state using force or threatening to breach international peace and security.

Although Article 39 states that the Security Council shall determine the existence of a threat to the peace, breach of the peace, or act of aggression, in practice the General Assembly has also considered that it has a right to make such a determination. In adopting the Palestine partition resolution, for example, the Assembly requested the Council to consider whether the situation in Palestine during the transitional period constituted a threat to the peace.[8] The Assembly has in the past attempted to induce the Council to apply sanctions against belligerent states and has also asserted its authority further by recommending collective measures in the event of a breach of the peace or act of aggression whenever the Council failed to exercise its primary responsibility. This was the case after the adoption, by the General Assembly in 1950, of the Uniting for Peace Resolution (see Appendix 4). The purpose of this resolution was to provide the General Assembly with responsibilty for collective security measures and at the same time to decentralize the UN system itself. The initiative to adopt the resolution was led by the US, France and Britain whose intention it was to have the General Assembly recommend collective security measures if the Security Council was unable to do so because of deadlock.[9] Adopted over the objections of the USSR and other Communist States, the Uniting for Peace Resolution has always been surrounded by controversy. The USSR maintained that the UN Charter, according to Article 11, Paragraph 2, prohibited any organ other than the Security Council from recommending forceful collective security measures. Despite these objections the resolution was used by the General Assembly to deal with a number of crises during the Cold War - such as the Suez in 1956 and Congo in 1960.

It is clear from the provisions set down in Chapter VII, however, that the potential power of the Security Council is enormous. Once the Council determines that there has been a threat to international peace, a breach or an act of aggression it may adopt any of a number of measures to restore the peace. Article 41 outlines various measures not involving the use of force. 'These may include complete or partial interruption of economic relations and of rail, sea, air, postal, telegraphic, radio, and other means of communication, and the severance of diplomatic relations.'[10]

Although during the first twenty years of the UN's existence (1946-1966) the Security Council did not actually enforce Article 41, it was first discussed in connection with a call upon Members to sever diplomatic relations with Franco's Spain. In 1946 the Security Council concluded that the way Franco's regime had gained power, its role during World War II and the concentration of troops on French borders meant that the Franco regime could no longer be regarded as an internal Spanish affair. Later in 1948, Article 41 was discussed again when the Council attempted to persuade Israel and its Arab neighbours to cease hostilities.[11] In addition, the Article's provisions have on a number of occasions been used without specifically citing the Article itself. In connection with South Africa, for example, the Council called upon UN Members to boycott South African goods, and the Assembly itself requested Members to take such measures against Korea in 1950.[12]

The Council's ultimate power, however, was contained in Article 42, which states,

> Should the Security Council consider that measures provided for in Article 41 would be inadequate or have proved to be inadequate, it may take such action by air, sea, or land forces as may be necessary to maintain or restore international peace and security. Such action may include demonstrations, blockade, and other operations by air, sea, or land forces of Members of the United Nations.[13]

By empowering the Security Council to take military action against belligerents the Charter went far beyond the system that had been established under the League of Nations Covenant. It is not clear, however, that Article 42 was ever applied by the Security Council during the Cold War. The ideological enmity between East and West prevented the Security Council from taking any form of action which would have had a Chapter VII mandate. Even in those cases where enforcement took place, such as during the Korean War between 1950 and 1953, and in the Congo between 1960 and 1964, there is debate over whether the action taken was explicitly under Article 42.[14] In fact only once was the application formally proposed. During the Suez crisis in 1956, the Soviet Union pushed for UN Members to provide naval, air and ground forces to assist the Egyptians. The action that was taken eventually, however, was not as outlined under Article 42.[15]

Article 43 is equally important in that it established the means of supplying the Security Council with the armed forces necessary for carrying out its decisions. Numerous options were put forward at Dumbarton Oaks and San Francisco. The first was to establish an international force under the complete jurisdiction of the Security Council. This was rejected, however, on the grounds that the watering down of sovereignty would not be accepted. A second option, that of leaving the enforcement of Security Council decisions to a coalition of national forces under some form of international direction, was very similar to the system that had existed under the League and so this was rejected since the founders did not wish to repeat the League's experience. Thirdly, the system that was eventually adopted also relied on national contingents, but with advance agreement by the Members as to the size and nature of the forces to be provided.[16] However, East and West collapsed into bitter ideological struggle before any agreement could be reached. Before descending into irrelevancy, however, the Military Staff Committee (MSC), discussed below, did report to the Council on the basic principles that should govern the UN's armed forces. One important area of agreement was that the Permanent Members should provide the initial contributions with other Members providing armed personnel at a later stage.[17]

The whole question of providing the Security Council with strength was dealt with by Article 47 which established the MSC. The Committee's purpose was to advise and assist the Security Council on all questions relating to the Council's military requirements. The idea of the MSC was unique since the framework of reference for the Committee, as a subsidiary organ of the UN, was provided for within the Charter itself.[18] It was anticipated, therefore, that the MSC would command land, air, and sea forces in order to maintain international peace and security.

Taken together Articles 39-51, at least on paper, portray the potential for the Security Council to be a very powerful executive committee of an embryonic world state. The failure of the MSC to assume any responsibility and the ultimate failure to realise the grandiose designs of the Security Council, were less to do with the provisions in the Charter and more to do with the emergence of the Cold War and the lack of consensus amongst the Permanent Members of the Council. It was inevitable, therefore, that the UN Charter would become increasingly inadequate in its response to the changing needs of its members.

The Security Council

The primary goal of the United Nations - to maintain international peace and security - is stated right at the start of the Charter in Article 1 Paragraph 1. Article 24 then goes on to confer this primary responsibility on the Security Council. Designated as a principle organ by Article 7 of the Charter the Security Council consists, following an amendment in 1965, of fifteen Members of which five are permanent and ten are non-permanent. The Permanent Members of the Council are named in the Charter as being the Republic of China (later the People's Republic of China), France, the United Kingdom, the USA and the USSR (later Russia). In accordance with Article 23, the non-permanent Members are elected by the General Assembly for a term of two years with 'due regard being specially paid, in the first instance to the contribution of Members of the United Nations to the maintenance of international peace and security and to the other purposes of the Organisation, and also to equitable geographical distribution'.[19]

The one crucial difference between the Security Council and the other UN bodies is that while other organs of the UN (General Assembly, Economic and Social Council, Trusteeship Council and International Court of Justice) may make recommendations to governments, only the Security Council has, under the Charter, the power to take decisions which all UN Members are obliged to accept. This essentially means that it is mandatory for the Members to abide by the terms of any resolution adopted by the Council. Under the Charter the Security Council was granted specific powers to facilitate the Pacific Settlement of Disputes (Chapter VI, Articles 33-38) and to take action with respect to threats to the peace, breaches of the peace and acts of aggression (Chapter VII, Articles 39-51).

In order to exercise its primary role the Security Council is organized in a manner which enables it to function continuously. For this reason a representative of each of its Members is present at the UN headquarters at all times. The principal officer of the Security Council is the President who, rather than being elected, is appointed monthly, in rotation, according to alphabetical order, thus giving each Member of the Council (non-permanent as well as Permanent) a chance to hold the Presidency. The President's functions range from arranging meetings on his own initiative or upon the request of the Secretary General or the Council. Meetings must also be convened by the President when a dispute is brought to the attention of the Council by the General Assembly or a Member State.[20]

Each Member of the Council has one vote and voting is generally carried out on two types of issues. First, decisions on matters of *procedure* are taken by an affirmative vote of at least nine of the fifteen Members. Decisions on *substantive* matters also require nine votes but in this case a resolution fails if any of the Permanent Members casts a negative vote. Therefore, these rules make the veto applicable to most decisions of the Security Council and the purpose behind them is to obtain Great Power unanimity on important Security Council matters - specifically those dealing with international peace and security. Procedural issues are concerned with questions such as the creation of subsidiary organs, the adoption of new rules, the place of meetings and the referral of a question to the General Assembly. Substantive issues, on the other hand, are ones where the veto power of the Permanent Members may be exercised and include important issues such as the determination of a dispute, the application of sanctions, the appointment of the Secretary General and the admission or expulsion of Members.[21]

Despite major power assurances during the San Francisco Conference that the veto would not be used unjustifiably, lack of cooperation, demonstrated by the extensive use of the veto, amongst the key decision makers during the Cold War prevented the Security Council from carrying out some of its major functions - particularly those that required a Chapter VII mandate.

As White observes, the number of vetoes in the period 1946-1986 were: China 22, France 16, Soviet Union 121, UK 26 and the USA 57. He goes on to emphasize the importance of the fact that the Soviet Union cast 77 of its vetoes in the first ten years when the UN was Western dominated, whereas the US cast 45 vetoes between 1976 and 1986, the period of the development of successful relations between the Non Aligned Movement and the Socialist bloc in the UN.[22] At San Francisco it had been hoped that the limited cooperation amongst the Great Powers during World War II would develop into something more fruitful. Much has been written on why the relationship did not take a positive route and it is not proposed to discuss the Cold War as a separate issue here.[23]

The Secretary General

Before discussing the concept of peacekeeping it is necessary to consider one further important component associated with the primary objective - that of the function of the Secretary General in relation to the maintenance of international peace and security. It is clear that this role developed significantly during the Cold War period. Article 97 of the Charter states that the Secretariat of the United Nations (the body responsible for assisting, in an administrative capacity, the other organs of the UN) shall 'comprise a Secretary General and such staff as the Organisation may require'.[24] From the start it was intended that the Secretary General of the UN would play a much greater role in international affairs than the League's rather anonymous Chief. As a result, a crucial role assigned to the position of Secretary General was enshrined within the Charter itself. Article 99 stated that 'The Secretary General may bring to the attention of the Security Council any matter which in his opinion may threaten the maintenance of international peace and security'.[25]

Clearly this authority is closely related to the primary responsibility of the UN itself. Even though the Article appears to be procedural in nature, in practice Article 99 has enabled the Secretary General to undertake a wide range of political and diplomatic initiatives for the purpose of maintaining international peace and security. By having the right to bring any matter to the attention of the Security Council which, in his opinion threatened peace, the Secretary General's position increased in importance as the UN became increasingly assertive in its peacekeeping role.

The responsibility given to the Secretary General under Article 99 (Appendix 3) meant that this function became an essential tool by which the UN could respond to the international situation at any given time. During the Cold War the Security Council was unable to adopt resolutions on numerous occasions due to unbridgeable divisions between its Permanent Members. In such cases the Secretary General was able to act as intermediary in order to help them to accommodate and reach agreement. In 1986, for example, the position of Secretary General was the only open channel of communication over questions relating to the Iran-Iraq war, Cyprus and Lebanon.

The Nature of Peacekeeping

Peacekeeping does not appear anywhere in the UN Charter. Adopted during the Cold War as a substitute for collective security and in response to the stalemate between the Permanent Members of the Security Council, peacekeeping was principally used as a means to prevent the two superpowers from becoming embroiled in localized disputes. As peacekeeping developed, it became clear that it did not refer to the authoritative or forceful maintenance of peace. Instead peacekeeping came to describe the help provided by the international community to disputing states to minimise violence. As an activity, peacekeeping is essentially responsible for bridging the gap between the will for peace and its actual achievement. As the Cold War progressed, states, primarily in their capacity as UN Members, established a number of operations which were viewed as having certain basic functions and characteristics in common. The mixing of these characteristics opened the way for the UN to embrace peacekeeping as its primary tool for maintaining international peace and security. The term did not come into general usage until the 1960s and by 1988 thirteen peacekeeping operations had been set up, and more than 600 men had given their lives in keeping peace for the UN.

Broadly speaking, peacekeeping operations during the Cold War may be classified into two categories: observer missions consisting of a group of military observers, and peacekeeping forces composed of national contingents. Although the mandates of operations falling under one category are distinct in nature from the other category, it is important to remember that the essential characteristics of both categories of peacekeeping are the same.

Alan James provides a useful insight into the concept of peacekeeping. He begins by stating that peacekeeping is composed of four essential elements which when taken together distinguish peacekeeping operations from enforcement and other forms of action. First, the personnel deployed as part of any peacekeeping operation have to be of a *military* nature.[26] In addition to numerous military observer missions during the Cold War - such as those deployed between India and Pakistan (UNMOGIP and UNIPOM) - there were a number of operations made up of military forces in the traditional sense composed of a number of battalions under the authority of a commander - such as UNEF I, UNFICYP and ONUC.[27]

The second characteristic of peacekeeping, is concerned with *values* of the operation itself. Obviously for a peacekeeping operation to be successful it has to gain the trust of all the disputants. For this reason, despite the fact that a peacekeeping operation is military in structure, it has to be non-threatening.[28] This is crucial for the simple reason that if the operation, for some reason or other, abandons its non-threatening posture then it will inevitably become party to the dispute and hence lose its claim to be a peacekeeping body. In such circumstances the mission will have crossed the fine line which separates peacekeeping from enforcement. A second value of importance is that all peacekeeping operations can only employ force for the purposes of self-defence. As long as the host(s) know that the peacekeeping mission's arms will only be used in self-defence then this value will successfully complement the non-threatening stance adopted by the mission. Thirdly, peacekeeping operations are distinct from enforcement measures in the *content* of their mandates. Impartial peacekeeping forces or military observers are well placed to potentially be able to defuse tensions in areas of crisis. Once defused they are responsible for the stabilization of the situation which may then enable political negotiation to take place.[29]

Finally, Alan James goes on to state that the characteristics of peacekeeping operations have to do with the *context* within which they take place. 'Together with the two values of peacekeeping, they constitute the very core and essence of the activity ...'[30] The context therefore includes the following provisions: first, the decision to establish a peacekeeping operation must be taken by a competent authority be it an international organisation - such as the UN - or a regional body. Second, the operation must have adequate support in the form of finances, personnel and equipment. Third, the operation can only be established if the host state(s) has granted their consent to the presence of foreign troops on their territory. It has to be accepted that the withdrawal of this consent effectively signals the termination of the operation which was the case in 1966 when President Nasser of Egypt withdrew his consent, thus prematurely bringing UNEF I's mandate to an end.[31]   Finally, a peacekeeping operation must have the political cooperation of all the parties to the dispute otherwise it is unlikely that it will complete its mandate successfully.   A clear example of the failure to cooperate with peacekeepers is provided by the case of UNYOM (1963-1964) when the Saudis and the Egyptians continued to violate their disengagement agreement, thus effectively preventing the mission to fulfil its mandate. In direct contrast to this was in the case of West Irian (UNTEA: 1962-1963) which was largely successful due to the cooperation extended by Indonesia to the Temporary Executive Authority.[32]

There are numerous other contributions to the concept of peacekeeping. Amongst them a notable addition is that of William Durch who states that 'peacekeeping supplements the self-help system of international politics with an element of disinterested outside assistance that can help the parties to a conflict disengage themselves from it'.[33] He goes on to state that peacekeeping operations may involve:

> ... uncovering the facts of a conflict; monitoring of border or buffer zones after armistice agreements have been signed; ... supervision of the disarming and demobilization of local forces; maintenance of security conditions essential to the conduct of elections; and even the temporary, transitional administration of countries.[34]

Other writers, such as Rikhye, while agreeing with the broad characteristics of peacekeeping, including the principles of consent, impartiality, mediation and persuasion, emphasize the fact that peacekeeping had, during the Cold War, become associated with the process of decolonization. This is certainly a valid argument as a significant number of crises were in countries that were being or had just been decolonized. The retreat by the European powers from their colonies after World War II resulted in the surfacing of previously suppressed rivalries. Conflicts in Indonesia, Palestine, Cyprus and between India and Pakistan are examples. Having said this, however, Rikhye goes on to state that it is important not to look at peacekeeping within the confines of this narrow framework. The significant number of operations launched during the Cold War stand testimony to the fact that peacekeeping forces and observer missions employed measures designed to be flexible, versatile and innovative. In this light peacekeeping must not be limited to the inflexibility in purpose and performance of the era of decolonization.[35]

Peacekeeping, therefore, is clearly a regulatory system. Its success during the Cold War overwhelmingly lay in the fact that it had limited objectives. It would, nevertheless, be inaccurate to state that peacekeeping had no failures. There have been instances when peacekeeping operations have failed to fulfil their mandates - such as in the case of the United Nations Yemen Observation Mission (UNYOM) amongst others. Reasons behind failures of specific operations are discussed in Chapter 2, here it is sufficient to state that for a peacekeeping operation to be successful all the elements outlined above have to be present. So, for example, one of the crucial elements outlined above was that of cooperation on the part of the disputants. The lack of this cooperation was one factor which greatly contributed to the failure of UNYOM. Another example is provided by the Congo situation in 1960. Initially, there was a danger that ONUC would not be able to fulfil its mandate as there was very little cooperation on the part of the Katanganese leadership. The situation deteriorated to such an extent that there was effectively no peace to keep. So peacekeeping gave way to more forceful methods. It is apparent, therefore, that peacekeeping operations will only succeed in completing their mandates if the conditions outlined above are met.

To summarize, peacekeeping operations during the Cold War are broadly classified into two categories; observer missions and peacekeeping forces. Both categories are included within the realm of peacekeeping since the same basic principles apply to either case. The UN's own definition of peacekeeping is

> ... a peacekeeping operation has come to be defined as an operation involving military personnel, but without enforcement powers, undertaken by the United Nations to help maintain or restore international peace and security in areas of conflict. These operations are voluntary and are based on consent and cooperation. While they involve the use of military personnel, they achieve their objectives not by force of arms, thus contrasting them with the 'enforcement action' of the United Nations under Article 42.[36]

Conclusion

Even though the Charter provided a theoretical framework for a system of collective security, the UN was unable to prevent conflict during the

Cold War, the onset of which successfully destroyed the myth of Great Power unity. Having invested so much in the international body, however, Members sought a new role for the UN. Peacekeeping, therefore, emerged in response to the lack of Great Power co-operation and became successful, to a degree, in bringing at least some order to the international system if not total peace.

The final judgement of the success of peacekeeping, however, can only be made once a detailed analysis of some of the operations is carried out, and that is done elsewhere in this volume. This chapter has concentrated upon the primary role of the UN and the various components that exist (in theory and in practice) to help fulfil that primary objective. Factors such as the Charter, specifically Chapters VI and VII (Appendix 1 and 2), the Security Council, the Secretary General and the concept of peacekeeping are all component parts the interaction of which enabled the UN to carry out a semblance of its primary role.

The end of the Cold War saw the emergence of a debate which sought to address the question of making the Security Council more effective. The debate appeared to be a reaction to the relative ineffectiveness of the Security Council during the Cold War. Conflicting interests combined with hostility between East and West during the Cold War had limited the executive functions of the Security Council whenever an issue threatened the vital interests of any one of the Permanent Members. Indeed, Permanent Member interests became so widespread that the veto effectively prevented the Security Council from taking action or even recommending measures to solve conflicts. The end of the Cold War and, in particular, the UN's success in the 1991 Gulf War, prompted consideration of reform of the Security Council. The two main issues centred around whether or not to abolish the veto power held by each of the Permanent Members and whether to increase the number of Council Members, thus making it more representative. It is recognized, however, that to improve the effectiveness of the Security Council the Permanent Members would have to commit themselves to decisions taken by the Council but the argument against the veto is that it has exempted the Permanent Members from this obligation. Eliminating the veto would mean abolishing the self-interest upon which its existence is based.

As regards the structure of the Security Council this was last changed in 1963 at a time when Third World countries had felt under represented. Consequently, four more non-permanent seats were added to the Security Council with 7 out of 10 being assigned to Third World states. The post-Cold War debate centred around the incompleteness of the Council. Two states (Japan and Germany) emerged as possible Permanent Members on the grounds that they were the second and third largest financial contributors to the UN. As Chicchanski observes 'denial of participation of these two powers in the decision-making in the Security Council was thus tantamount to taxation without representation'.[37]

Counter arguments against restructuring the Council and cancelling the veto have also been put forward. These include claims that increasing the size of the Council, with both permanent and non-permanent members, would naturally make the decision-making process more cumbersome and thus diminish its organisational capacity to operate. In addition, the composition of the Security Council has to be based upon a particular state's ability to exercise international responsibility. This argument, however, can only apply in cases where self-interest is not of paramount importance. No great power has been willing to bind itself to compulsory collective action. As such, it is possible to argue that when the interests of the Permanent Members have coincided with wider international interests then the Security Council has proved that it is capable of authorising UN action. In light of this, it is perhaps inappropriate to criticise the Security Council, and it would be more relevant to state that the effectiveness of the Council does not rest on its structure but rather on the commitment of its members, particularly its Permanent Members, to make the existing system work. The 1950 Uniting for Peace Resolution was one attempt to erect safeguards against the consequences of inaction. Despite being invoked on a number of occasions, however, this procedure was to remain surrounded in significant controversy.

Although individual Secretary Generals may have been criticized for particular policies and stances the actual position of Secretary General has not come under serious criticism. Indeed, there have been no formal proposals for reviewing the role. Instead, the role as the head of the UN and as a moderator in conflicts has won considerable praise though recently there has been speculation over both the reform of the selection process with emphasis being given on extending the period of office from the current five to seven years.[38]

The discussion of the nature of peacekeeping centres around breaking the concept into its various segments. From this it has been possible to see how different it is from what was envisaged in the Charter. Whereas Chapter VII of the Charter advocates the use of force for maintaining international peace for example, peacekeeping recommends mediation, impartiality, and persuasion. Even though the term 'collective security' was not used in the Charter, the same intention was expressed in the phrase 'to unite our strength to maintain international peace and security'.[39] In reality, however, unity and idealism gave way to second best - *peacekeeping*.

Suggested Reading

Baehr, P., & Gordenker, L., *The United Nations: reality and ideal*, New York, Praeger, 1984.

Bailey, S.D., *The procedure of the UN Security Council*, Second Edition, New York, Oxford University Press, 1988.

Bowett, D.W. et al., *United Nations forces: a legal study of United Nations practice*, London, Stevens and Sons Ltd., 1964.

Finkelstein, L.S., (ed.), *Politics in the United Nations system*, London, Duke University Press, 1988.

Goodrich, L.M., *The United Nations in a changing World*, New York, Columbia University Press, 1974.

Gross, E.A., *The United Nations: structure for peace*, New York, Harper & Brothers, 1962.

Hiscocks, R., *The Security Council: A study in adolescence*, London, Longman Group Ltd., 1973.

James, A., *Peacekeeping in international politics*, London, Macmillan Academic and Professional Ltd., 1990.

Peterson, M.J., *The General Assembly in world politics*, Boston, Allen & Unwin, 1968.

Pogany, I.S., *The Security Council and the Arab-Israeli conflict*, England, Gower Publishing Company Ltd., 1984.

Rikhye, I.J., *The theory and practice of peacekeeping*, London, Hurst, 1984.

Vincent, J.E., *International relations, United Nations*, New York, University Press of America Inc., volume 3, 1983.

Wiseman, H., (ed.), *Peacekeeping: appraisals and proposals*, New York, Pergamon Press, 1983.

Notes

1. For an account on the work of the League of Nations see the following: Webster, C.K., & Sydney, H., *The League of Nations in theory and practice,* London, George Allen and Unwin Ltd., 1933 and Zimmern A., *The League of Nations and rule of law, 1918-1935,* London, MacMillan and Co., Ltd., 1936.

2. cf.Declaration by Churchill, Roosevelt and Stalin quoted in Goodrich, L. M., *The United Nations,* New York, Thomas Y. Crowell Company, 1959, p.22.

3. For a detailed analysis of the origins of the UN see Eichelberger, Clark, M., *Organizing for peace,* New York, Harper and Row Publishers, 1977.

4. cf.Article 103, *UN Charter.*

5. cf.Article 2, *UN Charter.*

6. cf.Article 33, *UN Charter.*

7. White, N. D., *Keeping the peace: the United Nations and the maintenance of international peace and security,* Manchester University Press, 1993, p.6.

8. Goodspeed, S. S., *The nature and function of international organization,* New York, Oxford University Press, 1963, pp.208-213.

9. Ibid., p.162.

10. cf.Article 41, *UN Charter.*

11. Russell, R. B., *A history of the United Nations Charter,* Washington, Brookings Institution, 1958, pp.466, 676.

12. With regards to South Africa, the Security Council adopted resolution 181 on 7 August 1963 which called upon all states to cease the sale and shipment of arms, ammunition and other military equipment to South Africa. The call for an arms embargo against South Africa was reiterated in subsequent resolutions.

13.   cf.Article 42, *UN Charter*. For a more detailed account of the provisions relating to the Security Council's coercive powers see Articles 39-51 of the UN Charter. The Pacific Settlement of Disputes, contained in Chapter VI related to the steps to be taken prior to bringing an issue to the Council. This meant that disputing states had to seek a solution through peaceful means at their disposal before the Security Council took responsibility.

14.   For an account of the legal basis for international action in Korea see Bowett, D.W. et al, *United Nations forces: a legal study of United Nations practice,* London, Stevens & Sons, 1964, pp.29-47.

15.   The action taken by UNEF I was different to that of the Korean case. Whereas in Korea the main purpose was to drive out the aggressor from the invaded state and to restore the *status quo,* in the Middle East although the ultimate goal was the restoration of the position before the Israeli attack the primary function of UNEF I was to supervise the voluntary acceptance of the recommendations of the General Assembly by the belligerents.

16.   Article 43, *UN Charter.*

17.   White, op.cit, p.101.

18.   Article 47, *UN Charter.*

19.   cf.Article 23, *UN Charter.* The number of non-permanent Members was increased from six to ten by an amendment of the Charter which came into force in 1965.

20.   Bailey, S. D., *The procedure of the UN Security Council,* Oxford, Clarendon Press, second edition 1988, pp.20-35.

21.   Hiscocks, R., *The Security Council: A study in adolescence,* London, Longman Group Ltd., 1973, pp.84-92.

22.   White, op.cit, p.12.

23.   See for example Dockrill, M. L., *The Cold War: 1945-1963,* London, Macmillan, 1988; Brown, C., & Mooney, P. J., *Cold War to detente 1945-1980,* London, Heinemann Education Books, 1992; Crockatt, R., & Smith, S., (eds.), *The Cold War past and*

present, London, Allen and Unwin, 1987; Lefeber, W., *America, Russia and the Cold War 1945-1992,* New York, McGraw-Hill Inc., seventh edition 1993, first edition 1967; Halliday, F., *The making of the second Cold War,* London, Verso Editions and NLB, 1986.

24.   cf.Article 97, *UN Charter.*

25.   cf.Article 99, *UN Charter.*

26.   James, A., *Peacekeeping in international politics,* London, Macmillan Academic and Professional Ltd., 1990, p.1.

27.   The various acronyms stand for: UNMOGIP: United Nations Military Observer Group in India and Pakistan, UNIPOM: United Nations India Pakistan Observer Mission, UNEF: United Nations Emergency Force, UNFICYP: United Nations Force in Cyprus and ONUC: United Nations Operation in the Congo.

28.   James, op.cit, pp.2-3.

29.   Ibid., pp.4-5.

30.   cf.Ibid., p.5.

31.   Ibid., pp.6-7.

32.   The acronyms stand for: UNYOM, United Nations Yemen Observation Mission and UNTEA, United Nations Temporary Executive Authority.

33.   cf.Durch, W. J., 'Introduction', in *The evolution of UN peacekeeping: case studies and comparative analysis,* edited by idem, New York, St. Martin's Press, 1993, p.3.

34.   Idem.

35.   Rikhye, I. J., 'Peacekeeping and Peacemaking', in *Peacekeeping: appraisals and proposals,* edited by Wiseman, H., New York, Pergamon Press, 1982, p.18.

36.   cf.*The blue helmets: a review of United Nations peacekeeping,* United Nations, Second edition, p.4.

37.   Chiechanski, J., 'Restructuring of the UN Security Council', *International Peacekeeping*, vol.1, no.4, Winter 1994, p.415.

38.   Saksena, K.P., *Reforming the United Nations: the challenge of relevance,* London, Sage Publications, 1993, p.183.

39.   Preamble, *UN Charter.*

Chapter 2
The Evolution of UN Peacekeeping 1947-1987

Introduction

Chapter 1 established that peacekeeping emerged during the Cold War as the principal tool through which the UN attempted to fulfil its primary goal of maintaining international peace and security. This chapter will take the analysis a step further by determining at which points during the Cold War, these various characteristics were to materialise. However, it is important to reiterate that the concept of peacekeeping was not mentioned in the UN Charter. Instead, elements of peacekeeping began to be established once the basic observer missions were set up soon after World War II.

Further analysis shows that the progression of UN peacekeeping during the Cold War was not as uniform as it may seem. Instead, a comparison of early operations set up during the late 1940s, such as UNSCOB and UNTSO, with missions established in the 1950s and 1960s - UNEF I and ONUC for instance - clearly indicates different levels of UN assertiveness at various points during the Cold War.[1] This chapter, therefore, separates the Cold War into three distinct analytical periods: the birth of UN peacekeeping, 1947-1956; the assertive period, 1956-1974; and the quiescent period, 1974-1987.

As clarified in Chapter 1 peacekeeping was not mentioned in the Charter, instead it was established by the UN as part of a process for the management of conflict. It must also be understood that peacekeeping was not applied as a panacea to all conflict situations, instead its usage has been limited and had varying degrees of success. The observer missions of the 1940s were to formalize basic characteristics of peacekeeping such as monitoring, observing, reporting and persuading. Peacekeeping, however, was not fully utilised until the second, assertive period. This stage in the evolutionary process saw the establishment of the first sizeable peacekeeping forces in the form of missions like UNEF I and ONUC. These missions were infinitely more complex in structure and mandate than their predecessors had been. Marrack Goulding (formerly the UN Under-Secretary-General for Peacekeeping Operations) describes this period as the UN's 'golden age' during which time nine of the thirteen peacekeeping operations established during the Cold War were set up.[2] The third, quiescent, period saw the UN withdraw dramatically from the pattern it had instituted over the past eighteen years which resulted in only one new peacekeeping operation, UNIFIL, being set up in 1978. Though detailed in structure and mandate, UNIFIL was not as ambitious or perhaps even as successful as UNEF I, ONUC or UNTEA had been.

For the sake of completeness certain other not so obvious issues inherent within the practice of UN peacekeeping can be identified. The development of the roles played by the Secretary General and the General Assembly, for instance, are as important as the establishment of operational norms such as consent and impartiality. This chapter, therefore, will attempt to link the development of the principals of peacekeeping with a range of other diverse elements which all played an important role in the fulfilment of the UN's primary responsibility.

Dividing the Cold War into time-zones provides a useful method through which to address a number of other central issues. It becomes possible to compare the UN's performance in each of the time periods. Connected to this, it is also important to determine why some peacekeeping operations may have been more successful than others. From this it is possible to determine the conditions necessary for peacekeeping. In addition, it is possible to argue that the path taken by UN peacekeeping during the Cold War is almost certainly linked to its successes and failures. The success of the initial military observation missions during the first period for instance undoubtedly encouraged the setting up of much more ambitious missions during the 1950s and 1960s. The experience of operations such as ONUC and UNFICYP during the second, assertive, period, however, had an effect on the style of peacekeeping undertaken in the third, less ambitious, period of peacekeeping.

Missions which became established as peacekeeping operations are listed in the table below:

TABLE 2: Peacekeeping Operations during the Cold War, 1945-1987

Missions	Brief Explanation
UN Special Commission on the Balkans (UNSCOB) 1947-51	Inquire into foreign support for guerrilla fighters in Greece
UN Truce Supervision Organisation (UNTSO) 1948-present	Monitor ceasefire lines between Israel and its neighbours
UN Military Observer Group in India and Pakistan (UNMOGIP) 1949-present	Monitor ceasefire between India and Pakistan in Kashmir
UN Emergency Force I (UNEF I) 1956-67	Act as a buffer between Israeli and Egyptian forces in the Sinai
UN Observation Group in Lebanon (UNOGIL) 1958	Monitor movement of arms, troops and equipment into Lebanon
UN Operation in the Congo (ONUC) 1960-64	Provide military assistance to the Congolese Government and restore order
UN Temporary Executive Authority (UNTEA) 1962-63	Administer West Irian prior to transfer of territory to Indonesia
UN Yemen Observation Mission (UNYOM) 1963-64	Monitor movement of arms, troops and equipment into Yemen from Saudi Arabia
UN Force in Cyprus (UNFICYP) 1964-present	Maintain order prior to 1974 and monitor buffer zone after Turkish invasion
UN India Pakistan Observer Mission (UNIPOM) 1965-66	Monitor ceasefire between India and Pakistan after the 1965 war
UN Emergency Force II (UNEF II) 1974-79	Act as a buffer between Israeli and Egyptian forces in the Sinai
UN Disengagement Observer Force (UNDOF) 1974-present	Monitor the separation of Israeli and Syrian forces on the Golan Heights
UN Interim Force in Lebanon (UNIFIL) 1978-present	Act as a buffer zone between Israel and Lebanon

The Birth of UN Peacekeeping: 1947-1956

The three peacekeeping missions established during this period were reponsible for beginning the process through which peacekeeping became an established tool for the UN. They primarily focused upon observation, monitoring, establishing facts and reporting their findings. They were, firstly, UNSCOB, set up in 1947 to monitor and investigate the assertion made by Greece of the support being provided by Albania, Bulgaria and Yugoslavia, to insurrectionist communist guerillas in Greece who had vowed to overthrow the established government. Secondly, UNTSO was set up in 1948 to monitor the ceasefire lines between Israel and its neighbours. This organ is still in existence, as is the third operation set up during this period. UNMOGIP was established in 1949 to monitor and report on the situation along the ceasefire line within Kashmir over which India and Pakistan had fought between 1947 and 1949.

United Nations Special Commission on the Balkans (UNSCOB: 1947-1951)

There is some debate over whether UNSCOB was actually a peacekeeping operation. The argument that UNSCOB was not rests on the premise that there has to be some form of cooperation from the parties involved in the dispute. An analysis of UNSCOB, however, shows that there was never any chance of this from the communist states neighbouring Greece in the north. Nevertheless, UNSCOB is included as an example of UN peacekeeping in that it represented the first time that observation groups, made up of impartial military personnel, were used. This, in itself, established a central element for subsequent peacekeeping operations. In addition, the mission demonstrated the UN's first steps towards peacekeeping through the establishment of subsidiary organs.

Germany's occupation of Greece during World War II gave rise to an underground resistance movement known as the National Liberation Front (EAM). Although EAM and its military wing ELAS (the National People's Liberation Army) operated under the auspices of the Greek Communist Party (KKE) there were many non-communists in its ranks.[3] Diferences between communists and non-communists developed, from 1944, into open civil war.

As the civil war spread northwards the communist guerillas were to start receiving military help from the newly established communist states of Albania, Bulgaria and Yugoslavia. This had the effect of raising tensions to such an extent as to warrant UN action.[4] A study of the the Greek civil war is important in that it highlighted the emerging conflict between the West and the Soviet bloc which was to result in deadlock in the Security Council. The continuous use of the veto by the Soviet Union led to Britain and the USA removing the issue from the Security Council to the General Assembly (which was to later establish UNSCOB), thus illustrating early on the inevitability of an active Assembly role in peacekeeping. The functions and mandate of UNSCOB were limited to observation and information gathering by teams stationed near Greece's northern borders. Their role was to determine whether the Greek guerillas were being supplied with arms and other equipment by the communist states in the north.

It is important to remember that UNSCOB was the UN's first attempt at placing observers on the ground to determine facts. However, it was inevitable that the operation would not contain all the elements of what was later to be recognized as peacekeeping. The Cold War had manifested itself clearly in the Greek affair and UNSCOB was accused of biased reporting in favour of the Greek government. Further, although UN peacekeeping during the Cold War was to be based upon the principle of consent, Albania and Yugoslavia never allowed UNSCOB observers on their territory. Despite these and other problems UNSCOB did provide the UN with invaluable experience by successfully indicating how difficult it was to influence the activities of states. This, in itself, contributed greatly to the emergence of the element of impartiality in peacekeeping.

United Nations Truce Supervision Organisation (UNTSO: 1948-present)

The confusion surrounding UNSCOB's status as a peacekeeping operation has led some academics to regard UNTSO as actually being the first UN peacekeeping mission during the Cold War period.[5] UNTSO is particularly important as a peacekeeping operation as it was to become the forerunner of six other operations set up in the Middle East during the Cold War. Identified as an observer mission, UNTSO has, over the years, been responsible for observing and monitoring the ceasefire lines between Israel and its neighbours. One particularly important function that UNTSO has attempted to fulfil, however, and a new one for UN peacekeeping at the time, was its mandate to investigate local disputes and attempt to defuse situations along the ceasefire lines which may have escalated into violence. As such, persuasion and diffusion were to be added to UN peacekeeping's mounting characteristics.

Jewish immigration into Palestine before World War II set the scene for protracted hostility between Arabs and Jews and war between them resulted in the creation of UNTSO in 1948. Set up by the Security Council, its main function was to supervise a truce called for by the UN. The UN's initial proposals, made by the UN Special Commission on Palestine (UNSCOP), to partition Palestine into an Arab state and a Jewish state were rejected by the Arabs.[6] The Palestinians questioned the legality of the UN to recommend the partition of their ancestral home. Following this, UNSCOP was relieved of its responsibilities and the UN created the office of a UN Mediator for Palestine. Count Folke Bernadotte, selected for the post, began his task of trying to find common ground between the two sides. A Truce Commission, the precursor of UNTSO, was established to assist in the process.

The UN's proposals for partition were marked by two other significant events. First, Jewish authorities proclaimed the creation of the state of Israel and second, the proclamation prompted a number of neighbouring Arab states to invade Palestine/Israel on 15 May 1948.[7] However, in June Count Bernadotte managed to negotiate a truce though hostilities were to resume again in July.[8]

Apart from demanding a truce, the Security Council called for international supervision of its demands. It was, therefore, at this stage that UNTSO began to play an important role. Military observers were sought from Belgium, France and the United States. After hostilities were resumed in July the Security Council demanded an indefinite truce. By the end of 1948, however, the Jews had won the war and were thus able to force the Arabs into a series of Armistice Agreements in 1949.

Four Mixed Armistice Commissions were set up to overlook the Agreements and this was to radically alter UNTSO's functions. Its functions were to include functions such as assisting in prisoner exchanges and supervising demilitarized zones in accordance with the Armistice Agreements which had been set up. The Security Council now authorized the military personnel associated with UNTSO to assist the parties in *supervising* the application of the Agreements. In fulfilling its peacekeeping role UNTSO began to carry out its own investigations and attempted to defuse potential problem incidents.

UNTSO is particularly important for UN peacekeeping in that it played a wider role in the Middle East. Its lack of structural mandate has meant greater flexibility which has allowed it to adapt to special circumstances and get involved with other operations set up in the Middle East.[9] During all the Arab-Israeli wars, in 1956, 1967, 1973, and 1982, UNTSO observers remained on ceasefire lines, and at other times prevented isolated incidents from escalating into general conflict. UNTSO also provided a point of contact between states which did not have established diplomatic relations, thus being valuable in political as well as humanitarian terms.[10] It remains important to realise, however, that despite being able to secure agreements between local commanders UNTSO's observers inevitably found themselves powerless to prevent large-scale operations deliberately planned by the Israeli army or by various Arab groups.

United Nations Military Observer Group in India and Pakistan (UNMOGIP: 1949-present)

The third and final peacekeeping mission set up by the UN during the first period began in 1949 following an agreement between India and Pakistan to cease fighting. Its mandate was similar to that of UNTSO in that it was to oversee the ceasefire between the two ex-belligerents, to prevent minor incidents from escalating into major conflicts, and to report on each sides' compliance with the arms limitation agreement. UNMOGIP and UNTSO both demonstrated that without a lasting political settlement between the disputants themselves, peacekeeping operations have the potential for continuing for decades. In the case of UNMOGIP, settlement over the Kashmir issue has not been forthcoming since 1949.

With the conclusion of World War II, the decolonization process within the Indian Subcontinent came to be signified, as in other regions, by the emergence of territorial conflict. This conflict found expression in the way in which the partition of India and the independence of its constituent parts was handled. Both India and Pakistan gained independence from the British soon after the Indian Independence Act of 1947 was adopted. Pakistan was established predominantly as a Muslim state separate from India, which mainly comprised of Hindu provinces. This Act also provided a basis for the partition and established the independence of over 500 other princely states within what had been British India. Geography and religion made it relatively easy for most of the states to join either India or Pakistan. One of the most serious outstanding issues, however, was that of Kashmir.[11]

Failure on the part of Kashmir's Hindu ruler to take into account the wishes of the predominantly Muslim population, the majority of whom sought union with Pakistan, resulted in riots breaking out. This led to invasion by Pakistan, forcing Kashmir's ruler to turn to India for military assistance, which agreed on condition that the state accede. The subsequent accession of Kashmir to India resulted in war breaking out between India and Pakistan on 24 October 1947.[12]

UN involvement came about as a result of India's complaint to the Security Council in early 1948 that Pakistan was threatening international peace and security through its invasion of Kashmir. Apart from denying interference, however, Pakistan maintained that Kashmir's accession to India had been illegal and that a plebiscite was necessary. These differences of opinion set the basis for hostility for the next forty years. India has repeatedly accused Pakistan of interfering in its internal affairs whilst Pakistan remains consistent in its views over the illegality of Kashmir's accession to India.

As in the case of UNTSO, the UN facilitated the negotiation process by setting up the United Nations Commission on India and Pakistan (UNCIP) to mediate between the belligerents. Although both Indian and Pakistani positions diverged on a range of issues, UNCIP did manage to arrange for a ceasefire to take effect from 1 January 1949. In this way Kashmir came to be divided between India and Pakistan. At the same time the Commission acquired a military component later known as the United Nations Military Observer Group in India and Pakistan (UNMOGIP).

Alan James separates the mandate of UNMOGIP into two phases - the first one covering 1949-1971 and the second, 1972 onwards.[13] During the initial phase UNMOGIP was largely successful in fulfilling its mandate. The high degree of impartiality shown by the UN observers gained the respect of both India and Pakistan, thus ensuring continued cooperation. Also, in accordance with the principals of peacekeeping, they adopted a non-threatening stance, which meant that India and Pakistan continued to consent to their presence.

UNMOGIP served one other important function which demonstrated the flexible nature of peacekeeping operations. It served a particularly useful role when India and Pakistan fought on a wider front in 1965. The military group served as the basis for another UN peacekeeping mission, the United Nations India Pakistan Observer Mission (UNIPOM) which is discussed later.

It is possible to argue that UNMOGIP outlived its usefulness during what Alan James describes as phase two. Civil war in Pakistan in 1971 resulted in Indian military intervention, which facilitated the creation of Bangladesh out of what was East Pakistan. After this event India shifted its stance *vis à vis* Kashmir claiming that the issue no longer had an international element and that it had to be dealt with on a purely bilateral basis. At the same time India reiterated its claim to the whole of Kashmir, arguing that a plebiscite was no longer relevant. Consequently, India ceased cooperation with UNMOGIP and severely restricted its movement. Clearly, with one side no longer willing to cooperate UNMOGIP has diminished in value. Yet the UN has maintained the peacekeeping operation primarily in the hope that the presence of a moral authority will avert further serious confrontation between two powerful armies.

The Assertive Period: 1956-1974

Even though peacekeeping was not fully utilised until the late 1950s, by 1956 the international community had found a role for the UN. The three peacekeeping operations dealt with above had gone some way to provide a basis upon which the characteristics of peacekeeping could be formalized. The existence of host nation consent and impartiality among the military observers provided an adequate platform upon which the UN could launch observation missions. Initially concerned with reporting and observing, these missions later developed an investigative edge as part of their mandates and, as such, were successful in lowering tensions caused by minor disputes along ceasefire lines. This period also saw a number of other important developments which were to have a significant impact on the development of peacekeeping in later years. First, deadlock in the Security Council, in the case of UNSCOB, introduced the General Assembly into the area of defining mandates for peacekeeping operations. This set the precedent for Assembly involvement in later crisis. Also, considerable use was made of the Secretary General's good offices, which strengthened his position as being a central element in maintaining international peace and security.

Any analysis of peacekeeping operations established during the second, assertive, period must take into account the fact that the fundamental characteristics of peacekeeping and the problems associated with it became apparent during the years 1947-1956. It was in 1956, however, that the UN went a considerable step further as regards peacekeeping. The next eighteen years were to see the UN set up nine new peacekeeping operations which were both ambitious and diverse in nature. This period also saw the formalization of the characteristics of peacekeeping in the sense that the factors of consent, the non-use of force, and the use of military personnel evolved to become established principles of peacekeeping.

United Nations Emergency Force I (UNEF I: 1956-1967)

The July 1956 announcement by President Gamal Abdel Nasser of Egypt of the nationalization of the Suez Canal was to have serious repercussions. Angry that the United States had withdrawn its offer of assistance to build the Aswan Dam, Nasser decided to place the Suez Canal under Egyptian control and declared that Canal dues would be used to finance the project. This decision led to a series of events, the culmination of which was the establishment of a new type of UN operation, the *peacekeeping force*. There were significant differences between UNEF I and the peacekeeping operations which preceded it. The size and complexity of the force itself was suggestive of the magnitude of the problem.[14] As such, whereas UNMOGIP had been set up to observe the ceasefire line between India and Pakistan, UNEF I was established to *secure* the ceasefire - a considerable step forward for UN peacekeeping. It is important to point out, however, that the mandate of UNEF I did not go as far as to advocate the *enforcement* of the ceasefire.

Another example of the UN's strengthened objectives was that the role played by the Secretary General during this crisis far outweighed any functions that he fulfilled during the preceding years.[15] This was largely due to the fact that the need for careful diplomacy was much greater particularly as two Western members of the Security Council - Britain and France - had militarily invaded a Third World country, and in doing so had increased the potential for a direct confrontation between the Soviet Union and some Western nations.

Nasser's announcement provided Israel with the opportunity to denounce the 1949 Armistice Agreements and attempt to solve the increasing problem of Egyptian backed Palestinian raids into Israel from the Gaza strip. The declaration also provided two major European powers, Britain and France, the pretext to invade, with the assistance of Israel, due to their obligations in the Far East where the Suez Canal offered the shortest sea route. Closure of the Canal would also have threatened their economic interests as a major portion of their Middle Eastern crude oil came through it. Britain and France were also concerned with the rise of Nasser's pan-Arab rhetoric. In particular, in the case of France, there was suspicion that Nasser was aiding Algerian nationalists. Meanwhile, other events, such as the collapse of the Armistice Agreements between Israel and several Arab countries heightened tensions. Israeli-Egyptian relations, in particular, had become increasingly tense throughout the early 1950s in light of the continuing Egyptian raids on Israeli population centres.

American dissatisfaction with the Franco-British policy led to the ceasefire and the subsequent setting up of UNEF I. As on previous occasions, Security Council meetings failed to produce any resolutions since they were vetoed by both Britain and France. Therefore, the General Assembly once again contributed towards maintaining international peace through the use of the 1950 Uniting for Peace procedure.

On 1 November 1956 the General Assembly adopted a resolution which proposed an immediate ceasefire and instructed Israel to withdraw behind the Armistice lines. It also called upon Britain and France to halt their advance on Egypt. Other resolutions were adopted between 2 and 5 November which called upon the Secretary General to submit a plan for the setting up of 'an emergency international United Nations Force to secure and supervise the cessation of hostilities'.[16] Resolution 1000, adopted on 5 November, accepted the Secretary General's plan and established a United Nations Command. UNEF I was to supervise the withdrawal of foreign troops from Egypt, to patrol border areas and prevent military incursions, to secure a ceasefire by forming a buffer zone between Anglo-

French-Israeli and Egyptian forces, and finally to strengthen the provisions covering the Egypt-Israel Armistice Agreements of 1949.[17]

UNEF I is particularly important for UN peacekeeping as it established a number of principles which were used in subsequent operations including, amongst others, ONUC, UNIFIL, UNDOF and UNFICYP. These included questions concerning the status of the Force, privileges and immunities for the Force, civil jurisdiction, and freedom of movement. As regards to UNEF I itself, the Chief of Command for the force was to be appointed by the UN, and he was authorized to recruit officers from UNTSO. These conditions were designed to ensure that his position remained independent of the policies of any one nation. In addition, despite proposals that UNEF I guarantee the rights of passage through the Canal, its functions rested upon two basic factors: first that the Force be an emergency one and second, it was to be temporary in nature, as its mandate was not intended to influence the military balance in the region.[18] Another crucial factor was the consent of the host government. Since UNEF I was not an enforcement action under Chapter VII of the UN Charter, it could only operate with the consent of the Egyptian government. In order to obtain this, the UN had to assure Egypt that it would not be coerced into making a decision over the Suez Canal nor would its sovereignty be compromised in any way.

The central reason for UNEF I's deployment had been to secure the withdrawal of the invaders. Israel's retreat marked the successful conclusion of this part of its mandate. Following the withdrawal there was a marked shift in its operation from securing, to observing, the ceasefire. Israel, however, refused to allow international observers within its own borders and so UNEF I had to make do with setting up posts on the Egyptian side. The Force was to stay in Egypt until 1967 and during this period the Egyptian-Israeli border remained remarkably quiet. Although UNEF I would not have been able to prevent a determined attack by either state the very fact that it had created a buffer zone between Israeli and Egyptian troops lent credibility to its presence.

UNEF I's mandate came to an end in 1967 due to the general Arab-Israeli war. Armed hostility between Syria and Israel resulted in Egyptian demands for the withdrawal of UNEF I. The Secretary General's attempts at persuading Nasser to allow UN troops to remain proved fruitless and the UN had to comply. It is important to remember that UN peacekeeping operations were, by now, based on the principle of consent. As such, UNEF I's continued role was entirely dependent upon Egypt's consent and once this was withdrawn the operation had to cease. UNEF I did, nevertheless, successfully demonstrate both the importance of peacekeeping operations and its limitations, thus providing valuable lessons. On the one hand the UN presence helped maintain peace in what was otherwise a volatile situation. But in being unable to address the underlying reasons for conflict, however, the UN did not contribute to a lasting peace.

United Nations Observation Group in Lebanon (UNOGIL: 1958)

Domestic tensions within Lebanon during 1958 threatened to be compounded by the intervention of the United Arab Republic (UAR), consisting of Syria and Egypt. In response, UNOGIL was set up. However, it was different from other peacekeeping operations in one important respect. The mandate restricted it to merely ascertaining the facts prior to the UN adopting any further measures. Other peacekeeping operations, such as UNTSO, UNEF I and II and UNMOGIP had much wider roles including observing, reporting, and trying to defuse potential problem incidents (in the case of UNTSO and UNMOGIP).

From the time it gained independence from France, Lebanon consisted of a mosaic of religious and political groups each vying for influence and power. By 1958 the fragile peace in Lebanon came to be structured between pro-West Christian president Kamil Shamun and Muslim Druze supporters who aspired to Nasser's pan-Arabism.[19] Shamun sought to amend the constitution to enable himself to be re-elected for a second term, thus infuriating the Muslim opposition groups. This led to serious disturbances breaking out between supporters of both groups. Consequently, Shamun, fearful of external intervention, primarily from the UAR, lodged a complaint with the Security Council. The Secretary General, with Security Council backing, despatched a military observer group to ensure that there was no illegal infiltration of supply, materials or personnel across Lebanese borders. UNOGIL's 100 man team was, however, initially refused access to areas on the Lebanese-Syrian border. Despite this, the observation group's initial report indicated that there was no evidence of mass foreign infiltration. This, understandably, infuriated Shamun who then turned to the United States for help which took the decision to intervene militarily.

The American intervention, however, coincided with UNOGIL gaining access to all areas of Lebanon's borders. This was immediately followed by a reassessment which downgraded the importance of external factors in Lebanon's crisis. The conflict now came to be seen as a result of domestic religious and political rivalries. Even these problems subsided when a widely accepted candidate, General Fouad Chehab, was elected as the next president, thus removing the controversial issue of Shamun's second term.

It is important not to overlook the importance of both UNEF I and UNOGIL for UN peacekeeping as a whole. Both operations, though significantly different from each other, were to provide a set of guidelines and principles upon which subsequent peacekeeping operations could be formed. In addition to formalizing the principles of host nation consent and the use of armed force only in self defence, other factors were to become peculiar to peacekeeping during and after the 1950s. Amongst these were rights conferred upon UN personnel which made them immune from prosecution in local courts. Connected to this was a provision which ensured freedom of movement for UN personnel within the area of operation. As mentioned earlier, one crucial development for peacekeeping had been the principle of maintenance of strict impartiality. In order to ensure this neutrality, units from Permanent Member states were excluded from field operations.[20]

United Nations Operation in the Congo (ONUC: 1960-1964)

UN peacekeeping operations before 1960 had included monitoring ceasefires along tense though structured ceasefire lines and borders - such as those in the Middle East and between India and Pakistan. Also peacekeeping had, in most cases, revolved around keeping two belligerents apart. The Congo presented a much more complex and rapidly changing environment with little or no structure with the function of ONUC to be to save a country from disintegration in the face of an imperfect decolonization effort.

The UN operation in the Congo between 1960 and 1964 was one of the largest undertaken by the Organisation comprising, at its peak strength, nearly 20,000 troops. In addition to this force, it included an important Civilian Operations element. Apart from being one of the most complicated of all peacekeeping operations it cost the UN dearly in terms of finances and lives, including that of the Secretary General Dag Hammarskjöld.[21] More than any other operation the UN's involvement in the Congo clearly isolated certain elements of great importance for the development of the Organisation.

Hammarskjold saw the crisis in the Congo as an opportunity to test the principle of preventive diplomacy which, in his opinion, was of special significance in areas where the crisis was said to be the direct result of the creation of a power vacuum.[22] The Congo presented just such an example where the termination of the colonial system was leading to serious conflict and a breakdown of society. The UN's institutional intervention, therefore, was aimed at temporarily filling the power vacuum created by the withdrawing colonial power thereby giving the newly independent state time to develop its own political, economic and geographical cohesion.[23]

The crisis in the Congo had its roots in the country's complex tribal structure. Increased political awareness and the emergence of key figures facilitated the creation of political groups with varying loyalties. One group of significance was Patrice Lumumba's nationalist, centrist party known as the *Mouvement Nationale Congolese* (MNC). Another important party was Moise Tshombe's federalist *Confederation des Association Tribales du Katanga* which belonged to the rich southern Katanga region and was interested in achieving greater financial and political autonomy from any Congolese government.

CONAKAT

Despite political victory over the Belgians in 1960 the various Congolese leaders had differing political motives and as a result their alliance proved to be too fragile. Before long it became clear that the Congo was not adequately prepared to assume responsibilities of independence. Law and order under Belgian rule had been maintained by the *Force Publique,* known as the *Armee Nationale Congolese* (ANC) after independence. The ANC, however, became a poorly-disciplined force, and a worsening situation persuaded Belgium to consider military intervention to safeguard European lives. Despite Lumumba's opposition, Belgian troops began to land in Katanga on 10 July 1960 in clear violation of a Treaty of Friendship between the two countries. At the same time Tshombe, president of the provincial government in Katanga, exacerbated tensions by declaring independence and placing Belgian individuals in official public posts. This convinced Lumumba that Belgium was preparing to take over the country, and so he turned to the international community for military help against the armed intrusion.

Following Lumumba's request, Hammarskjold invoked Article 99 of the Charter and informed the Council that the events in the Congo were a threat to international peace and security. This initiative was formally exercised for the first time in the history of UN peacekeeping and was meant to emphasize the gravity of the situation. The Security Council reacted to the warnings and adopted Resolution 143 on 14 July 1960 which authorized the Secretary General to provide the Congolese Government with '... such military assistance as may be necessary ...'.[24] This resolution provided the grounds upon which ONUC was established, to assist the Congolese Government to maintain law and order until 'with the technical assistance of the United Nations, the national security forces may be able, in the opinion of the Government, to meet fully their tasks'.[25] Hammarskjold appointed Ralph Bunche (a senior UN official) as Special Representative and Commander of the UN Force in the Congo. The establishment of this office itself was a new invention for UN

Congo: had to remain united

peacekeeping. Peacekeeping missions had initially been headed by government representatives answerable to the Security Council but in the Congo since the task had been entrusted to the Secretary General by the Council, his representative was answerable to him alone.[26]

The principles which had governed the peacekeeping action taken by UNEF I were to form the basis for ONUC. UNEF I had set the pattern for preventive diplomacy through peacekeeping. By entering the Suez Canal the UN sought to protect a vital waterway and at the same time divide the Israeli and Egyptian forces. In addition UNEF I denied the Anglo-French forces the opportunity to fulfil their goals. In the Congo the Secretary General concluded that despite the Belgian Government's announcements that its troops were there for the protection of life and property, their presence was a source of internal and international tension. This meant that the UN had to provide Belgium the opportunity (as UNEF I had done for the Anglo-French force) to withdraw - thus acting as a stop-gap arrangement whilst waiting for the re-establishment of order by the Congolese forces. Thus in both cases preventive diplomacy sought, without condemning, to create the conditions necessary by which any violation of international law could cease.[27]

Other principles of peacekeeping which had been established in preceding operations were invoked by the Secretary General. These included the following factors: first, ONUC was to have the status of a temporary security force deployed with the consent of the host state. Second, the UN was to retain command of the Force and even though it was to aid the Congolese Government in the maintenance of law and order, it was not to become involved in any internal conflict, thus maintaining an air of impartiality.[28] Third, other important factors included the provisions that ONUC was to have free access to areas of operation and the normal rules of engagement (use of force only in self-defence for instance) were to apply.[29]

In the light of deteriorating circumstances, however, the principles on which the UN operation was based were to change. While its original mandate - to help in the restoration of law and order and bring about the withdrawal of Belgian troops - remained valid ONUC was given additional tasks and responsibilities which, it can be argued, took it outside the realm of peacekeeping.

One of the main problems faced by the UN was how to find a balance between the Mission's functions of restoring law and order and overseeing Belgian withdrawal while at the same time adhering to the principle of non-interference in the internal affairs of the Congo. The UN was to become increasingly concerned with assisting the Congolese Government to maintain territorial integrity and political independence.[30] Much greater emphasis was placed upon this function as the question of Katanga's secession came up. This aspect, more than any other, revealed the extent of differing opinions amongst the various actors which not only increased the levels of tension within the Security Council, but contributed to the deteriorating relations between the UN and the Congolese Government itself.

The Secretary General had hoped for a peaceful UN entry into Katanga. The Soviet Union and the Congolese Government, on the other hand, insisted that the UN had, if necessary, to force itself into the province - clearly a Chapter VII operation. The Secretary General, however, viewed ONUC as being similar to UNEF I - that of an interpositional and consensual peacekeeping force established under the recommendatory powers of Chapter VI.[31] The situation in the Congo was to deteriorate to such an extent, however, that ONUC had to invoke Chapter VII principles.

Constitutional crisis followed by Lumumba's death and Tshombe's belligerency threatened to plunge the country into unmanageable civil war. It quickly became clear that the UN's success overwhelmingly depended upon the question of Katanga. Hammarskjold, although clear in his conviction that Belgian troops in Katanga were the cause for continued danger, became convinced that their withdrawal would not be sufficient to end the crisis. Resolution 161 of 21 February stressed the threat to international peace and security and advocated, as a last resort, the use of force.[32] The deteriorating situation in Katanga was to turn international opinion against Tshombe and particularly the foreign mercenaries aiding him. Resolution 169, adopted on 24 November 1961, reaffirmed the Council's commitment to maintaining the Congo's territorial integrity and political independence and went on to completely reject Tshombe's claim that the Katanga was a soveriegn state. It also authorised the Secretary General to use force if necessary to end Katanga's seccession and expel any foreign military personnel not operating under UN authority.[33] By the end of December 1962 Tshombe renounced his goal of making Katanga independent. With the authority of the Congolese Government extended over the whole of the Congo the new Secretary General, U Thant, announced that the majority of ONUC's mandates had been fulfilled, following which the Operation began a phased withdrawal which ended on 30 June 1964.

Despite the many criticisms of Hammarskjold and the way in which ONUC operated, it did manage to preserve the territorial integrity and political independence of the Congo. To do so, however, ONUC had to step outside the bounds of what had by now become established as peacekeeping: impartiality, use of force only in self-defence, and host consent. In addition to some of the factors mentioned earlier, peacekeeping

developed a number of other characteristics after the Congo which are
perhaps not so obvious. One of these was that subsequent peacekeeping
operations had very short mandates usually lasting only a matter of months.
This meant that their mandates have had to be periodically renewed by the
Security Council which, therefore, has had the effect of providing the
Permanent Members with the opportunity to veto any extension. Another
crucial development for peacekeeping was the central role played by Dag
Hammarskjold. As Secretary General Hammarskjold did much to develop
the position and this was facilitated by the importance attached to his role
during the crisis.

Time has to be considered

cannot understate! (Mazower)

United Nations Temporary Executive Authority (UNTEA: 1962-1963)

Though very different from each other in structure and mandate UNTEA
and ONUC had unique features. While in the Congo the use of force
provided ONUC with its unique characteristics, under UNTEA, for the
first time in its history, the UN had complete authority over a vast territory
under the jurisdiction of the Secretary General. To facilitate this
unprecedented level of authority the Secretary General placed a UN
Security Force (UNSF) at the disposal of UNTEA to maintain internal law
and order. As such the functions of UNSF related directly to UNTEA in
that it was set up to be the police arm of the Executive Authority.

The status of West New Guinea (hereafter West Irian) remained
unresolved after Indonesia gained independence from the Netherlands in
1949. Claims that West Irian was legally a part of Indonesia were disputed
by the Dutch who viewed themselves as an administrative authority over
a colony awaiting self-determination. As such their readiness to make
West Irian independent was based upon the premise that the territory would
be placed under temporary UN control.

Indonesia, however, refused to agree to the proposal stressing that West
Irian was legally a part of Indonesia. Increased tensions resulted in a naval
clash and a campaign of armed intervention into West Irian by the
Indonesians. At this point the Dutch accused Indonesia of aggression and
requested the UN to provide military observers. The Secretary General,
however, in clinging to the principle of consent, refused on the grounds
that UN troops could only be sent if both the Netherlands and Indonesian
governments had made the request.

The negotiated settlement between the Dutch and Indonesia which
established UNTEA and UNSF agreed that after a period of UN
administration there was to be a transfer of control to Indonesia which
agreed to provide certain guarantees for the population, including

provisions for self-determination. Therefore, since UNTEA was to emerge out of a bilateral agreement between the Dutch and the Indonesians (as UNMOGIP had in the case of India and Pakistan) it met the condition of consent. The bilateral agreement also meant that the issue was kept outside the Cold War boundaries of the Security Council and as a result these factors combined to give UNTEA and UNSF the reputation of being the UN's most ambitious and successful peacekeeping ventures.[34]

The UN operation proceeded in three stages. First, it provided administration and security for the territory during a seven month transition period starting in October 1962 and ending in April 1963. This was followed by a transfer of administration to Indonesian authorities and the local police force. The third stage concerned Indonesian obligations. With UN assistance, Indonesia was to provide guarantees for self-determination to the population of West Irian.[35]

In accordance with the Dutch-Indonesian accord full administrative authority was transferred to Indonesia in May 1963. By this stage UNSF, predominantly made up of UN troops from Pakistan, had successfully fulfilled its mandate. It had maintained law and order effectively during the transition period and had also managed to construct a viable local police force which was able to take over the role of keeping order upon UNTEA's withdrawal. The third stage of UN's involvement in West Irian was characterized by providing assistance to the Indonesian Government to fulfil its own obligations. Under UN auspices the population of West Irian were given the choice between severing or retaining ties with Indonesia. In 1969 the territory decided to remain with Indonesia, thus bringing UN involvement in West Irian to an end.

United Nations Yemen Observation Mission (UNYOM: 1963-1964)

Despite its very limited success, UNYOM remains an important part of UN peacekeeping in that it clearly highlighted the central role played by the Secretary General. The position of Secretary General had acquired an important level of personal authority over the years which, contributed much to U Thant's ability to set in motion such an operation. This level of independence for the Secretary General had also been shown in West Irian and the Congo. The operation in Yemen also reaffirmed that for a peacekeeping operation to be successful there had to be a combination of local consent and co-operation and it had to be backed up with adequate resources. These were just some of the assets which the observer mission in Yemen lacked.[36]

UNYOM was authorized by the Security Council in June 1963 to assist in the disengagement of forces involved in the civil conflict in Yemen. This conflict involved nationalist Republican forces supporting secular pan-Arab nationalism supported by Egypt and conservative Royalist forces receiving support from Saudi Arabia. There was a fear that there was a real danger of conflict spilling over into Saudi Arabia, and therefore, both the US and the UN Secretary General took steps to involve the UN in the crisis. The Secretary General's Special Representative, Ralph Bunche, was able to work out a disengagement agreement between Egypt and Saudi Arabia under which the Saudi Arabian government undertook to halt its support for the Royalists in Yemen while at the same time prohibiting the use of its territory by Royalist forces, while the Egyptians agreed to suspend aid to the newly established government in Yemen and to begin withdrawing their troops.

As in the case of West Irian, agreement for the disengagement and for the presence of a UN observer mission was reached through bilateral negotiations outside the Security Council. The USSR raised objections, however, on the grounds that since it was a matter of international peace and security only the Security Council could establish the peacekeeping operation. The Soviet Union appeared determined for a time that the Secretary General should not be in a position to authorize peacekeeping operations of this kind without the explicit authority of the Security Council. But since the two parties concerned, Saudi Arabia and Egypt, had agreed to finance the cost of the mission themselves, the USSR was forced to withdraw its objections, though it abstained from voting for the resolution which established the mission. In this way the Secretary General was, once again, instrumental in establishing a peacekeeping operation.

UNYOM's mandate, established on 11 June 1963, was to remain very limited. The observers were merely to report on the status of the disengagement agreement between Egypt and Saudi Arabia. Therefore, its functions were clearly limited to observing, certifying and reporting on whether Saudi Arabia ceased its support for the Yemeni Royalists and whether Egyptian troops were being withdrawn. A ground patrol of 100 Yugoslav troops were transferred from UNEF for the purpose and a 20-mile wide demilitarized zone on either side of the Saudi-Yemen border was established.

Ultimately UNYOM failed to fulfil the provisions of its mandate for three main reasons. Firstly, the area which was being patrolled by the UN observers remained very unsettled. The Saudis and Egyptians continued to accuse each other of violating the disengagement agreement. The Saudi government even went as far as to threaten to withdraw its funding of UNYOM as it became increasingly disenchanted with Egypt's promises of

withdrawal. In consequence, Saudi Arabia refused to stop aiding the
Royalists. Secondly, it was clear that even though both Egypt and Saudi
Arabia had expressed a willingness to co-operate with UNYOM there was
a reluctance on the part of both sides to fulfil their obligations before the
other side had done so. This in turn seriously frustrated UNYOM's
efforts. Thirdly, the resources available for UNYOM for even its limited
mandate of observation were far from adequate. A much bigger force was
required to ensure the detection of movement of men and equipment from
Saudi Arabia to Yemen.[37]

United Nations Force in Cyprus (UNFICYP: 1964-present)

The role played by UNFICYP can be divided into two periods of
operation: the first period, between 1964 and 1974, presented UNFICYP
with a different set of problems to those which it faced in the second period
initiated by the Turkish invasion in 1974. Any analysis of UNFICYP must
therefore, take these differences into account. Between 1964 and 1974 the
UN was to have no clear dividing lines along which it could separate both
the Greek and Turkish Cypriot communities. Rather, as in West Irian, it
had to act more like a police force to prevent clashes and negotiate disputes
at a local level. Since the Turkish invasion in 1974, however, UNFICYP's
role has been to create and maintain a buffer zone between the two
communities.
  Cyprus became independent in August 1960 on the basis that it would
become a republic with a government that was specially formed to take into
account the ethnic and cultural mix of the population (approximately 80 per
cent Greek Cypriot and 20 per cent Turkish Cypriot). Intent on preserving
the rights of the minority the colonial power, Britain, formed a constitution
which was heavily weighted in favour of the Turkish Cypriots. Whilst
comprising only 20 per cent of the population, they were given 40 per cent
of the army, 30 per cent of the legislature, civil service and police and the
Vice-President, always to be a Turk, was given a veto in matters of
defence and foreign policy.[38] It is possible to argue that rather than
safeguarding the Turkish Cypriots' position this arrangement exacerbated
the divisions between the two comunities, particularly as the majority of
Greek Cypriots favoured *Enosis* (union with Greece), thus setting into
motion a decline into inter-communal violence.[39] This violence came to
a head after Archbishop Makarios (the first President of Cyprus) proposed
a set of constitutional changes in 1963 which would have minimized
Turkish Cypriot rights.

The UN was not directly concerned with this initial crisis. Instead the British provided a force which managed to deter further violent clashes, but this clearly was not an acceptable long-term solution. Inevitably, in February 1964, the worsening situation came before the UN Security Council which adopted Resolution 186 establishing UNFICYP, initially for a period of three months.[40]

The overall function of UNFICYP was to interpose itself between the Greek and Turkish communities and at the same time avoid any action which may influence the political situation. It is important to remember that the UN was, at the start of the Cyprus crisis, still involved in enforcement action in the Congo from what had started as a very neutral position in 1960. Nevertheless, the one crucial factor which distinguished the Cypriot crisis from the Congo was the Secretary General's own interpretation. The Congolese crisis had, to Hammarskjold, been a serious threat to regional peace as underlined in Article 39 of the Charter.[41] U Thant's interpretation, however, made it possible for UNFICYP to have a mandate similar to that of UNEF I - that of consensual type peacekeeping.

The UN's peacekeeping efforts in Cyprus are also important for another crucial factor. In addition to providing a force to maintain peace, the Secretary General undertook steps to provide a mediator for the purpose of promoting a peaceful solution to the crisis in parallel with the peacekeeping operation itself. This was an important development for UN peacekeeping since rarely had the UN sought to pursue political settlements in the past. However, it was becoming recognized that peacemaking efforts were as important as the establishment of peacekeeping missions themselves. The UN's efforts in Cyprus were frustrated, however, due to the deep-seated antagonism between the two communities. Despite this volatile mix, UNFICYP did manage to maintain overall peace until 1974 when the situation changed drastically due to Turkey's invasion of Cyprus.

When the new ceasefire came into effect in mid-August 1974 the Turkish and Turkish Cypriot forces were in control of the northern half of the country. UNFICYP was now faced with a very different set of circumstances to those which prevailed prior to the invasion. Since 1974 UNFICYP has maintained a buffer zone between the areas controlled by the opposing forces. The ceasefire line was now to extend 180 miles across the island, and strict adherence to the military status quo in the buffer zone became a vital element in preventing a recurrence of fighting. It can be argued that since 1974 the situation on the ground has been calmer partly due to the fact that the UN had interposed itself between the two sides over a relatively well-defined area. Humanitarian duties were also entrusted to UNFICYP during and after the 1974 invasion and the Force endeavoured to protect civilians caught up in the hostilities. This was important since nearly one-third of the population of Cyprus became homeless as a direct result of the invasion.

Since 1974, in the absence of a formal ceasefire agreement and political settlement, UNFICYP has continued to separate the two communities. Little progress towards a long-term political solution has been made, however, and it is even possible to argue that by interposing itself between the two communities the UN has reduced any chances of achieving a lasting peace.   In light of these developments a clear lesson for UN peacekeeping efforts has been reaffirmed by the Cyprus saga. That is the importance of combining peacekeeping activities with the continued and viable search for a durable peace.

United Nations India Pakistan Observer Mission (UNIPOM: 1965-1966)

The ongoing hostility between India and Pakistan provides a classic example of the failure of both the disputants and the Security Council to address long-term issues.   Mediation efforts during the 1965 war clearly indicated how long-term solutions were overlooked in exchange for short-term gain in the form of a ceasefire. The intention here is not to place the blame on the UN but, rather, to point out how weakly placed the Security Council was, during the Cold War, to coerce the disputants to compromise.

As noted earlier, UNMOGIP was largely successful in carrying out its functions until 1965. Then, however, increased tensions between India and Pakistan led to hostilities across the line patrolled by UNMOGIP in Kashmir.   This time, wider factors contributed to full scale war.   These centred primarily around conflicting claims over territory at the southern point of the two states' common international border. Unable to reach a compromise over the issue, tensions steadily rose during 1965 leading to war in August.

Unlike conflicts elsewhere, such as those which resulted in the setting up of UNSCOB and UNEF I, this time the Security Council demonstrated that it could put up a front of unity.   During September 1965 the Security Council adopted three resolutions which called upon the opponents to cease all hostilities and return to the positions occupied before 5 August 1965.[42] Another tougher resolution, Resolution 211, adopted on 20 September, took into account the fact that the hostilities had spread along the whole Indian-Pakistani border and consequently demanded that a ceasefire take effect immediately.[43] This resolution also requested the Secretary General to provide the necessary assistance to supervise the withdrawal of troops from both sides. Unable to either take Kashmir by force or induce the Security

Council to force a long-term solution in favour of a plebiscite in Kashmir, Pakistan informed the Security Council that it would agree to a ceasefire.

The Security Council established another observer mission to complement the work of UNMOGIP. UNIPOM was established as a temporary measure for the purpose of supervising the ceasefire along the border between India and Pakistan, outside the state of Kashmir, and to supervise the withdrawal of Indian and Pakistani troops and equipment. Despite numerous ceasefire violations during the course of its existence UNIPOM reported, on 26 February 1966, that the disputants had completed their withdrawal on schedule. Consequently, having fulfilled its mandate successfully UNIPOM was terminated on 22 March 1966 leaving UNMOGIP to continue to function as before.[44]

The 1973 Arab-Israeli War: United Nations Emergency Force II (UNEF II: 1974-1979) and United Nations Disengagement Observer Force (UNDOF: 1974-present)

UNEF II

A detailed analysis of the events between the years 1967 and 1973 is beyond the remit of this book. Yet one event in particular is important as it clearly demonstrated the weaknesses of peacekeeping. Two more Arab-Israeli wars were to start and finish between 1967 and 1973. The first came about as a result of increased hostility between Syria and Israel, prompting Egypt to demand the withdrawal of UNEF I which then paved the way for armed conflict between Egypt and Israel. The fact that UNEF I had to withdraw upon Egypt's insistence conclusively illustrated the limitations of peacekeeping.

This, and the failure to address the underlying problems between Israel and its neighbours, meant that conflict was always conceivable. This included the bitter artillery exchanges between Egypt and Israel during the lengthy War of Attrition.[45] The second war, which resulted in the creation of UNEF II and UNDOF began when Syria and Egypt launched surprise attacks against Israel in October 1973. In the Israeli-Egyptian sector, UNEF II was not only important in re-establishing a buffer zone between Israel and Egypt but it also helped to diffuse a crisis which had threatened to bring about a direct superpower confrontation in the Middle East. Hailed as the most serious threat to world peace since the Cuban Missile Crisis, the 1973 war between Egypt and Israel had to be diffused quickly and so UNEF II was to concentrate on consolidating short-term peace by interposing itself between the Egyptian and Israeli forces, setting up observation posts, and investigating complaints. Consequently, the acceptance by Israel and Egypt of a UN presence not only had the effect of diffusing the local crisis but also helped reduce superpower tensions.

Following the Israeli withdrawal from much of Egyptian territory in the Sinai desert UNEF II assumed the longer-term functions in its mandate, successfully performed now that a much wider UN buffer zone had been established. Military Observers from UNTSO also worked with UNEF II to observe at the various checkpoints. The Force continued to fulfil its functions until 1979 when the Camp David agreement between Israel and Egypt rendered its mandate redundant.

UNDOF

UNDOF was the second peacekeeping operation to emerge out of the 1973 Arab-Israeli war. Whereas UNEF II was deployed between the Egyptian and Israeli armies in the Suez Canal area, UNDOF was established to supervise the implementation of a disengagement agreement between Israeli and Syrian forces in the Golan Heights. Although the tension in the Israeli-Egyptian sector was diffused rapidly with the arrival of UNEF II, the tensions in the Israeli-Syrian sector remained high and even increased in March 1974. At this time the United States turned its attention to the war between Syria and Israel and a round of diplomatic initiatives began which concluded on 31 May 1974 with an Agreement on Disengagement.

Apart from calling upon Israel and Syria to observe a ceasefire the Agreement proposed the establishment of a buffer zone between the two sides to be patrolled by a UN force. UNDOF was initially authorized for a period of six months, but continued to have its mandate renewed periodically. Following the ceasefire, the Golan Heights was separated into two zones. The first, known as the area of separation, was a completely demilitarized buffer zone. The other zone, an area of limitation, lay on either side of the demilitarized buffer zone in which both the Israelis and Syrians are permitted to have limited amounts of personnel and equipment. UNDOF's mandate contained provisions which related to the patrolling of these two zones. As part of its mandate the Force was authorized to investigate alleged violations by either side. UNDOF undoubtedly contributed greatly to the calm situation which has prevailed since 1974. Since its deployment neither the Israelis nor the Syrians have made any military moves to upset the status quo and conditions were created for a peace process to develop in the 1990s.

The Quiescent Period (1974-1987)

Once UNDOF had been set up, the UN withdrew considerably from new peacekeeping operations. From 1974 to the end of the Cold War only one new operation, in the form of UNIFIL, was created even though other missions such as UNTSO, UNMOGIP, and UNFICYP remained in existence. This significant withdrawal from peacekeeping appeared to be a reaction to the fact that the UN had overstretched itself considerably. Financial crises and disenchantment on the part of contributing states had set in. UNIFIL itself demonstrated all that had gone wrong with UN peacekeeping. High costs, refusal on the part of Member states to pay their assessments, lack of consent and co-operation on the part of the disputants all showed that peacekeeping operations could only fulfil their mandates successfully if most of the criteria for peacekeeping were present.

UNIFIL was set up in order to supervise the withdrawal of Israeli forces from Lebanon and restore peace. The Palestine Liberation Organisation (PLO) repeatedly conducted raids into Israeli territory from bases in surrounding countries. Lebanon, itself a highly unstable state was ill-placed to play host to a powerful organisation, and the presence of the PLO had the effect of exacerbating the already tense conditions throughout the country. Civil war in 1975 between Christian and Muslim groups introduced Syria into the highly complex equation when it sent troops into Lebanon claiming that its intention was to stabilize the situation. However, the Syrian action did nothing to limit the PLO's attacks on Israel from Lebanese territory.

With the situation tense and Jewish deaths high, Israel decided to invade Lebanon on 14 March 1978 with the intention of destroying PLO bases. This unilateral action, however, considerably concerned the US which feared that the invasion would upset the chances of concluding a peace treaty with Egypt.[46] Consequently, the US turned to the UN and within four days the Security Council adopted Resolutions 425 and 426 which called upon Israel to immediately cease all military activity and withdraw its forces from Lebanon. The Security Council also decided

> ... in light of the request of the Government of Lebanon, to establish immediately under its authority a United Nations interim force for Southern Lebanon for the purpose of confirming the withdrawal of Israeli forces, restoring international peace and security and assisting the Government of Lebanon in ensuring the return of its effective authority in the area ...[47]

The first UNIFIL troops arrived on 23 March 1978. Between 1978 and 1982, however, UNIFIL was unable to fulfil its mandate for a number of reasons. Resolution 425 of the Council had not addressed the civil war in Lebanon which had meant that the Lebanese Government had not been able to control Southern Lebanon for a number of years, and was in no condition to assume responsibility. Also, both the PLO and Israel did not accept UNIFIL's mandate. Given, in particular, the Israeli attitude UNIFIL was unable to deploy in areas evacuated by Israel as it began its withdrawal. In fact, the Israeli army was to hand much of the control of Southern Lebanon to allied Christian militias which refused to co-operate with either the Lebanese government or UNIFIL.

As such, this region in Southern Lebanon was to remain under Israeli control, thus frustrating UNIFIL's chances of fulfilling its mandate. The UN mission found that it could not move freely and its troops were regularly fired upon by members of numerous different factions. There were also differing interpretations of UNIFIL's mandate. The Israelis justified their own continued presence in South Lebanon on the grounds that UNIFIL had failed to clear the area of PLO fighters. The PLO on the other hand, continued to maintain that the Cairo Agreement of 1969 had allowed them a semi-autonomous regime in the refugee camps in Southern Lebanon and that UNIFIL had no mandate superior to this.[48]

The PLO continued to attack Israeli settlements in Northern Israel which prompted the latter to launch its second invasion of Lebanon in June 1982 this time determined to expel the PLO fighters. Israeli troops overran UNIFIL positions entirely and reached the outskirts of Beirut in early July. It would be inappropriate to blame UNIFIL for not stopping the Israeli invasion as it neither had the mandate nor the means with which to oppose a large force. The invasion drastically altered UNIFIL's position because for the next three years the UN operation was to remain *behind* Israeli lines.

In 1985 the Israelis did begin a partial withdrawal but continued to maintain a so-called security zone in the border area. This has meant that UNIFIL was still unable to complete its mandate. As a peacekeeping force, UNIFIL's record has not been good. Nevertheless, even in this case, its failure has been less to do with its own ability to carry out its functions, and it should be judged within the context of existing conditions. Despite being able to return some areas to Lebanese authority, the security zone in the south, in particular, remained under Israeli control and so UNIFIL has not been in a position to occupy this region. Another major problem during the 1980s was the Lebanese Government's own inability to manage and administer. Without effective central control UNIFIL's mandate did not have a chance of being fulfilled. As such, UNIFIL has clearly demonstrated that peacekeeping operations can only be successful if the appropriate conditions exist. Conditions such as cooperation among the disputants, which UNIFIL has lacked, are essential.

Conclusion

Analysis of the various peacekeeping operations during the Cold War shows that the different time periods are closely linked to each other. The *Birth of Peacekeeping*, depicted by the establishment of observer missions, provided the basis upon which the much larger and more ambitious operations of the *Assertive* period could develop. Operational norms such as impartiality and consent certainly emerged during the *Birth of Peacekeeping* but were not formalized until the establishment of UNEF I and UNOGIL in 1956 and 1958 respectively. UNEF I itself was the first mission of its kind consisting of a sizeable peacekeeping force whose job was to *secure* the ceasefire, as opposed to merely *observing*.

Links between the *Assertive* and *Quiescent* period can be made. During this final period only one new peacekeeping operation was set up, in many ways due to the experiences of the *Assertive* period. UNIFIL clearly highlighted the problems with peacekeeping that had begun to emerge during the *Assertive* period in particular. The mission demonstrated that for a peacekeeping operation to be successful the appropriate conditions have to exist and conditions such as cooperation among the disputants, Great Power interest, adequate resources and financial backing are as important for UN peacekeeping as the operational norms themselves.

Closely linked to the evolution of peacekeeping have been the roles played by the Secretary General and the General Assembly. As numerous case studies have shown the Secretary General has been instrumental in instituting a number of peacekeeping operations. This has clearly shown the close link between the position of Secretary General and the primary goal of the UN - that of maintaining international peace and security. The Secretary General's role emerged during the first period, and developed considerably later on, as shown by UNTEA, for instance. In West Irian the UN was to have, for the first time in its history, complete authority over a vast territory under the jurisdiction of the Secretary General. Other operations such as UNYOM and ONUC have also illustrated that the role played by the Secretary General was central.

Similarly, it was realised early that due to the high potential for deadlock within the Security Council the General Assembly would play an active role in adopting resolutions which established peacekeeping operations. On numerous occasions issues were removed from the Security Council under the Uniting for Peace resolution and placed before the General Assembly. Under this resolution the General Assembly had been given an increased role in the area of maintaining international peace and security. In this way, Cold War hostilities could be minimised, but it also enabled newly independent states to be introduced to peacekeeping issues.

A final issue of great importance which emerged during the Cold War was the extent of the Security Council's weakness in coercing disputants to compromise. As such the UN failed in its mediation efforts during numerous crises by overlooking long-term solutions for short-term gain in the form of signed ceasefires. This failure is demonstarted by the large number of long-standing disputes such as those in the Middle East, Cyprus and the Indian Sub-continent. However, peacekeeping was to be viewed in a completely new light as the Cold War came to an end, and it is to this period that the analysis now turns.

Suggested Reading

Abi-Saab, G., *The United Nations Operation in the Congo 1960-1964*, Oxford University Press, 1978.

Barker, A.J., *Suez: the seven day war*, London, Faber and Faber Ltd., 1964.

The blue helmets: a review of United Nations peacekeeping, United Nations, 1990.

Crawshaw, N., *The Cyprus revolt: an account of the struggle for union with Greece*, London, George Allen & Unwin, 1978.

Dayal, R., *Mission for Hammarskjold: the Congo crisis*, London, Oxford University Press, 1976.

Durch, W.J., *The evolution of UN peacekeeping*, New York, St. Martin's Press, 1993.

Higgins, R., *United Nations peacekeeping, documents and commentary, IV, Europe 1946-1979*, Oxford University Press, 1981.

Higgins, R., *United Nations peacekeeping, documents and commentary, III, Africa 1946-1967*, Oxford University Press, 1980.

Higgins, R., *United Nations peacekeeping 1946-1967, documents and commentary II, Asia*, London, Oxford University Press, 1970.

James, A., 'The Congo controversies', *International peacekeeping*, vol.1, no.1, Essex, Frank Cass and Company Ltd., Spring 1994.

James, A., *Peacekeeping in international politics*, London, Macmillan, 1990.

Kanza, T., *The rise and fall of Patrice Lumumba: conflict in the Congo*, London, Rex Collings, 1978.

Pappe, I., *The making of the Arab-Israeli conflict, 1947-51*, New York, I.B. Tauris and Co. Ltd., 1992.

Notes

1. The various acronyms stand for, UNEF - United Nations Emergency Force, ONUC - United Nations Operation in the Congo, UNSCOB - United Nations Special Commission on the Balkans, UNTSO - United Nations Truce Supervision Organization.

2. Goulding, M., 'The evolution of United Nations peacekeeping', *International Affairs,* vol.69, no.3, July 1993, p.452.

3. Higgins, R., *United Nations peacekeeping, documents and commentary, IV Europe 1946-1979,* Oxford University Press, 1981, pp.5-7.

4. Birgisson, K. Th., 'United Nations Special Committee on the Balkans', in ed., Durch, W. J., *The evolution of United Nations peacekeeping,* New York, St. Martin's Press, 1993, pp.77-79.

5. Liu, F.T., *United Nations peacekeeping and the non-use of force,* London, Lynne Rienner Publishers Inc., 1992, p.13.

6. Pogany, I. S., *The Security Council and the Arab-Israeli conflict,* England, Gower Publishing Company Ltd., 1984, pp.21-22.

7. Ibid., p.35.

8. Cattan, H., *Palestine, the Arabs and Israel: the search for justice,* London, Longmans, 1969, pp.34-36.

9. Wiseman, H., 'United Nations peacekeeping: an historical overview', in *Peacekeeping: appraisals and proposals,* edited by Idem, New York, Pergamon Press, 1982, p.28.

10. James, A., *Peacekeeping in international politics,* London, Macmillan, 1990, pp.154-156.

11. James, A., ibid., p.158.

12. Karl, Th. B., 'UN Military Observer Group in India and Pakistan' in ed., Durch, *The evolution of peacekeeping,* op.cit, p.274.

13. James, op.cit, pp.158-163.

14. The size of the force was gradually increased to around 6,000. See Burns, A. L., and Heathcote, N., *Peacekeeping by UN forces,* London, Pall Mall Press Ltd., 1963, p.9.

15. Wiseman, op.cit, p.32.

16. cf.*Resolution 998 (ES-1) in Official Records of the General Assembly, First Emergency Special Session, Supplement No.1 (A/3354),* p.2, 4 November 1956.

17. Idem.

18. *Official Records of the General Assembly, First Emergency Special Session, Annexes,* document *A/3302,* 1956.

19. Salibi, K. S., *Crossroads to civil war: Lebanon 1958-1976,* London, Ithaca Press, 1976, p.13.

20. Burns and Heathcote, op.cit, p.19. The only time when a Permanent Member was involved as part of a UN peacekeeping operation during the Cold War was in the case of the UN mission in Cyprus which contained British soldiers.

21. Secretary General Dag Hammarskjold was killed in a plane crash on his way to meet President Tshombe of Katanga. This was to further complicate the UN's efforts in expelling foreign mercenaries from the Congo.

22. Abi-Saab, G., *The United Nations Operation in the Congo: 1960-1964,* Oxford University Press, 1978, p.2.

23. Ibid., p.5.

24. cf.*Security Council document, S/4387, Resolution 143,* 14 July 1960.

25. cf.Idem.

26. Dayal, R., *Mission for Hammarskjold: the Congo crisis,* London, Oxford University Press, 1976, p.7.

27. Abi-Saab, op.cit, pp.12-13.

28. This was to change later, however, as the question of the succession of Katanga came before the Council.

29.   *The blue helmets: A review of United Nations peacekeeping,* United
      Nations, second edition, p.220.

30.   *Security Council document, S/4405, Resolution 145,* 22 July 1960.

31.   White, N.D., *Keeping the peace: the United Nations and the
      maintenance of international peace and security,* Manchester
      University Press, 1993, p.236.

32.   James, op.cit, p.295.

33.   White, op.cit, pp.235-236.

34.   Durch, W. J., 'United Nations Temporary Executive Authority', ed.
      Durch, *The evolution of UN peacekeeping,* op.cit, p.285.

35.   Ibid., pp.288-289.

36.   Birgisson, Karl Th., 'United Nations Observation Mission', in ibid.,
      p.215.

37.   Ibid., pp.210-211.

38.   Vernier, op.cit, pp.80-81.

39.   For a detailed account of the Cyprus issue see Crawshaw, N., *The
      Cyprus revolt: an account of the struggle for union with Greece,*
      London, George Allen & Unwin, 1978.

40.   *Security Council document, SC Res.186 (1964),* 4 March 1964.

41.   Article 39 states that 'The Security Council shall determine the
      existence of any threat to the peace, breach of the peace, or act of
      aggression and shall make recommendations, or decide what
      measures shall be taken ...'.

42.   The Security Council adopted Resolution 209 on 4 September 1965.
      Resolution 210 was adopted two days later. Both Resolutions called
      upon the states to agree on a ceasefire and Resolution 210
      specifically provided for the strengthening of UNMOGIP. See *The
      blue helmets,* op.cit, pp.162-163.

43.   Idem. The date from which the Security Council demanded that the
      ceasefire take effect was 22 September.

44. *The blue helmets,* op.cit, pp.165-166.

45. The War of Attrition lasted for almost two years. The fighting, although intense, was limited to artillery exchanges as opposed to troop movements.

46. James, op.cit, p.340.

47. cf.*Security Council document, S/RES/425 (1978),* 19 March 1978.

48. Evron, Y., *War and intervention in Lebanon,* London, Croom Helm Ltd., 1987, p.8.

Chapter 3
The Rebirth of Peacekeeping

Introduction

As the 1980s began, few people could have predicted the dramatic changes which were to take place within the international political system by the end of the decade. The election of Mikhail Gorbachev as General Secretary of the USSR in 1985 heralded an end to over four decades of ideological conflict and effectively eradicated the risk of military confrontation. Spurred on by domestic financial problems, both superpowers sought peace dividends by ending overtly expensive support for regimes in areas of the world which they no longer deemed to be in their national interest. The international community, caught up in the euphoria brought about by the expectation of a new peaceful age, hoped that all that would be required was a method of overseeing the conclusion of conflicts, which had resulted from, and been sustained by, a now defunct global rivalry. It was in this context that the United Nations, after over ten years of quiescence, was to experience a renaissance unprecedented since its inception in 1945.

The requests for the United Nations to become involved in helping the superpowers disengage and assist the conflict ridden nations left behind find lasting peace, were to provide badly needed opportunities for the UN to renew peacekeeping's visibility and perceived workability in the international arena of conflict resolution.[1] These opportunities were not to go to waste. Before the end of 1991 the UN had established ten new peacekeeping operations covering all areas of the globe. This rapid expansion, however, was to be the Organisation's undoing. Less than ten months later the UN had realised that its resources for planning, deploying and maintaining operations in the field were totally inadequate for the number, size and complexity of the operations which the international community had called upon it to conduct. During 1993, therefore, the UN was again to experience a crisis of credibility, as the unforeseen humanitarian catastrophes in the former Yugoslavia and Somalia overwhelmed the Organisation, bringing it ever closer to breaking point. Less than seven years after UN peacekeeping had been awarded the Nobel Peace Prize, the international community began to reassess its understanding of the nature of conflict and the UN's ability to resolve it.

The remainder of this book will, therefore, attempt to understand the evolution of peacekeeping in the post-Cold War period. It begins with the contention that the successes of the peacekeeping operations in the renaissance period of 1988-91 caused the UN to overlook the inherent inadequacies in its ability to conduct large multi-dimensional peacekeeping operations. This oversight led the Organisation to commit itself to ever larger and more complex operations, until the realisation of its weaknesses was driven home by the failure of the second Angolan operation in October 1992. This expansion of UN peacekeeping will be covered in Chapter 4. The crisis in the UN's credibility will be discussed in Chapter 5. This chapter will show how the realisation of the UN's lack of resources and its failure to predict the consequences of the use of force in peacekeeping operations during 1993, caused many to question the UN's role in conflict resolution. And the final chapter will show how the international community's reaction to the UN's problems were to have horrific consequences in Rwanda and leave the UN looking both ineffectual and irrelevant.

The following chapters will, therefore, take the relevant period in peacekeeping's post-Cold War evolution and describe the background and mandates of the operations established within that period. After assessing the successes it will continue to describe the problems experienced in each operation and within the Organisation itself. Finally, each chapter will include a discussion of the factors which helped the UN succeed or fail during its operations. For the sake of clarity, a distinction has been made between the operations established to help implement negotiated peace settlements and those which emerged on an *ad hoc* basis in reaction to humanitarian crises. For this reason each chapter will end with both a description and discussion of events in the UN's role in humanitarian operations.

TABLE 3: Peacekeeping Operations established 1988-1991

Mission	Brief Explanation
UN Good Offices Mission in Afghanistan and Pakistan (UNGOMAP) 1988-90	Monitor Soviet withdrawal from Afghanistan
UN Iran-Iraq Military Observer Group (UNIIMOG) 1988-91	Monitor ceasefire at the conclusion of Iran-Iraq war
UN Angolan Verification Mission (UNAVEM I) 1988-91	Monitor Cuban withdrawal from Angola
UN Transitional Assistance Group (UNTAG) 1989-90	Supervise transition to independence from South African rule in Namibia
UN Observer Group in Central America (ONUCA) 1989-91	Monitor compliance with Esquipulas II agreement and assist in demobilisation of Nicaraguan Contras
UN Angolan Verification Mission II and III (UNAVEM II and III) 1991-95	Monitor ceasefire and creation of new army and holding of elections
UN Iraq-Kuwait Observer Mission (UNIKOM) 1991-present	Monitor buffer zone between Iraq and Kuwait after Gulf War
UN Mission for the Referendum in Western Sahara (MINURSO) 1991-present	Conduct, organise and verify referendum on independence from Morocco
UN Observer Mission in El Salvador (ONUSAL) 1991-95	Monitor human rights; ceasefire; demobilisation and reintegration of forces; monitor elections
UN Advanced Mission in Cambodia (UNAMIC) 1991-92	Advance planning for UNTAC
UN Transitional Authority in Cambodia (UNTAC) 1992-93	Supervise government functions and elections; disarmament and demobilisation; repatriation and rehabilitation of refugees

United Nations Good Offices Mission in Afghanistan and Pakistan (UNGOMAP: 1988-1990)

The first three new peacekeeping operations established by the UN in nearly ten years were all to be observer missions and the first of these was

UNGOMAP. As such, UNGOMAP was to be the first ever UN mission to be conducted in a conflict which had involved either of the Cold War superpowers. In this case, the Soviet Union, which had invaded the country in 1979, ostensibly to aid the nominal government of Afghanistan maintain law and order, had redefined its geo-political goals and sought to extract itself from a conflict which had brought heavy casualties and increasing domestic unrest. On the basis of the Geneva Accords, signed on 14 April 1988, the Secretary General, Javier Perez de Cuellar, dispatched a group of 50 military observers to Afghanistan and Pakistan, to monitor the implementation of the agreements which became operational on 15 May. The Geneva Accords, formally known as the Agreements on the Settlement of the Situation Relating to Afghanistan, consisted of four instruments. The first was a bilateral agreement between the governments of Afghanistan and Pakistan on the principles of mutual relations, particularly the principles of non-interference and non-intervention; the second consisted of a declaration on international guarantees, signed by the USSR and US; the third was another bilateral agreement between Afghanistan and Pakistan, this time on the voluntary return of refugees; and the final and most important instrument was the agreement on the inter-relationship for the settlement of the situation relating to Afghanistan, signed by Afghanistan and Pakistan and witnessed by the USSR and US.[2] This final instrument was the most important for the UN because it covered the provisions for the phased withdrawal of approximately 103,000 Soviet troops, based in 18 garrisons in 17 of the 30 Afghan provinces.[3]

Perhaps the most complicating factor of the Geneva Accords was that the various mujahideen, which together had formed the vast bulk of the Afghan resistance, had not been party to their negotiation. They did not, therefore, feel obliged to allow the Soviet forces to withdraw peacefully, or to end their campaign against the nominal Afghan government, simply because the Soviets were leaving. The result was an effective postponement of Soviet withdrawal from mid-August to late January 1989, whilst the Soviets brought in reinforcements to ensure that the Kabul regime could defend against guerilla attacks from areas the Red Army had recently vacated and the mujahideen had subsequently recaptured. Withdrawal did eventually take place, however, with the last soldiers leaving in mid February. With withdrawal complete, UNGOMAP's mandate was terminated on 15 March 1990.

United Nations Iran-Iraq Military Observer Group (UNIIMOG: 1988-1991)

The second observer mission, the UN Iran-Iraq Military Observer Group, was established pursuant to Security Council Resolution 598 on 8 August

1988, to monitor the ceasefire which had been accepted by both sides at the culmination of the eight year old Gulf war. The mandate of UNIIMOG included the establishment of ceasefire lines in co-operation with the parties; monitoring compliance with the ceasefire; investigation of violations; prevention, through negotiation of any other change in the *status quo* pending withdrawal of their respective forces to internationally recognised boundaries; to supervise, verify and confirm the withdrawal of all forces to these internationally recognised boundaries; and to obtain the agreement of the parties to other arrangements which, pending negotiation of a comprehensive settlement, could help reduce tension and build confidence between them.[4] UNIIMOG consisted of 350 observers from 26 countries with 105 international and 93 local staff, together with 53 military staff.

The success of UNIIMOG was, as in all observer missions, totally dependent on the co-operation of both parties. Worries were, therefore, increased when several hundred prisoners of war were captured by Iraq on 23-24 August 1989, only days after UNIIMOG had deployed. Violations of the agreements did continue, but apart from the flooding of an area of no-mans land in the Kursk region by the Iranians, in order to create a water obstacle between the two opposing armies, the majority were to be only minor contraventions.[5] As UNIIMOG's mandate also included the oversight of exchange of POW's this initial action did not bear well for the mission's future. However, subsequent co-operation allowed UNIIMOG to acquit its mandate successfully, although the final momentum to seek a permanent peaceful solution was only to be provided by Iraq's need to pacify the border so that it could transfer troops to fight the coalition forces during the Second Gulf War of 1990-91. It was, therefore, a little ironic, that whilst the UN was mandating a coalition of multinational forces to urge Iraq to withdraw behind its border with Kuwait, it was also monitoring the peaceful withdrawal of Iraqi troops behind its internationally recognised border with Iran.

United Nations Angolan Verification Mission (UNAVEM I: 1988-1991)

The third observer mission was to have a similar mandate to that of UNGOMAP. As will be discussed in greater detail later in this chapter, UNAVEM was to take place as the first stage of a comprehensive political settlement designed to bring independence to the South-West African state of Namibia. Few regions of Africa were ever free of the ideological conflict of the Cold War, and Southern Africa was among the worst affected. With support from the Soviet Union and Cuba, the *Movimento*

Popular de Lieragao de Angola (MPLA) finally succeeded in winning the civil war which had begun in 1975, after the transitional government leading Angola out of Portuguese dependence collapsed in August of that year. With the South African government attempting to destabilise the country by conducting raids into Angolan territory, ostensibly to capture SWAPO guerillas escaping from Namibia, the MPLA government requested an increase in the number of Cuban troops deployed on its territory. By 1988 the number of Cuban troops was estimated at 50,000.

UNAVEM's mission began after the signing of peace agreements among the states of South Africa, Angola and Cuba on 22 December 1988, and was mandated through SC Resolution 626 (1988) of 20 December to 'verify the redeployment northwards and the phased and total withdrawal of Cuban troops from the territory of Angola in accordance with the timetable agreed between Angola and Cuba'.[6] At its peak UNAVEM consisted of 70 unarmed military observers, 22 international and 15 local staff.

The Bilateral Agreement signed between Angola and Cuba established a 27 month long four phased withdrawal. The first phase lasting from April to October 1989 was to see 50.3 percent or 25,181 combatants repatriated at a rate of over 3,600 per month. The second phase, covering October to 30 March 1990 ended one month late due to the actions of the resistance group *Uniao Nacional para a Independencia Total de Angola* (UNITA).[7] As had been the case in Afghanistan, the resistance faction in Angola, UNITA, which had previously been supported by South Africa and the US, was not party to the settlement negotiations. It therefore, on occasions, continued to attack Cuban troops. On 23 January 1990, the Cuban military authorities in Angola informed the Chief Military Observer that withdrawal of their troops would be suspended in reaction to a UNITA attack two days earlier against a Cuban water purification plant near Lobito in which four Cuban soldiers had died. However, it was obviously not in UNITA's long term interests to prevent the Cubans from leaving and so a resumption of the process took place on 25 February 1990 after an agreement mediated by the Secretary General.[8] By the end of April, 33,048 troops, or 66 percent of the total number had been withdrawn. By the end of the third phase in September 1990 76 percent had been repatriated, and by the culmination of the final phase in May 1991 the total had reached 47,090. The final Cuban soldier left on 25 June 1991 with the Cuban authorities declaring that: 'On that date, the government of the People's Republic of Cuba and the government of the Republic of Angola will have honoured in exemplary fashion, 36 days before the deadline, the bilateral commitment which they undertook before the UN and the international community'.[9]

United Nations Transitional Assistance Group (UNTAG: 1989-1990)

The first major peacekeeping operation to be undertaken by the UN in the post-Cold War period was to be the effective 'decolonialisation' of South West Africa into the independent state of Namibia. The first suggestions for the UN to become involved in Namibia were made as early as 1978 when the group of states known as the 'Western Five', including West Germany, Canada, France, Britain and the US, proposed a settlement plan to the Security Council which envisaged the creation of a UN peacekeeping body to supervise free and fair elections of a Constituent Assembly. The democratically elected Assembly would then be mandated to construct a constitution for the newly independent state. Although this plan was approved by the Security Council in Resolution 435 (1978) it was not to be until ten years later that the plan could actually come to fruition. With the election of Ronald Reagan, the US negotiation team, headed by then Assistant Secretary of State Chester A. Crocker, broke away from the Western Five negotiations and attempted to negotiate a settlement unilaterally. Due to the more confrontational stance of the new Reagan administration with its perceived communist enemies, the US began to link the prospect of an independent Namibia with the requirement of Angola to remove its Cuban troops. Although, in the beginning, the South Africans had not themselves made this linkage, they soon realised that by making it a prerequisite of their acquiescence for the creation of UNTAG, they could effectively stall the settlement negotiations.[10] Crocker himself proposed the linkage, citing his belief that 'the prospects for reconciliation and negotiated political change within states (in this case Angola, Namibia and South Africa) was directly affected by the climate of security (or insecurity) between them'.[11] The Security Council and General Assembly, however, opposed the linkage, the former rejecting in Resolution 566 (1985), 'South Africa's insistence on linking the independence of Namibia to irrelevant and extraneous issues as incompatible with Resolution 435'.[12] It was not, therefore, to be until the relaxation of tensions between the superpowers that the Cuban withdrawal was made politically possible, leading to the signing of the trilateral Namibian Accords (Angola, South Africa and Cuba) on 22 December 1988. This allowed the implementation of Resolution 435 to proceed, although by now it had been extended and modified substantially.

On 16 January 1989 the Security Council adopted Resolution 629 specifying that the implementation of Resolution 435 should begin on 1 April.[13] On its establishment UNTAG was given three main objectives; to monitor democratic elections; to monitor the actions of the South West African Police (SWAPOL); and to monitor the ceasefire. These duties were to be the respective responsibility of UNTAG's civilian electoral personnel, civilian police monitors and military component.[14] Although the elections were to be under the 'supervision and control' of the SGSR, they were still to be 'organised and conducted' by the South African Administrator General. Technically this meant that the SGSR had at 'each stage, level and place [to] satisfy himself that the conduct and the procedure of the election, including the establishment of the list of candidates, the taking of the poll, the determination of the results of the poll, and the declaration of the results of the election are fair and appropriate.'[15] The elections for the Constituent Assembly were held from 7 to 11 November 1989 and were declared free and fair by the SGSR on 14 November.

The monitoring of the SWAPOL was the responsibility of the UN police monitors (CIVPOL), one of six elements within UNTAG's civilian component.[16] The importance of this role was increased when, after the UN had supervised the retention of all military personnel to base, SWAPOL became the only effective means of intimidation left available to the South African authorities. When as a result of this, complaints about SWAPOL conduct in the north of the country began to intensify, the UN responded by steadily enlarging its CIVPOL contingent to an eventual size of 1,500. As the elections approached, however, most of the CIVPOL's were assigned to election related duties.

The military component of UNTAG was charged with the duty of monitoring the ceasefire which included the responsibility of restricting the South African troops to recognised bases and eventually overseeing their phased withdrawal; monitoring the conduct of those South African military personnel who continued to perform civilian duties; dismantling the command structures of citizen forces, commando units and ethnic forces and confinement of their arms; disarming SWAPO guerillas before their repatriation and the restriction of remaining SWAPO troops to bases in Angola and Zambia. It was also responsible for monitoring the border to prevent infiltration and for the protection of entry points and reception centres for returning refugees. As will be discussed in greater detail later in this chapter, although the original plans for UNTAG had envisaged a military force of 7,500, the greater political nature of the operation which had evolved over the ten years after 1978 caused the Security Council to seek a reduction in the number of troops deployed. The number eventually deployed was 4,493.

United Nations Observer Group in Central America (ONUCA: 1989-1991)

Negotiations between the five Central American states of Honduras, Nicaragua, Guatemala, Costa Rica and El Salvador eventually produced an agreement signed in August 1987 which committed each of them to a number of pledges. In this agreement, known as the *'Esquipulas II'*, the five states promised to work towards national reconciliation; the cessation of hostilities; democratisation including freedom of the press and political pluralism and the ending of states of emergency; the holding of free and fair elections; ending support for irregular and insurrectionist forces and the prevention of the use of their territory for attacks on other states; and finally, to provide support for refugees and displaced persons.[17] Implementation of the agreement was to be frustrated, however, by the continuing hostilities between Nicaragua and Honduras over the presence of Nicaraguan Resistance members (commonly known as 'Contras'). Refusing to lay down their arms, the Contras were continuing to attack Nicaraguan held territory from bases in Honduras, causing the Sandanista government to attempt legal action against Honduras in the International Court of Justice. It was clear that no progress could be made on *Esquipulas II* whilst this action was pending.

The lack of adequate conditions to verify the implementation of the *Esquipulas II* was recognised by a joint UN/Organisation of American States (OAS) inspection team which had been sent to Central America following the signing of the agreement. In light of this the Secretary General refused to instigate a peacekeeping mission until circumstances produced a more conducive environment. The situation was to change, however, after a meeting held at Tesoro Beach in El Salvador in February 1989. At this meeting an agreement was reached to hold democratic elections in Nicaragua no later than 25 February 1990. In response to this the other four states agreed to develop a plan within 90 days for the voluntary demobilisation, repatriation or relocation of the Nicaraguan resistance and their families.[18] The Secretary General responded to the Nicaraguan government's request for the UN to monitor the elections by establishing the United Nations Observer Mission to Verify the Electoral Process in Nicaragua (ONUVEN) which became operational on 25 August 1989.

Earlier the same month, at a summit in Tela, Honduras, the Presidents of the five Central American states issued a Declaration and 'Joint Plan for the voluntary demobilisation, repatriation or relocation of the members of the Nicaraguan Resistance and their families, as well as assistance in the demobilisation of all those involved in armed actions in the countries of the region when they voluntarily seek it'.[19] To provide support for this process the Secretary Generals of the UN and OAS were requested to create an International Support and Verification Commission (CIAV). The establishment of the CIAV was announced on 25 August and was to take effect from 6 September. Also at Tela an agreement was struck between the governments of Nicaragua and Honduras with regard to the pending litigation at the ICJ. With this last obstacle out of the way, the Secretary General recommended the establishment of ONUCA to the Security Council on 11 October 1989.

ONUCA, established pursuant to Security Council Resolution 644 (1989) of 7 November 1989, was mandated only to conduct on-site verification of the security undertakings contained in the *Esquipulas II* Agreement. It could not proceed with the demobilisation of the Contra rebels until the Resistance members themselves agreed to it. This willingness was not shown until after the defeat of the Sandanista government in the elections of February 1990. ONUCA's mandate was subsequently expanded on two occasions, the first to accommodate demobilisation within Honduras, and the second to allow it to occur within Nicaragua itself. ONUCA was to be responsible for implementing the military aspects of the demobilisation process, i.e. taking delivery of the weapons, material and military equipment, including military uniforms, whilst all the civilian aspects of the process, including the repatriation, relocation and resettlement and subsequent monitoring of the welfare of members of the Resistance, were to be the responsibility of the CIAV[20]. To accommodate for the creation of five 'security zones' within Nicaragua, within which the Contras would demobilise, the Secretary General sought approval for an expansion of ONUCA's mandate. This approval was granted through SC Resolution 653 (1990) of 20 April 1990.

United Nations Iraq-Kuwait Observer Mission (UNIKOM: 1991-present)

The first mission to be instigated in the 1990s was to be the mission requested to monitor the border between Iraq and Kuwait after the Second Gulf War ended in March 1991. As the only peacekeeping operation to emerge from a Chapter VII enforcement action, UNIKOM, pursuant to SC Resolution 689 of 9 April 1991, was requested to monitor a de-militarised zone (DMZ) covering an area of the Iraq-Kuwait border. Created through SC Resolution 687 on 5 April, the de-militarised zone covered an area approximately 200 kilometres in length, stretching 10 km into Iraqi territory and 5km into Kuwait. UNIKOM was also requested to monitor the *Khawr 'Abd Allah* waterway which ran for about 40km between the two countries. UNIKOM was mandated to deter violations of the Iraq-Kuwait border through its presence in, and surveillance of, the de-militarised zone, and to observe any hostile action mounted from the territory of either state. Although created on an open-ended mandate, UNIKOM was to be reviewed every six months by the Security Council.

Throughout the operation UNIKOM has been careful not to create the impression that the de-militarised zone has come under UN authority, thereby attracting refugees seeking international protection. The responsibility for the maintenance of law and order has remained with the governments of the respective areas. UNIKOM, therefore, needed to post only one observer for every ten kilometres, with only the most basic of equipment, usually a pair of binoculars and a passive night vision device for each fixed observation post.[21]

United Nations Mission for the Referendum in Western Sahara (MINURSO: 1991-present)

As the first mission instigated in 1991, MINURSO was mandated to conduct, organise and verify a referendum designed to decide the political future of the indigenous population of the north-east African territory of Western Sahara. As colonial rulers since 1884, the Spanish, under pressure from both the international community and the internal liberation group *Frente Popular para la Liberacion de Saguia el-Hamra y de Rio* (POLISARIO), had decided to allow a referendum to take place in 1975 so as to resolve the question of the future status of the territory. For this purpose the Spanish administration conducted a population census which stated that, in 1974, Western Sahara had 95,019 residents of which 73,497 were indigenous.[22] The validity of this census has created the greatest debate and formed the major stumbling block of the whole MINURSO operation.

Before the Spanish sanctioned referendum could take place, however, Morocco conducted a 'Green March', in which 350,000 'volunteers' crossed into Western Sahara in order to reclaim the territory on 'historical' grounds. Whilst Morocco invaded from the north, Mauritania invaded from the South. This 'joint' invasion seemed to be the result of secret negotiations between the three countries which compensated the Spanish with special trade agreements for its withdrawal from the territory.[23] Supported by Algeria, Libya and Cuba, POLISARIO continued its fight for independence against the two invaders, a war which by February 1976 had incurred enough financial and material losses for Mauritania for it to relinquish all claims on Western Saharan territory. Morocco's response, however, was to invade the third of Western Sahara that Mauritania had subsequently relinquished.

In 1985, despite the acceptance by the Moroccan authorities, in principle, to hold a referendum on the future status of the territory, the Secretary General ruled out UN mediation of the conflict because of the lack of direct talks between the parties involved. However, Morocco's unwillingness to talk directly with POLISARIO was overcome by a compromise deal in which direct talks took place, although they were not officially recognised as such. With proposals for a UN role being made throughout 1988-91, the Security Council finally adopted Resolution 690 (1991) of 29 April 1991 establishing MINURSO.

The architecture of MINURSO was to be one of a 'quasi-governor-in-trust, responsible for administering-in-transition the last colony of Africa.'[24] As such MINURSO was to be the first UN operation charged with the authority to restrain local forces, identify and register voters; conduct a referendum; certify the results and supervise the losing side's withdrawal or disarmament. On 24 May 1991, in accordance with the plan, the Secretary General proposed that the ceasefire should enter into effect on 6 September. However, it soon became clear that MINURSO would not be able to complete a number of tasks, including the preparation of a list of voters, the confinement of combatants to barracks and the repatriation of refugees, before the ceasefire was to take effect. Despite violations of the informal ceasefire which had held for over two years, the Secretary General insisted that the settlement plan ceasefire should still come into effect on 6 September, although the transition period leading to the referendum would not begin until the outstanding tasks were completed. Despite the effective stability of the ceasefire from this date the referendum, initially planned for January 1992, has not been held. This has been due to the lack of cooperation which the UN has received from both parties, and the wide divergence of opinion between the Moroccan authorities and POLISARIO on the criteria which should be applied for voter eligibility.

United Nations Observer Mission in El Salvador (ONUSAL: 1991-1995)

In contrast to the conflict in neighbouring Nicaragua, the civil war in El Salvador was to see an American supported nominal government fighting against a leftist resistance faction, the FDR-FMLN (Democratic Revolutionary Front-Farabundo Marti Front for National Liberation). With both sides unable to make significant military advances, a stalemate had been reached on the battlefield by the mid 1980s. However, despite the willingness of the FDR-FMLN to seek a negotiated settlement, the influence of the US was to prevent any form of compromise until the demise of the Reagan administration in 1988. By that time the FDR had split with its former ally to form the *Convergencia Democratica* and entered democratic politics, and the right-wing *Alianza Republicana Nacionalista* (ARENA) had won an impressive victory in the legislative elections of the same year. Together with the election of the ARENA party leader, Alfredo Cristiani, to the presidency in 1989, these victories were to greatly enhance the confidence of the Right to enter some form of democratic political system. Equally, the FMLN's 'increased awareness of the possible loss of prestige and support that would ensue from the continuation of a civil war with little prospect of success', helped encourage the faction to enter into negotiations.[25] Despite these incentives a deep mistrust remained between the parties.

UN involvement in the conflict began in early 1990 when it organised secret meetings between the government and FMLN which eventually led to formal talks in April 1990.[26] On 26 July 1990, an Agreement on Human Rights signed between the two parties in San Jose, Costa Rica, provided for the establishment of a UN verification mission to monitor nationwide respect for, and guarantee of, human rights and fundamental freedoms. Although the agreement envisaged the mission would begin at the cessation of the armed conflict, the Secretary General was requested by both parties to send a preliminary mission to assess the feasibility of deployment before fighting had actually stopped. This mission was sent in March 1991 and the UN Operation in El Salvador (ONUSAL) was officially launched on 26 July 1991 pursuant to Security Council Resolution 693. Its initial mandate was to verify the parties' compliance with the commitments made under the San Jose Agreement.

To complete the peace negotiations three other agreements were signed between the parties. The Mexico Accord, signed on 27 April 1991, envisaged both the creation of a Truth Commission to investigate human rights violations since 1980, and the introduction of important reforms to the nation's Constitution. The second agreement, the New York Accord, was signed on 25 September 1991, and included provisions for the establishment of a National Commission for the Consolidation of Peace (COPAZ), a multiparty organ charged with the supervision of the peace agreements. And finally, the Chapultepec Agreement, signed on 16 January 1992 in Mexico City, which 'brought the parties to the end of more than a decade of internal conflict.'[27] This final agreement required a substantial enlargement of ONUSAL's mandate so as to include the verification of all aspects of the ceasefire and the separation of forces, and the monitoring of the maintenance of public order during the transition period whilst the new National Civil Police was being established. This enlarged mandate was accepted by the Security Council through resolution 729 two days before the Chapultepec Agreement was signed.

United Nations Angolan Verification Mission (UNAVEM II: 1991-1995)

The resistance groups which had fought to end Portuguese colonial rule in Angola had already turned on each other before independence was declared in 1975.[28] For 16 years the nominal government of Angola led by the MPLA, backed by the Soviet Union and Cuba, fought a bloody civil war with the US and South African supported UNITA. A combination of military stalemate and the cessation of military and financial support at the end of the Cold War persuaded both parties to engage in dialogue leading to a negotiated peace settlement in 1991. On 31 May, President Jose Eduardo dos Santos and Jonas Savimbi, the respective heads of the MPLA government and UNITA, signed the Peace Accords for Angola which, after establishing a ceasefire, included plans for democratic elections and the integration of MPLA and UNITA forces to create a unified Angolan army.

Recommended by the Secretary General, the Security Council adopted Resolution 696 (1991) on 30 May entrusting a new mandate to the UN (already present in Angola with UNAVEM) establishing UNAVEM II for a period of 17 months. This period was to end in November 1992 with the holding of democratic elections. The role of UNAVEM II during this time, however, was to be extremely limited. The Joint Political-Military Commission, established by the Accords and composed of equal numbers of MPLA and UNITA observers, together with representatives of Portugal, the US and USSR, was charged with the job of monitoring the assembly and demobilisation of troops, the Angolan police and the creation of the integrated army. The task of the UN was only to verify that the joint monitoring groups, which were responsible for on-the-spot monitoring, carried out their duties. UNAVEM II was not, therefore, to have a direct role in the implementation of the Peace Accords, but was intended to monitor the monitors.

Working closely with these joint monitoring groups UNAVEM II verification teams provided support in the investigation and resolution of alleged violations of the ceasefire. They responded to requests for assistance and used their good-offices to resolve problems within monitoring groups. In addition, UNAVEM II took the initiative in monitoring some aspects of the Accords, such as the regular counting of troops and weapons in the assembly areas, as well as monitoring of unassembled troops, demobilised troops, and troops selected to join the new Angolan army. On many occasions UNAVEM II conveyed to both sides suggestions to overcome difficulties related to the assembly and the demobilisation of troops, the proper custody of weapons and the monitoring of the Angolan police, as well as other matters. The UN also helped with the provision of food in the assembly areas.

On 5 September 1991, the Secretary General received a request from the Angolan government for the UN to provide technical expertise to help it prepare for and conduct the elections which it later announced would be held at the end of September 1992. An agreement on technical assistance for the first ever Angolan democratic elections was signed in January 1992.

United Nations Advanced Mission in Cambodia and United Nations Transitional Authority in Cambodia (UNAMIC/UNTAC: 1991-1993)

If the end of the Cold War and the proposed creation of a 'New World Order' heralded hope for any nation, Cambodia was it. Torn apart for over twenty years by despotic rule and civil war, Cambodia had long been a playpen for international Great Power rivalry and petty vendettas. Despite a population of only nine million, the perceived strategic importance of Cambodia was such that within thirty years, the French, the US, the Chinese and the Soviet Union had all attempted to control it through their respective puppet regimes. Perhaps the worst of these was the Chinese backed Khmer Rouge, who having seized power in 1975 when the North Vietnamese captured Saigon, continued on a series of purges, forced collectivisation and urban expulsions, which in their four year tenure left an estimated two million fatalities.

As was typical of the period, the 1979 Vietnamese invasion of Cambodia left the international community divided and diplomatically strained. The Chinese, the US and the majority of UN members manifestly refused to recognise the new Vietnamese installed regime. In line with this the General Assembly voted to maintain a coalition of parties loyal to the past President, Prince Sihanouk, including the Khmer Rouge, as the legitimate incumbents of the UN Cambodian seat. Despite this situation a number of attempts were made by the UN to negotiate a peace between the nominal Cambodian government and the three internal resistance factions within the country. By 1988 the Secretary General had invited his Special Representative to travel to South East Asia to relay to the Cambodian parties concerned, and to regional governments, 'certain concrete ideas which might serve as a framework for a comprehensive settlement plan'. These ideas it was hoped would lead to the establishment of an 'independent, neutral and non-aligned Cambodian state'.[29]

The first face-to-face talks involving all of the Cambodian parties took place in Jakarta, Indonesia, in July 1988. In juxtaposition with the continuing meetings of the Cambodian factions, the five Permanent Members of the Security Council held high level talks in order to discuss a potential settlement for Cambodia. The Five eventually announced that they had reached an agreement on a framework for a comprehensive political settlement after their sixth meeting in August 1990. Over the following year talks between the four Cambodian factions and the Permanent Five continued under the joint chairmanship of France and Indonesia, in order to find solutions to problems which had arisen because of the newly proposed UN role. These eventually culminated in the Paris Conference on Cambodia in October 1991, at which eighteen nations, together with Cambodia, signed the Comprehensive Political Settlement of Cambodia (CPSC) on October 23 1991.

Commonly known as the Paris Peace Accords the CPSC comprised four documents: the Final Act of the Paris Conference on Cambodia; the Agreement on a Comprehensive Political Settlement of the Cambodian Conflict; the Agreement Concerning the Sovereignty, Independence, Territorial Integrity and Inviolability, Neutrality and National Unity of Cambodia; and the Declaration on the Rehabilitation and Reconstruction of Cambodia. The Accords committed the four Cambodian factions to a ceasefire, an end to their acceptance of external military assistance, the cantonment and disarmament of their military forces, the demobilisation of at least 70 percent of such forces prior to the completion of electoral registration, demobilisation of the remaining 30 percent or their incorporation into a new national army immediately after the election, and the release of all prisoners of war and civilian political prisoners. Each faction was to retain its own administration and territory pending the election and the formation of a new national government.[30] The agreement also stipulated that all foreign forces were to be withdrawn and that the 'sovereignty, independence, territorial integrity, inviolability, neutrality and national unity' of Cambodia was to be respected.[31]

During the transitional period between the entry into force of the Accords and the formation of a new government, the UN was to create a 'neutral political environment' conducive to free and fair elections. To achieve this all '... administrative agencies, bodies and offices which could directly influence the outcome of elections [were] placed under direct United Nations supervision or control.' In that context special attention was to be given to 'foreign affairs, national defence, finance, public security and information.' To prevent the impression that Cambodia had become a UN trusteeship, and to help form a single Cambodian voice, the Accords created a Supreme National Council (SNC) formed on a quadripartite basis from the four Cambodian factions. Under the Agreements the SNC became the 'unique legitimate body and source of authority in which, throughout the transitional period, the sovereignty, independence and unity of Cambodia [would be] enshrined.' Although the United Nations was endowed by the SNC with 'all powers necessary to ensure the implementation of [the] Agreement', in recognition of the SNC as the principle 'source of authority', the Organisation agreed not to act in any manner in which consensus within the SNC wished to prohibit.[32]

UNTAC's mandate, apart from the traditional role of supervising the ceasefire, also included the supervision, monitoring and verification of the withdrawal and non-return of foreign military forces; the cantonment, disarmament and demobilisation of the four factions' armed forces (Phase II); the location and confiscation of caches of weapons and military supplies; the conduct of a free and fair election; the promotion and protection of human rights; the oversight of military security and civil administration and of the maintenance of law and order; the repatriation and resettlement of Cambodian refugees and displaced persons; assistance with mine clearance and the establishment of training programmes in mine clearance and awareness; and the rehabilitation of essential infrastructure and the commencement of economic reconstruction and development. To implement this mandate UNTAC was composed of seven components. These were the military, police, human rights, civil administration, electoral, rehabilitation and repatriation components. Together they were to require the deployment of over 20,000 UN personnel. However, recognising that the deployment of these components would take some time, the Secretary General recommended to the Security Council the establishment of a United Nations Advance Mission in Cambodia (UNAMIC) which would be able to conduct assessments of UNTAC's future requirements and represent his good-offices to the Cambodian parties. On 16 October 1991 the Security Council adopted Resolution 717 establishing UNAMIC.

Successes

The successes of the UN in the renaissance period of 1989-91 were numerous. With UNGOMAP, its first new peacekeeping operation for nearly thirteen years, the Organisation conducted an observation mission with the direct involvement of one of the superpowers, heralding a new age of Security Council consensus. UNAVEM, established under SC Resolution 626 (1988), 20 December 1988, to 'verify the redeployment northwards and the phased and total withdrawal of Cuban troops from the

territory of Angola', as the first stage in the regional peace settlement to
bring independence to South-West Africa (Namibia), even managed to
complete its mandate two months ahead of schedule.[33] Angola's energetic
compliance with its commitments was mainly due to the fact that the
maintenance of the Cuban troops was costing it approximately $20 million
a year, a price it could no longer afford. Therefore, even before the
schedule was under way, 3,000 troops were repatriated to Cuba between
January and April 1989 ostensibly as a 'goodwill gesture'. UNAVEM then
continued to verify the withdrawal of a further 47,000 Cuban troops over
four phases, with Cuba completing the withdrawal on 25 June 1991. For
the Secretary General the success of UNAVEM demonstrated just 'what
can be achieved by a UN peacekeeping operation when it receives the full
co-operation of the parties concerned'.[34]

As the second stage of the regional peace agreement, UNTAG became a
ground-breaking operation in more ways than one. As the first major
peacekeeping operation of the post-Cold War period, UNTAG oversaw the
effective 'decolonialisation' of a South African protectorate into the
independent state of Namibia. In this respect UNTAG was the first ever
mission to prepare a nation for elections and independence. Although
UNTAG was only mandated to 'supervise and control' the elections and not
run them, a task undertaken by the South African Administrator General,
the daunting nature of its mandate was not underestimated. To be a true
success UNTAG had to transform the political atmosphere of a country
which had suffered under South African repression for over one hundred
years, and which had subsequently failed to gain any democratic
experience, into an atmosphere conducive to democracy and the protection
of human rights. As Chester Crocker noted, UNTAG was, therefore, not
peacekeeping 'in any normal sense of the term'. Rather, the UN played
a role of 'joint governor with the South African' authorities, to show how
in situations of deep polarisation, an institution such as the UN can
legitimise a political process.[35]

During a period of four days, from 7 to 11 November 1989, UNTAG
supervised and controlled elections for the 72 members of the Constituent
Assembly. Covering some 358 polling stations (215 fixed location and 143
mobile) the SGSR Marti Ahtisaari was assisted in his task by 800 troops
from the military component, together with 1,700 electoral supervisors
drawn from 27 member states. 1,023 police monitors also participated in
the exercise. UNTAG's electoral personnel supervised some 2,500
counterparts appointed by the Administrator General in connection with the
poll.[36] With a massive 97.04 percent of registered voters having cast
their ballots, the SGSR informed the Secretary General on 14 November
that the elections had been both free and fair. Recognising the turnout as

'an impressive demonstration of the importance [Namibians] had attached to the electoral process', the Secretary General noted that 'with these events, a most significant phase in the process of bringing Namibia to independence [had] been accomplished'.[37] And equally as profoundly, having witnessed the operation's overwhelming success, the UN felt able to declare that 'the practicability of physically putting a solution in place through the management of the UN, given the requisite support of member states, need no longer be in question'.[38]

Initially created to verify compliance of the five Central American governments with the security undertakings each of them had given under the *Esquipulas II* Agreement, ONUCA's mandate was enlarged in 1990 so as to 'enable it to play a part in the voluntary demobilisation of the members of the Nicaraguan Resistance'.[39] Although the *Esquipulas II* Agreement had provided *inter alia* for the voluntary demobilisation, repatriation or relocation of the members of the Nicaraguan resistance and their families, the resistance members themselves had not expressed a willingness to proceed until after the surprise defeat of the Sandanista government in the elections of February 1990. To accommodate their demobilisation, four locations were established in Honduras, together with eight 'security zones' inside Nicaragua itself. To increase security for the demobilising soldiers the establishment of the 'security zones' called for the forces of the Nicaraguan government to withdraw from an encircling area of 20km around each of them. ONUCA's mandate was expanded so that it could monitor the ceasefire and the separation of forces which resulted from this requirement. Demobilisation began on 16 April 1990 and 8 May 1990 in Honduras and Nicaragua respectively and the process was essentially completed by 28 June. By this date ONUCA had successfully demobilised a total of 21,963 members of the Nicaraguan resistance (nearly twice the number first envisaged) and collected over 17,000 pieces of ordnance, including small arms, missiles and grenade launchers. Although the 'security zones' had shut down by the end of June, individuals and small groups continued to present themselves for demobilisation over the proceeding month, totalling a further 510 members by 6 July. Once the Resistance members had handed over their weapons, military equipment and uniforms (not every member possessed each or all of these) they immediately became the responsibility of the CIAV, which was responsible for the civilian aspects of the demobilisation process.[40] Once the military aspects of demobilisation were completed, ONUCA reverted to its original mandate of verifying compliance to the *Esquipulas II* Agreement, although for a couple of months also maintained a presence in areas in which large numbers of demobilised soldiers and their dependents had settled, 'so as to help to encourage a sense of security and confidence among the population'.[41]

So, as the first peacekeeping operation in the western hemisphere ONUCA had been successful in not only overseeing a ceasefire during an election period, but also in redeploying to assist in the demobilisation of the Nicaraguan Resistance, 'the final step in the pacific settlement of the war'.[42] It was also to be the first time the UN had been involved in physical disarmament, experience which was to come in useful in later operations. ONUCA's peacemaking strategy successfully mediated between an antagonistic government and resistance faction to enable agreements to be struck which allowed former guerillas to lay down their weapons and repatriate themselves into civilian life. As the UN's first observation of elections inside an internationally recognised state, ONUCA also had a civilian composition which changed the content of peacekeeping's definition by blurring the distinction between civilian and military operations and between security and human rights.[43]

Problems

By the end of 1991 the confidence of the Organisation was riding high. All of the operations established by the Organisation in 1988-89 had ended, or were about to end, as unqualified successes. And by the close of the year the number of operations under way had doubled. However, the confidence created by the UN's success in conducting these early operations of the 1988-91 period caused it to overlook the inherent inadequacies in its methods of operation. These inadequacies ranged from the manner in which peacekeeping operations were funded, to the planning and conduct of operations in the field. When the international community eventually called on the UN to conduct the large peacekeeping operations of 1992-93, therefore, the Organisation was to find that these selfsame inadequacies were to manifest themselves in a much more severe way, threatening to unhinge all the good work the UN's peacemaking strategies had achieved. So what exactly were these inadequacies?

Funding

The most serious emerging problem for the United Nations at the end of the 1980s was its dearth of peacekeeping funds. The failure of the international community to pay its assessed and voluntary contributions had forced the Secretary General on a number of occasions to express his growing concern at the Organisation's financial situation. Matters were only to get worse. As the next chapter will elucidate, the cost of UN peacekeeping was to grow exponentially over 1992-93, with the member states' failure to pay their contributions causing disastrous results in the UN's operations. Yet even while the UN's budget deficit remained relatively low, the inertia of the UN's budget processes was to nearly derail the operation in Namibia.

The planning for the deployment of UNTAG, which took place after the Security Council adoption of Resolution 435 in 1978, had originally perceived the operation to be essentially military in nature. It had, therefore, envisaged the deployment of around 7,500 troops. However, by the time the operation had become politically possible, ten years later, the nature of the operation had changed. Cuban troops had been withdrawn from Angola, the South African government was expected to be more co-operative in the restraining of its forces within designated areas and incursions by SWAPO forces were, therefore, deemed unlikely. As a consequence of this the Security Council requested a restructuring of UNTAG personnel to reflect the more political role involved, asking the Secretary General to 'identify wherever possible tangible cost-saving measures without prejudice to his ability fully to carry out [UNTAG's] mandate'.[44] Financial haggling in New York over the extent of the reduction in military personnel, however, was to delay the deployment, even of the reduced force, with unforeseen consequences for the operation.[45]

Despite the fact that the UNTAG operation had been expected to begin on 1 April 1989, by this date only the SGSR and a number of military monitors and observers had actually deployed. Few military or civilian personnel had arrived and there was a severe lack of vehicles and communications. When the SGSR was informed by the South African Administrator General on his arrival on 31 March, that a number of heavily armed SWAPO forces had begun to cross the border from Angola and that many were poised to follow, he could only send a team of UNTAG officials to investigate. Unable to deal with the situation properly in the absence of military troops, the SGSR had little option but to acquiesce with the request by the South African Foreign Minister to release a number of South African Defence Force troops from the bases to which they had been confined. Helpless to intervene, the UN watched as South African troops attacked SWAPO forces, crossing the Angolan border and killing over 200 people. When UNTAG was finally able to interview captured SWAPO forces, they found that they had originally crossed the border with the strict instructions to avoid South African forces if possible, in order to establish bases in Namibia under United Nations' supervision.

Although UNTAG criticised the South African interpretation of the SWAPO action for presuming a hostile intent, it was obvious that the SWAPO forces had moved across the border, after the operation starting date, in the expectation that the UN would be already deployed.[46]

As such, this initial incident in Namibia was to be the most serious of the whole operation. For the first time the UN was to witness the horrific consequences which could result from the failure of the Organisation to fulfil the promises it had made to the parties with which it had negotiated. Although in this case the SGSR was able to negotiate for the eventual deployment of UNTAG forces, the fighting could have easily escalated and the operation could have faltered even before it had properly begun.

In the ONUCA operation the UN was able to avoid the start up delays which had caused such serious problems in Namibia through budgeting for a larger civilian and military personnel than were actually deployed. However, such 'balloon budgeting' is criticised by member states and can have a detrimental effect on other operations as contributing states readjust their funding proposals to take account of the presumed excess the Secretariat has included. In the case of ONUCA itself, an amount totalling around $19 million was repaid to member states as unspent assessments. Despite this the operation was still technically $9 million short at its termination.[47]

Planning

The formal responsibility for the 'planning, organising, mounting, sustaining and accounting for duly authorised UN operations' lies with the UN Secretariat in New York.[48] Although the Secretariat had already gained experience in pre-operational planning and logistical supply with the UN peacekeeping missions during the Cold War, nothing was to prepare it for the scale and complexity of the operations which it was about to conduct in the post-Cold War era.[49] As the proceeding chapters will elucidate, the UN's ability to prepare for, deploy and sustain its missions in the field has been totally inadequate for the role it has been expected to play in the management and control of armed conflict. And the failure of the UN and international community to adapt to the planning and logistical demands of large-scale multi-dimensional peacekeeping operations was to cause serious hindrance to the effectiveness of future missions. Although the operations during 1988-91 did not overwhelm the UN Secretariat in the manner subsequent operations were to do, they nevertheless exhibited problems which at least indicated the insufficient capability of the Secretariat in this regard. Unfortunately, neither the UN nor the international community were to realise the seriousness of failing to react quickly enough to provide the Secretariat with the specialised personnel and resources required.

One of the most fundamental requirements of the Secretariat's pre-operational planning is for it to assess the number of personnel which will be required to carry out the proposed operation effectively. As noted earlier, in the case of UNTAG, this assessment had originally envisaged a force of around 7,500. Under pressure to cut potential costs, the Secretariat had re-examined its estimation of troop requirements in light of the more political role which had evolved for UNTAG. Although the Secretary General had been expressly requested not to let any reduction in personnel prejudice the operation's ability to carry out its mandate, doubts remain over the effectiveness of the lower number deployed. Paul Diehl posits that the force, which eventually numbered approximately 4,500, was insufficient even to monitor the actions of the 1.5 million Namibians, never mind the South African security forces in the country. And with the enormous area which UNTAG had to cover, it was often unable to verify whether the South African forces had been confined to base, relinquished their weapons, or even released political prisoners. 'In some cases the South African forces moved troops, weapons and prisoners from location to location, several steps ahead of a peacekeeping force that could not monitor the whole country.'[50] Even an increase in the number of Civilian Police (CIVPOL) from 300 to 1,500 at the peak of the operation failed to solve all UNTAG's problems. Charged with ensuring that the South West African Police (the last means of the South African government to intimidate voters after its troops had been confined to base) did not abuse their position, South African troops continued under the guise of the police force to intimidate the public and pass weapons to groups opposed to SWAPO.

Diehl also believes that inherent flaws existed in both the nature of the elections and the means of the UN to supervise them. With the peace agreement specifying that the elections were to be run by the South African Administrator General, the control of the election machinery was to remain in the hands of one of the interested parties. With such control there is always room for abuse. When, therefore, claims were made accusing the South African government of manipulating the elections to prevent SWAPO from achieving the two-thirds majority it required to re-write the constitution, UNTAG was powerless to investigate. As well as its lack of investigative powers, the operation was also to remain devoid of the mechanisms required to deal with such disputes between the parties.[51]

The operation in Central America (ONUCA) was also to find that expectations of its ability to investigate violations of the *Esquipulas II*

Agreement were to be over optimistic. In the words of the Secretary General: 'It was originally thought that ONUCA might have some capacity to detect violations of the security undertakings, which it could then take up with the Government or Governments concerned. In practice, however, it quickly became apparent that ONUCA's detective capacity [was] very limited'.[52] This was partly due to the nature of the terrain, climatic conditions and other topographical factors, but it had been mainly due to the fact that 'an international peacekeeping operation cannot undertake the detection of clandestine activities without assuming functions that properly belong to the security forces of the country or countries concerned - not least because they require armed personnel to carry them out'.[53] ONUCA therefore concentrated its observers in regions where breaches of the agreement were most likely to occur, hoping that by familiarising itself with the normal pattern of activities of the areas concerned would mean that any untoward or suspicious activity would be spotted. This, however, 'was never envisaged as physical prevention or deterrence; the idea was, rather, that ONUCA's presence would make it more difficult for activities contrary to the *Esquipulas II* Agreement to be carried out'.[54]

The ONUCA operation was to experience start up problems caused mainly by a lack of pre-operational co-ordination between planning personnel. The military component of the operation was only supplied with the Field Operations Division's (responsible for logistics and communications support within the Secretariat) 'standard operations document' after it had actually deployed. Thus, the failure to communicate properly before deployment meant that new plans had to be drawn up, delaying the deployment of the observer teams, after the FOD decided that much of the initial operational planning had to be scrapped to meet evolving field conditions.[55]

Personnel and Equipment

As well as experiencing difficulties in predicting field requirements in its pre-operational planning, the Secretariat was also to encounter problems in procuring adequately trained personnel and field equipment. Although, as with all the problems which emerged in the early post-Cold War operations, the severity of the Secretariat's difficulties was to become more acute in future operations, the early post-Cold War operations were once again to provide early warnings of impending inadequacies.

In the first operation to be instigated in the 1990s, UNIKOM observers were sent into the field with little more than tents to mark out their observation posts. Despite being deployed in the hottest months of the year, these tents contained no air-conditioning. Air-conditioned trailers did not become available until September 1991.[56]

In the case of UNTAG, logistical planning was extremely limited. With no more than four personnel working on UNTAG's planning at any one time, it could hardly have been anything else. The situation was to be made worse, however, by the shortened preparation time caused by the quibbling over the operation's reduced budget. When two US military transport specialists assigned to UN Headquarters decided to transport UNTAG's vehicles by sea rather than air, in order to reduce costs, the increased travelling time resulted in UNTAG beginning its operations with a lack of equipment. Planning oversight on more minor, but equally essential details, also meant that UNTAG personnel had to manage for the first two months with maps they had bought from local bookstores.[57] UNTAG also suffered from a lack of personnel who could speak the local language and the South African authorities questioned the ability of the mission to patrol the northern territories when its vehicles had engines and tyres unsuited for Namibian terrain.

Both UNTAG and ONUCA were also to experience the great divide which exists between the training and logistical supplies of the national contingents.[58] This problem was to emerge in the ONUCA operation when the Venezuelan battalion, chosen to help demobilise the Nicaraguan Resistance, failed to deploy with its own transport as the UN had requested it to do. Improvisation and borrowing from other companies helped overcome the problem. However, 'logistical problems encountered when the operation's mandate changed were indicative of deeper problems with the UN's antiquated supply system and its lack of either material or personnel reserves'.[59]

As will be seen in the following chapters, the Secretariat's cumbersome procurement system, together with shortages of adequately trained personnel and equipment, have combined to exacerbate the UN's already substantial problems in planning and conducting field operations.

Cooperation as the essential ingredient of success

Of the three principles on which peacekeeping was founded during the Cold War, perhaps the most important was the need for host state consent. It was this principle which helped assure the UN that its peacekeeping operations would always retain the co-operation of the parties concerned. If a state did not wish to co-operate, it need only request the UN to leave its territory. The increasing number of operations in the post-Cold War era dealing with internal conflict was, however, to raise a question over the nature of consent. In the three operations in Afghanistan, Angola and Nicaragua, the UN continued to negotiate peace settlements with the states concerned, but had little if any dealings with the internal resistance factions. Throughout the operations described earlier, it was noted that these internal resistance factions were not party to the settlement negotiations. This was the case with the various mujahideen in Afghanistan, UNITA in Angola and with SWAPO in Namibia. The fact that the respective resistance factions were not involved in negotiations did cause problems for the implementation of the agreements. Soviet and Cuban forces withdrawing from Afghanistan and Angola both came under fire from resistance members, resulting in a temporary suspension of the operations. In Nicaragua, having not been party to the regional negotiations, the Contras staged attacks designed to interrupt voter registration causing the Sandanista government to eventually break its ceasefire agreement.[60]

When the active participation of the resistance members was required, as it was when UNTAG and ONUCA became involved in disarmament, the cessation of superpower support, together with regional peace settlements between the neighbouring states, left them with little option. In essence, the UN had not dealt with an internal faction which had either the will or the means to continue operations. When in the case of Afghanistan the UN would have faced such a situation, it left, leaving behind only a political office in the hope of helping the remaining factions negotiate. The UN therefore, failed to gain experience of negotiating and dealing directly with autonomous internal factions. As the following chapters will show, the Organisation was to find out to its own detriment, especially in its operations in Cambodia and Somalia, that it was misguided to expect these internal factions to act within the expectations of inter-state diplomacy.

Conclusion

The first three years of the post-Cold War era were an unqualified success for UN peacekeeping. Having lain relatively dormant for over ten years, peacekeeping once again emerged as a relevant and successful means of resolving long standing and seemingly intractable conflicts. So confident had the Organisation become by the end of 1991 that it was willing to commit itself to the largest and most costly operation ever undertaken, in Cambodia. This operation represented the tenth established in the post-Cold War era, only three less than in the whole of the Cold War.

The Organisation's confidence, however, only served to mask inherent problems in its ability to operationalise the highly complex mandates which these new multi-dimensional peacekeeping operations required. As this chapter has demonstrated, these problems ranged from the lack of pre-operational planning; its dearth of peacekeeping funds; its anachronistic procurement processes; and the manner in which the UN must rely on the willingness of its member states to fulfil the promises they so readily make before operations begin. The failure of the Organisation to take full account of these problems before committing itself to even more operations was to have catastrophic consequences for the future of peacekeeping.

Suggested Reading

The blue helmets: a review of United Nations peacekeeping, United Nations, 1990.

Bourantonid, D., and Wiener, J., *The UN in the New World Order,* London, Macmillan Press, 1994.

Crocker, C., 'Southern African peacemaking', *Survival,* vol.32, no.3, May/June 1990.

Diehl, P., and Kumar, C., 'Mutual benefits from international intervention: new roles for United Nations peacekeeping forces', *Bulletin for Peace Proposals,* vol.22, no.4, 1991.

Donald, D., and Brad, H., *Beyond traditional peacekeeping,* London, Macmillan Press, 1995.

Durch, W.J., *The evolution of UN peacekeeping,* New York, St. Martin's Press, 1993.

James, A., *Peacekeeping in international politics,* London, Macmillan Press, 1990.

Parsons, A., *From Cold War to Hot Peace*, London, Penguin, 1995.

Russel, B., and Sutterlin, J.S., 'The UN in a new world order', *Foreign Affairs,* vol.70, no.2, Spring 1991.

Urquhart, B., 'Beyond the sheriff's posse', *Survival,* vol.32, May/June 1990.

White, N.D., *Keeping the peace: the United Nations and the maintenance of international peace and security,* Manchester University Press, 1993.

Notes

1.	See Weiss, T, G., and Forsythe, D., *The United Nations and changing world politics*, Oxford, Westview Press, 1994.

2.	'The United Nations Good Offices in Afghanistan and Pakistan', in *The blue helmets, a review of United Nations peacekeeping,* United Nations, 1990, p.316.

3.	Birgisson, K., 'United Nations Good Offices Mission in Afghanistan and Pakistan', in ed. Durch W., *The evolution of UN peacekeeping,* St. Martin's Press, 1993, p.305.

4.	White, N, D., *Keeping the peace: The United Nations and the maintenance of international peace and security*, Manchester University Press, 1993, p.224 and 'UNIIMOG' in *The blue helmets*, op.cit, p.328.

5.	Ibid., *The blue helmets,* p.332.

6.	cf.*United Nations document, S/20338*, 17 December 1988.

7.	*United Nations document, S/22644*, 28 May 1991.

8.	*United Nations document, S/21246*, 12 April 1990.

9.	cf.*United Nations document, S/22644*, 28 May 1991.

10.	Parsons, A., *From Cold War to Hot Peace*, London, Penguin, 1995, p.118.

11.	cf.Wendt, D., 'The peacemakers: lessons of conflict resolution for the post-Cold War world', *Washington Quarterly*, vol.17, no.3, Summer 1994, p.167.

12.	cf.'UNAVEM' in *The blue helmets*, op.cit, p.335.

13.	*United Nations document, A/45/997*, 16 April 1991.

14.	Fortna, V, P., 'Success and failure in Southern Africa: peacekeeping in Namibia and Angola', in ed., Donald D., and Hayes, B., *Beyond traditional peacekeeping,* London, Macmillan, 1995, p.284.

15.   cf.*United Nations document, S/20967,* 14 November 1989.

16.   The other elements were i) the Special Representative's Office ii) the Independent Jurist iii) the Office of the United Nations High Commissioner for Refugees (UNHCR) iv) the Electoral Division and v) the Division of Administration.

17.   White, op.cit, p.226.

18.   Smith, B., and Durch, W., 'ONUCA', in ed. Durch, W., op.cit, p.442.

19.   'ONUCA' in *The blue helmets,* op.cit, p.392.

20.   *United Nations document, S/21194,* 15 March 1990.

21.   Durch, W., 'The Iraq-Kuwait Observation Mission', op.cit, p.267.

22.   Chopra, J., 'Breaking the stalemate in Western Sahara', *International Peacekeeping,* vol.1, no.3, Autumn 1994, p.310.

23.   Durch W., 'Building on sand: UN peacekeeping in the Western Sahara', *International Security,* vol.17, no.4, Spring 1993, p.155.

24.   cf.Chopra, op.cit, p.308.

25.   Munck, L G., and Kumar, C., 'Civil conflicts and the conditions for successful international intervention: a comparative study of Cambodia and El Salvador', *Review of International Studies,* vol.21, no.2, 1995, p.170.

26.   Idem.

27.   cf.See Flores, T., 'ONUSAL - a precedent for future UN missions?', *International Peacekeeping,* vol.2, no.1, December 1994-January 1995, p.5.

28.   Fortna, op.cit, p. 288.

29.   cf.*The Comprehensive Settlement Plan for Cambodia* (CSPC), 23 October 1991.

30.   Findlay, T., 'Cambodia: the legacy and lessons of UNTAC', *SIPRI Report,* no.9, Oxford University Press, 1995, p.11.

32. cf.Idem.

33. cf.See *United Nations Document S/20338,* 17 December 1988 and Fortna, V, P., 'United Nations Angola Verification Mission I' in ed. Durch, *The evolution of UN peacekeeping,* op.cit, p.380.

34. cf.*United Nations document, S/21246,* 12 April 1990 and *S/20783,* 11 August 1989.

35. cf.Crocker, C., 'Southern African peacemaking', *Survival,* vol.32, no.3, May/June 1990, p.222.

36. See *United Nations document S/20967,* 14 November 1989 and Fortna, 'United Nations Transition Assistance Group', in ed. Durch, *The evolution of peacekeeping,* op.cit, p.365.

37. cf.*United Nations document S/20967,* 14 November 1989.

38. cf.Fortna, 'UNTAG' in Durch, *The evolution of UN peacekeeping,* op.cit, p.372.

39. cf.*United Nations document, S/21194,* 15 March 1990.

40. See *United Nations documents, S/21194,* 15 March 1990; *S/21194,* 2 May 1990; *S/21379,* 29 June 1990; *S/21909,* 26 October 1990.

41. *United Nations document, S/21909,* 26 October 1990.

42. White, op.cit, p.226.

43. Weiss and Forsythe, op.cit, p.67.

44. cf.'United Nations Transition Assistance Group in Namibia', in *The blue helmets,* op.cit, p.384.

45. See Diehl P F., *International peacekeeping,* Baltimore and London, The Johns Hopkins University Press, 1994, p.160.

46. 'UNTAG' in *The blue helmets,* op cit, pp.364-5.

47. Smith and Durch, 'United Nations Central America Observer Group', in Durch, *The evolution of UN peacekeeping* op.cit, p. 447.

48.   Berdal, M., 'Whither UN Peacekeeping', *Adelphi Paper 281,* October 1993, Brassey's for the International Institute for Strategic Studies, p.32.

49.   Logistics is traditionally defined as the 'science of planning and carrying out the movement and maintenance of forces'. See Berdal, ibid., p.32.

50.   cf.Diehl, op.cit, p.160.

51.   Idem.

52.   cf.*United Nations document, S/21909,* 26 October 1990.

53.   cf.Idem.

54.   cf.Idem.

55.   Smith and Durch, 'ONUCA' in Durch, *The evolution of UN peacekeeping,* op.cit, p.448.

56.   Durch, 'The Iraq-Kuwait Observation Mission', in Durch, ibid., p.265.

57.   Fortna, 'UNTAG' in Durch, ibid., p.367.

58.   Contingents which participate in peacekeeping operations are required to arrive with a first line of logistical support, defined as the daily requirements of supply, maintenance, transport and medicine, for a period of 60 days. The second and third lines of support - which include the resupply of petroleum, oil, lubricants and spare parts and the provision of heavy transport and advanced medical support - are in theory to be provided by the UN. See Berdal, op.cit, p.35.

59.   cf.Smith, and Durch, 'ONUCA' in Durch, *The evolution of UN peacekeeping,* op.cit, p.457.

60.   Ibid., p.443.

Chapter 4
The Expansion of Peacekeeping

Introduction

The first ever meeting of the Security Council at the level of heads of state and government was to take place in January 1992. Less than one year after the successful execution of the first ever Chapter VII enforcement action (with the expulsion of Iraq from Kuwait in the Gulf Crisis of 1990-91) by a United Nations mandated coalition of forces, and less than one month after the official dissolution of the Soviet Union, this meeting was designed to symbolise the new expectations which the international community held for the future role of the United Nations in the post-Cold War world. With five peacekeeping operations instigated in the previous three years, and with the last veto cast on 31 May 1990, the Security Council looked forward to an era in which Great Power co-operation could finally allow the United Nations to ensure the international peace and security which had for so long remained elusive. It was with this in mind that the Security Council, in its concluding statement of 31 January 1992, invited the Secretary General, Boutros Boutros-Ghali, to prepare by 1 July 1992 'analysis and recommendations on ways of strengthening and making more efficient within the framework and provisions of the Charter the capacity of the United Nations for preventive diplomacy, for peacemaking and for peacekeeping'.[1]   The report which the Secretary General subsequently produced, *An Agenda for Peace*, was indicative of the changing nature of United Nations action in the post-Cold War world. Rather than being satisfied with the simple prevention of escalation of conflict, which had been its major objective during the Cold War, the 1990s were to witness the emergence of peacekeeping as one of a number of strategically applied conflict resolution tools which the Security Council and Secretary General called preventive diplomacy, peacemaking, peacekeeping and post-conflict peacebuilding.   No longer limited to maintaining ceasefires, the goals of peacekeeping had now become the attainment of 'far reaching, just and long-term political solutions'.[2]

As demonstrated in the previous chapter, the growth of peacekeeping in the post-Cold War era was to take place with little analysis of how the problems posed by operations might affect future, more ambitious, missions. This was once again made evident by the fact that the United Nations had, in the twelve months previous to the Security Council request to the Secretary General, committed itself to another five operations, including the largest and most costly operation at that time, in Cambodia. As Adam Roberts noted, the request of the Security Council to find ways of 'strengthening and making more efficient' the concept of peacekeeping, rather than exploring its problems and questioning its traditional prescriptions, set the tone for the immediate future of peacekeeping in the 1990s.[3]   Therefore, with five successful operations under its post-Cold War belt, and the pervasive feeling after the Gulf War crisis of 1990-91 that consensus between the superpowers could allow force to be used in order to restore peace, *An Agenda for Peace* reflected the changing attitude of the Security Council towards conflict resolution.   The Secretary General's definition of peacekeeping within the report, as a 'United Nations presence in the field, *hitherto* with the consent of all the parties concerned …', was a fundamental deviation from the principles of peacekeeping developed during the Cold War.[4]   Consent of the host state for the deployment of peacekeeping forces had been a pre-requisite of UN intervention. Changing the definition of peacekeeping, however, allowed the introduction by the Secretary General of a new concept of so-called 'peace-enforcement units', which, under his command, could be used to enforce a ceasefire by taking coercive action against any party which happened to violate it. (See Appendix 6.)[5] The discussion of the feasibility of the whole issue of peace-enforcement was to continue throughout 1992, although its enactment was not to be seen until a year or so later in the crises in the former Yugoslavia and Somalia.

The Somalian and Yugoslavian crises themselves represented the beginning of a new realisation amongst the international community that the

'New World Order' which President Bush had called for after the Gulf Crisis of 1990-91, was not coming to fruition. Rather than opening up new opportunities for peace, the disengagement of the superpowers from their Cold War 'client' states in some cases simply left a political vacuum, in which historical animosities, nationalistic, cultural, religious and tribal rivalries subsequently competed for power. In Yugoslavia, the forces which had maintained the federation for over forty years, were no longer strong enough to do so after the death of President Tito in 1980. With the collapse of communism at the end of the decade and a new climate of freedom sweeping across Eastern Europe, national identity once again emerged as a powerful political force in the formation of new independent nations. It was equally as powerful in the destruction of the Yugoslav federation.

The crisis in Somalia was also to pose serious questions for the creation of President Bush's new post-Cold War order. In many cases the perpetuation of ancient tribal and religious beliefs precluded the introduction of democracy into non-western societies, which continue to be ordered by their own cultural traditions. When, therefore, the 'state' as a unit of political organisation was introduced into these societies, government control often passed to whichever tribe or faction was the most powerful. Supported by one or other of the superpowers the controlling regimes of these countries have tended to rule by force. However, when the superpowers began to disengage, discontinuing their political, military and financial support, many of these regimes found their ability to hold on to power disappearing. In the case of Somalia this led to a state of anarchy as the regime of Siad Barre collapsed leaving the remaining warlords vieing to take his place.

United Nations action in these so-called 'failed states' has been two-fold. In cases such as Angola and Mozambique, in which military stalemates between governments and resistance factions have created conditions for peace, the UN has established peacekeeping forces to help implement negotiated agreements. In Somalia and the former Yugoslavia, however, no such settlement seemed possible. Without even a viable ceasefire to maintain the UN can only hope to provide humanitarian comfort to those civilians suffering as a consequence of the violence, whilst using its diplomatic weight to encourage local co-operation. This type of 'humanitarian intervention', which was first used after the Gulf crisis to protect the Kurdish minority in northern Iraq, has had unpredictable consequences for the future of UN peacekeeping. By October 1992, in the absence of any real local co-operation, the Security Council, encouraged by the Secretary General himself, was edging ever closer to exercising more coercive action to force aid through to beleaguered civilians. As the next chapter will show, this policy was to be severely flawed.

Between 1988 and October 1992, therefore, the UN had instigated twelve new operations, five of which had already been concluded and disbanded (UNGOMAP, UNIIMOG, UNAVEM, UNTAG, ONUCA). Except for UNIKOM, all the UN peacekeeping operations instigated in 1991 had been created to implement negotiated settlements of long standing conflicts (UNAVEM II, ONUSAL, MINURSO, UNAMIC/UNTAC). And with the UN response to the problems in Yugoslavia and Somalia the UN, since 1988, had become involved in only one less operation than it had in the whole of the forty years previous. Commensurate with the expansion of the number of operations, 1992 witnessed a   fourfold increase in the costs of UN peacekeeping, and saw the number of peacekeepers on the ground increase to over 50,000. This period of expansion was also to be the United Nations' last expression of unwavering optimism.

TABLE 4: Peacekeeping Operations established 1992

Mission	Brief Explanation
United Nations Operation in Somalia I (UNOSOM I) 1992-93	Monitor ceasefire and assist in provision of humanitarian relief
United Nations Protection Force (UNPROFOR) 1992-95	Monitor ceasefire in Croatia; supervise withdrawal of JNA; de-militarisation and protection of UNPAs; support UNHCR delivery of humanitarian relief in Bosnia; ensure security and functioning of Sarajevo airport; protection of UN personnel; preventive deployment in FYROM

Ongoing operations

In Cambodia, despite establishing the United Nations Transitional Authority in Cambodia (UNTAC) through Security Council Resolution 745 of 28 February 1992, the UN was facing mounting problems. The creation of UNAMIC had not been able to alleviate the UN's lack of preparation and the Organisation's lack of funding and resources were to cause serious delays in UNTAC's deployment. The situation was to deteriorate in May when the Party of Democratic Kampuchea (PDK, commonly known as the Khmer Rouge) effectively withdrew its co-operation from the mission and refused to allow UNTAC to deploy in its areas of control. The PDK cited the UN's failure to dissolve the main institutions and structures of the

Phnom Penh authorities, and its failure to verify the withdrawal of Vietnamese forces, as the reasons for its actions. The Secretary General, however, stated that the PDK had begun to introduce 'its own interpretations of provisions of the Paris Agreements relating to the withdrawal of Vietnamese forces' and reiterated that UNTAC's mandate was to exercise control through the 'existing administrative structures' of each of the four factions.[6] As the Phnom Penh authorities formed part of these 'administrative structures' they could not, therefore, be either abolished or dismantled. Besides which it was obvious, to the UN at least, that UNTAC did not have either the staff or the expertise to establish and run a transitional government itself.

At a Ministerial Conference on the Rehabilitation of Cambodia, held in Tokyo on 22 June, an informal 'proposal for discussion' was drawn up by representatives of the five Permanent Members, and other participants, including the SGSR, in an attempt to overcome the objections of the PDK. This move, however, failed to achieve its objective, leading to the Security Council adoption of Resolution 766 (1992) on 21 July 1992 demanding that the PDK (although not actually named) permit the deployment of UNTAC in the areas under its control. It also demanded that the PDK implement Phase II (cantonment, disarmament and demobilisation of the respective armed forces) of the operation, which should have begun on 13 June. In a letter dated 27 July 1992 the SGSR wrote to the Secretary General expressing his fears that the refusal of the PDK to begin Phase II, whilst the other three factions were proceeding, was 'creating a [power] vacuum' which could be exploited by the PDK when UNTAC left. He was, therefore, having to be both 'selective and flexible' with the tempo of cantoning non-PDK affiliated troops. By the end of September 1992, UNTAC was close to full deployment, and the SGSR was still hopeful that 'external pressures, ... a combination of UNTAC's even-handed approach and the solid common front of the three factions', may eventually change the PDK's refusal to co-operate.[7]

With the failure of the operation in the Western Sahara even to get off the ground, the Secretary General in a report in February 1992 gave strong indications that the patience and resources of the international community were finite, and warned that a policy reassessment would be appropriate should the lack of progess in the operation continue into late Spring.[8] Moroccan violations of the ceasefire became more numerous throughout 1992, with MINURSO's movements being restricted in Moroccan-held areas. In response to its intransigence over the operation as a whole, the US Congress voted to reduce military assistance to Morocco from $144 million to just $52 million in late 1992.

Initially composed of only a human rights division, the first expansion of
ONUSAL was to take place in January 1992. On 14 January Security
Council Resolution 729 (1992) established both the Military and Police
Divisions, the former to oversee the agreed ceasefire and other military
aspects of the agreement (including demobilisation and reintegration of
former government and guerilla forces), and the latter to supervise the
maintenance of public order by the already existing National Police (NP)
during a transition period culminating in the creation of the new National
Civil Police (NCP). By mid-1992, however, questions were beginning to
be raised over the sincerity of the El Salvadorian government's
implementation of the agreements. Although it had announced the
dissolution of the National Guard and Treasury Police, it had become
evident that the government had simply transferred their personnel into the
Army, in direct contravention of the Agreements.[9] The lack of progress
on the government's commitment to land reform led the FMLN to inform
the Secretary General in September, that in order to maintain the link in the
original timetable between the key undertakings of the two parties, it would
suspend the demobilisation of its troops until new dates had been set for the
transfer of land.

Successes

The only unquestionable successes of 1991-92 were concerned with the
operations of UNIKOM and ONUSAL. The former, as a traditional style
peacekeeping operation, was always unlikely to fail, especially with the
overwhelming support of the Security Council after the Gulf War. The
latter, as the second stage of the regional peace agreement which had begun
with the ONUCA operation two years before, had a more testing mandate.
Within its first year, ONUSAL's role had the effect of increasing global
public perception of the importance of human rights as it monitored and
verified the compliance of the parties to human rights agreements and the
final peace agreements signed in January 1992. ONUSAL's military
component also collected and destroyed many of the opposing armies'
weapons, and helped oversee the creation of a new national army staff
college, where former adversaries mingled as students.[10] As such,
ONUSAL, like its regional predecessors ONUVEN and ONUCA, gave
independent credibility to the on-going peace process, leading in January
1993 to a request for the UN to supervise a national election.
Of the other four operations initiated before mid-1992, (UNAVEM II,
MINURSO, UNAMIC/UNTAC) the UN could claim some success in
having negotiated peace agreements between long standing adversaries, but

as time was to tell, even this assumption was tenuous. The difficulty of maintaining compliance with previously agreed commitments was to see UNAVEM II end in the resumption of civil war, MINURSO fail even to get off the ground, and UNTAC suffer serious delays in implementing essential elements of its mandate. Despite the intransigence of the Khmer Rouge, however, UNTAC had by September 1992 achieved the adoption of the electoral law (with the registration of voters planned to begin in October), returned more than 115,000 refugees and displaced persons and cantonned nearly 53,000 troops, collecting over 50,000 weapons.[11]

By the end of October 1992 the operations in Somalia and Yugoslavia had achieved few successes. The UN had managed to negotiate for the deployment of a number of UNOSOM troops around Somalia, but their security, and the delivery of humanitarian aid, remained precarious. Although the Security Council had agreed to an extension of UNOSOM's mandate in August 1992 to include assistance in establishing a police force and the creation, under UN auspices, of a disarming force to carry out a food for arms exchange, the deteriorating security situation at the end of the year meant that its implementation was not possible. In the former Yugoslavia international pressure had helped prevent a protracted war over Slovenian independence, and the UN had created United Nations Protected Areas (UNPAs) to ease tension in Croatia. As will be elucidated later, however, these UNPAs were to cause new tensions of their own. In Bosnia, constant negotiations were enabling some humanitarian relief to be supplied to besieged cities, but the UN was increasingly resorting to threats of force to encourage the Serbians to acquiesce in its provision.

So as 1992 came to an end it was evident that the massive expansion in the number, size and complexity of peacekeeping and humanitarian operations was beginning to threaten the UN's ability to conduct either role effectively. However, only the Angolan operation had, as yet, failed completely. The UN's largest operations, although facing serious problems, were continuing to operate as best they could and were achieving substantial successes nonetheless. It was not to be until 1993 that the optimism of the UN was to be severely dampened.

Problems

As noted in the previous chapter, the problems which were to manifest themselves in the peacekeeping operations after 1991 had virtually all been present, in a comparatively minor capacity, in the operations conducted in the first three years of the post-Cold War period. However, the failure of the international community to heed these warning signs, allowed unrealistic expectations to grow about the capacity of the UN to orchestrate the multi-dimensional peacekeeping operations which the Organisation was increasingly being called to conduct. With the euphoric optimism created at the end of the Cold War, the new consensus within the Security Council, and the sense of triumph after the Gulf War, the international community continued to view UN peacekeeping as a panacea for all the crises for which the 'New World Order' required a cure. By mid-1992, therefore, a dangerous divide had developed between the willingness of the Security Council to commit the UN to ever more ambitious peacekeeping operations, and the ability of the UN as an organisation to operationalise the subsequent mandates.

As in the previous three years the most serious problems which the operations were to face in 1992 were concerned mainly with the UN's peacekeeping funds; the Organisation's time consuming and complex budgetary processes; its equally as inefficient procurement procedures; and the desperate lack of pre-operational planning. The UN also suffered from a curious absence of any institutional learning process.   When the unexpected crises occurred in Somalia and Yugoslavia, therefore, an already extended organisation was stretched to breaking point.

Funding

By the beginning of 1992 the Secretary General, in *An Agenda for Peace*, had already recognised the 'chasm' which had developed between the tasks being entrusted to the United Nations and the financial means provided to it. Matters were only to get worse. Even before the operations in Somalia and Yugoslavia were to begin, the costs of peacekeeping in the first half of 1992 were to increase fourfold, from $700 million to approximately $2.8 billion.[12] By the end of the year, the UN had deployed over 50,000 peace-keepers in thirteen operations, at an annual cost of $3 billion.[13] This exponential increase in costs was exacerbated by the reluctance, and in some cases refusal, of member states to pay their dues. By the end of 1991 only 60 percent of the assessments of the regular budget had been paid.   As of June 1992, 35 percent of the 1991 assessments remained outstanding, together with 65 percent of the dues for the first half of 1992. This, therefore, meant that as of mid-1992 the United Nations was short by an amount equivalent of a full year's funding. The story in peacekeeping assessments looked equally as bad. By June 1992 only 25 percent of that year's 'heavy' peacekeeping dues had been paid, although the US had paid nearly 85 percent of its assessments by this time. The capriciousness of members' payments was symbolised by Japan, which as the UN's second largest contributor refused to pay 85 percent of its assessment until the end of 1991, and only then began to pay after acquiring a seat on the Security Council in January of the following year. Japan's contributions, however, remained strategic. Although it felt obliged to pay its assessment for the Cambodian operation in full by June (UNTAC had a Japanese Special Representative), it paid only a third of its assessments for Lebanon and Angola, and nothing towards the costs of the UNPROFOR operation in Croatia.[14]

Faced with increasing shortages of cash, the Organisation attempted to cut corners, riding its luck to an extreme. No more was this the case than in the Angolan operation UNAVEM II. With a territorial expanse the size of Western Europe and with a practically non-existent infrastructure, the Angolan mandate was a daunting task even to a well equipped and properly manned operation. To monitor the elections however, the UN deployed only 400 observers, despite there being no less than 6,000 polling stations. As a result UNAVEM II resorted to 'sample observation' in which teams of two observers spent an average of twenty minutes at each station, enough time to observe approximately four votes.[15] Even with this hectic timetable observers only visited 4,000 of the 6,000 polling stations. With the Electoral Law also requiring the count to take place at these polling stations, the farcical nature of the operation was made even more apparent. Even with one observer at each station it would only ever have been physically possible to cover less than 7 percent of the counts. Also, due to the low number of observers and the wide distribution of nationalities from which they had been composed, the operation suffered from an extreme shortage of Portuguese speakers, exacerbating the already overwhelming difficulties UNAVEM II faced. When the results of the election were unfavourable to UNITA, therefore, UNAVEM II was not really in a position to refute categorically the accusations of its leader Savimbi, when he claimed that there had been irregularities in the voting.

Both UNAVEM II and UNAMIC/UNTAC also suffered from the effects of the inefficient manner in which the UN approves the budgets for peacekeeping operations.[16] In the case of UNAVEM II, its budget was not approved for a period of nearly three months after the operation had begun, contributing to a slower than planned start and delaying the purchasing of essential equipment such as prefabricated buildings, generators and communications equipment.[17] The consequences of a lack of funding and delays in organising and approving the budget for UNTAC had equally regrettable consequences. Four months after deployment UNAMIC was still working on a miniscule budget of $45 million, most of which was supposedly allocated to de-mining, which could have swallowed ten times that amount alone.[18] The Bush administration did not pay its initial start up contribution of just $60 million until 1 May 1992, and even then it still owed a total of $112.3 million for past operations.[19]   Only on 14 February 1992 did the General Assembly approve an emergency request by the Secretary General for an advance appropriation of $200 million to help with the 'smooth and timely deployment of UNTAC'. The actual dispatch of UNTAC personnel, however, was still not possible. A prerequisite of such deployment is an overall budget prepared by the UN Secretariat and approved by the Security Council; a budget which was very slow to materialise.   Even Yashushi Akashi, the Secretary General's Special Representative, who himself was not appointed until two months into the operation, stated quite bluntly that despite the problems evident in the country, '... our main problems are not in Cambodia but here in New York over money and equipment'.[20]   It must have been one of the saddest ironies of the whole Cambodian operation, that having persuaded four civil warring factions to sign an agreement to cease military operations and partake in a democratic electoral process, that the UN needed Hun Sen, the leader of the Phnom Penh regime, to visit Congress in March 1992 and beg the US to release the money required to put the plan into effect. As Hun Sen told a Washington forum at the same time; '... once the peace accord was signed, governments (which had pressed for a UN role) became reluctant to pay.   They have placed the Cambodian people in a very dangerous situation.'[21]   Even Khieu Samphan, the nominal leader of the Khmer Rouge, and representative on the SNC, asserted that the absence of UNTAC on the streets of Phnom Penh during the initial months of the operation created a danger to the peace process in itself.[22]   The lesson of delayed deployment which the early days of the Namibian operation had taught seemed lost on the Security Council at least.   The sight of UN troops, together with a credible police force, could have instilled at least some confidence and hope.   Nor can it be said that the expectations of the Cambodians were too high.   During the crisis in the Congo in the early 1960s, over 18,000 troops were deployed within a week of the Security Council's decision.   Deployment in the Middle East in 1973 took only eighteen hours.

By the end of April 1992, however, UNTAC had only deployed 3,694 of a projected 15,900 troops, nearly five months after the operation had officially begun.   The delay in funding exacerbated the problem by postponing deployment until the beginning of the rainy season in late April. Despite the obvious climatic and topographical problems, the Force Commander drew up plans for Phase II of the operation (cantonment and demobilisation of the armed forces) which was approved in late May. This plan envisaged the deployment in their respective areas of at least eight battalions by the beginning of Phase II, on 13 June 1992. By that date, however, only four battalions had been fully deployed with complete equipment and personnel. These were the Bangladeshi, French, Indonesian and Malaysian battalions. Of the other battalions, the Dutch, assigned a north-eastern stronghold, were never able to fully deploy; the Pakistanis owing to heavy rain on 5 June were unable to cross the Dangrek mountain range, and did not reach full deployment until 6 July, a month behind schedule; the Tunisians arrived on 28 June; and the Ghanaians, who were assigned the Phnom Penh Special Zone, failed to arrive with complete stores and equipment.[23] Even by September 1992, virtually one year after the initiation of the operation, the Secretary General noted that the UNTAC military component was 800 troops short of its full contingent. Although in James Schear's view this delay in deployment did not affect adherence to the overall settlement timetable, it did,

> ... deny the operation early momentum, and it dampened the desired positive psychological impact upon domestic public opinion. It also, most damagingly, contributed to a sense of political drift and disarray allowing the four Khmer factions, in particular the Khmer Rouge and the Hun Sen regime, to hedge positions on full compliance with the Accords.[24]

By failing to implement its authority in a more assertive and forceful manner, UNTAC failed to take advantage of the element of surprise arising from the unfamiliarity of the combatants with the workings of the UN, the deterrent effect of its technical capabilities and the moral and political authority inherent in its mandate.[25] It was perhaps, therefore, his experience of the initial months of the Cambodian operation which prompted the Secretary General to state in *An Agenda for Peace*, that, '... our vision cannot really extend to the prospect opening up before us as long as our financing remains myopic.'[26]

Planning

Funding, however, although at the heart of most of the UN's problems, could not explain all of the UN's organisational inadequacies. Many of the complications which arose in the operations to this time could have been averted with adequate pre-operational planning, yet the UN system for planning and supporting field operations remained largely unchanged since the end of the Cold War. As such, it relied unduly on improvisation and *ad hoc* arrangements, both for organising operations and for managing the working relationships between members of the Secretariat and between officers and civilian personnel in the field. In order to strengthen the Secretariat's planning and managerial capabilities a Department of Peacekeeping Operations (DPKO) was established in February 1992. This department was to be headed by an Under-Secretary General and would consist of four divisions, covering Europe and Latin America, Asia, the Middle East, Africa and Electoral Assistance. The Department was also to include an Office of Planning and Support which, consisting of the Planning Division and the Field Administration and Logistics Division, would eventually 'serve as a centre of institutional memory and ... develop and maintain a ready capacity to act for future peacekeeping operations.'[27] Such a capacity, it was hoped, would prevent a repeat of the disarray caused in the UNTAC operation, in which each distinct component of the mission conducted a survey mission and formulated plans of its own, resulting in ridiculous situations such as the refugee repatriation programme beginning before the military component had deployed in sufficient numbers to designate minefields and provide the necessary security.[28]

This lack of strategic planning was also evident in New York. When Lieutenant General Sanderson, head of the military component of the UNTAC mission, travelled to UN headquarters in order to help speed up the deployment of troops, he discovered that not only did the UN lack any maps of Cambodia (as had been the case with Namibia), but that it also lacked any Khmer speakers, had no operations room, no team of UN military advisers to brief him on the UN's plans, no one able to brief contributing countries on what was expected of them, and no concept of how UNTAC's mandate might be translated into operational military terms. As Findlay states, it was obvious that the UN secretariat lacked the 'experience, resources and qualified personnel to organise a mission of such complexity, magnitude and novelty at such short notice'.[29] Its response to the lack of planning was to create UNAMIC, a hastily assembled good offices mission mandated to liaise between the conflicting parties whilst organising an operational assessment for UNTAC. Sanderson believed that the creation of UNAMIC lulled the Secretariat into a false sense of security. As he explained of the Secretariat's reaction to the realisation of the inadequacies of its preparation; 'The response to the deteriorating situation was to stick new pieces on to UNAMIC when it was not organised even to look after itself. UNAMIC therefore staggered from one crisis to another as it attempted to react to circumstances for which it was ill-prepared, leaving it unable to execute the important task of planning for UNTAC.'[30]

In Angola, the SGSR at the time of the elections, Margaret Anstee, complained that many of the problems which UNAVEM II had encountered had been rooted in the nature of the Peace Accord. As such, she complained that the UN had been given only a marginal role in the formulation and implementation of the peace plan. Although the reason for the UN's limited role lay at the doors of the Security Council and the Angolan parties themselves, Anstee had nevertheless found herself in control of institutional structures which relied too heavily on the 'good faith' of the parties concerned, and a timetable for demobilisation of their respective forces which was hopelessly unrealistic.[31]

The case of Western Sahara, and later Cambodia, also highlighted the problems which can arise in the separation of the UN's peacemaking and peacekeeping strategies. With little understanding of the complexities of conducting the kind of mandate upon which the negotiators had agreed, the UN peacemaking team had failed to separate the 'real from the fanciful'. As later analysts were to indicate, MINURSO failed even to begin with the necessary prerequisites for a successful peacekeeping mission. Although both contending parties had pledged their co-operation and support for the UN plan, there was no legally binding agreement for Western Sahara comparable to the 1991 Cambodian Settlement which had been signed by all four warring parties. Therefore, when Morocco failed to co-operate, Western powers such as the US and France, distracted by the events occurring in the former Soviet Union and Middle East and looking upon Morocco as an Arab moderate in the fight against fundamentalist Islam, refused to apply the diplomatic weight necessary to assure compliance. As no legally binding agreement had been signed, the US pressed only for the reduction of military trade with Morocco, whereas it had lobbied heavily for the introduction of comprehensive economic sanctions in the case of the Khmer Rouge. In the case of Cambodia the separation of the Organisation's peacemaking and peacekeeping strategies had come with the replacement of key personnel after the Paris Agreement, partly due to the recently appointed Secretary General Boutros Boutros-Ghali. Unlike the UNTAG operation in which the main negotiators of the UN role continued to be directly involved in its later implementation, UNTAC personnel had little knowledge of the negotiations which had led to their deployment. Warner cites this discontinuity of UNTAC mission personnel as being responsible for 'maybe half of the difficulties the mission faced in 1992'.[32]

Personnel and Equipment

The Secretary General also drew attention to the growing number of bottlenecks in the supply of personnel and equipment. The failure of the UN to establish an integrated logistics system had already left both the

UNTAC and UNPROFOR operations relying largely on national logistical capabilities. And although a UN system of procurement and contractor support was gradually evolving, it was quite obviously unable to cope during 1992. The Secretariat had, however, been involved in discussions leading to a United Nations involvement in Cambodia since at least 1990, and it would, therefore, seem unclear 'whether the Secretariat requested additional resources to enable it to manage the operation and was refused', or whether its initial logistical problems were caused by it being 'simply caught up unthinkingly in the UN's post-Cold War leap into nation-building'.[33]

The difficulty in procuring equipment for peacekeeping operations had already led the Secretary General to ask member states to establish reserves of stock, such as vehicles, radios, generators and prefabricated buildings, in different sites around the world, which could be released to the UN when required. As late as July 1992 the Secretary General reported that the shortage of radio-equipped vehicles had so far made it 'virtually impossible ... to fulfil adequately the mandate conferred upon UNPROFOR in the political and police areas'. In fact, when the Secretariat argued in the same month against the expansion of the operation into Bosnia and Herzegovina, one of the reasons cited by the Secretary General was that 'in spite of repeated requests to the General Assembly' he had not been 'authorised to establish a reserve stock of peacekeeping equipment which would enable [him] to respond quickly to new requirements of this kind'.[34]

Competition for specially trained personnel between the five operations being conducted through 1992 had also resulted in a shortage of qualified personnel for UNTAC's civil component. This had left it unable to assert sufficient control over the administrations of the warring factions, an essential element of the 'neutral' political environment UNTAC was required to produce. Seven months after the operation began, Girard Porcell, as head of UNTAC's civil component, felt obliged to confess that the UN's control over corruption within the Phnom Penh administration was so poor that; 'If I hear a complaint that someone is selling public property, I don't have the staff to send to the field to see if an official put the money in his pocket.'[35]

As well as a reserve stock of equipment, suggestions were also being made at this time for a reserve stock of personnel. Joseph S. Nye advocated a rapid deployment force of 60,000 troops built around a core group of around 5,000 professional UN soldiers, and even President Clinton proposed the establishment of a small standing 'rapid deployment force' to conduct operations, including the prevention of violence against civilians, providing humanitarian relief, guarding borders of countries threatened by aggression and combatting aggression. The French government also offered, within certain conditions, to make available 1000 troops to the Security Council on 48 hours' notice, and another 1000 within a week.[36]

UN Peacekeeping and the provision of Humanitarian Relief

As the relevant case studies have testified many of the peacekeeping operations conducted by the UN, both during and after the Cold War, have contained substantial elements of humanitarian work. Once deployed, peacekeepers are more than likely to be called upon to provide some kind of humanitarian comfort, whether it be to teach and monitor human rights in transforming states, provide food and shelter to victims of civil strife and natural disaster, or to facilitate prisoner exchanges and infrastructure building. In fact, in the post-Cold War operations covered in this section, the implementation of humanitarian elements of peacekeeping mandates, such as the return and repatriation of refugees and displaced persons; demobilisation and reintegration of former soldiers; demining and reinstitution of law and order; the restoration of essential supplies, such as education, water and power; have become as essential to the success of UN operations as the 'traditional' objective of separating belligerent forces. This is without doubt a consequence of the greater intra-state role which peacekeeping has adopted over the past seven years.

In the UN operations in the former Yugoslavia, Somalia and Rwanda, however, the integration of peacekeeping and the provision of humanitarian aid has had unexpected consequences. Firstly, the delivery of humanitarian aid in situations of political fluidity can jeopardise one of the fundamental precepts of UN Chapter VI operations: impartiality. As the UN has found out to its detriment, in intra-state conflict, as in all wars, preventing the enemy's access to food is a strategic objective. In the former Yugoslavia and Somalia, therefore, the UN has found that paramilitaries constantly block its attempts to deliver food, and on those occasions when the UN is successful, it is on many occasions perceived as having helped the opposing party. The second consequence of the fusion between peacekeeping and humanitarian aid is also concerned with a loss of impartiality, although this time it is caused through the use of force to protect relief convoys and civilian enclaves. 'Mission creep' is a phrase coined to describe how the UN has incrementally become ever more involved in operations which it began with only limited objectives. As one official described it in Bosnia:

... there was no political objective in our mandate when the operation began, but it was very quickly clear to us that we had to assume far wider responsibilities, including political and military negotiations at a much higher level than had ever been intended. We were, therefore, thrown into peacemaking whether we liked it or not because without some form of peace we could not possibly get the humanitarian convoys through.[37]

In the former Yugoslavia and Somalia, therefore, 'mission creep' occurred because the UN was forced to negotiate for the delivery of humanitarian aid and because it decided to enact Chapter VII mandates when these negotiations failed to produce the conditions it desired. Once again, however, the UN was unprepared for the consequences of such a use of force. As occurred in both operations, if one or more sides is deemed to be the aggressor, whether officially or unofficially, it is almost always impossible to remain impartial.

It is, therefore, because of the particular idiosyncrasies of these types of 'humanitarian' operations that this book has separated their analyses from those operations which have begun with 'comprehensive' negotiated settlements which the UN has helped in one way or another to implement.

The former Yugoslavia

Although the Secretary General remained cautious about the safety of a UN peacekeeping force in a situation in which the co-operation of all parties was not forthcoming, his fear that a failure to deploy might cause a breakdown of the latest ceasefire caused him to recommend the establishment of the United Nations Protection Force (UNPROFOR) in early February 1992. On 21 February the Security Council through Resolution 743 (1992) approved the establishment of the operation for an initial twelve month period. Under the criteria elucidated by the 'Vance plan', UNPROFOR, composing military, civilian police (CIVPOL) and civilian elements was to be deployed in the three so-called United Nations Protected Areas (UNPAs) in Croatia. These UNPAs, covering Eastern Slavonia, Western Slavonia and Krajina, were chosen due to their majority, or large minority, of Serbians resident within them. In this regard UNPROFOR was to help create the conditions of peace and security required for the negotiation of an overall settlement of the situation in former Yugoslavia.[38] Full deployment of UNPROFOR in these areas, however, was to be delayed by several months, the late arrival of some elements caused both by financial bickering in New York and complications produced through the outbreak of war in Bosnia. According to one human rights group this delay allowed ethnic cleansing in the UNPAs to go virtually unchecked, and stated that by the time UNPROFOR was fully operational in late June 1992 'most of the area's non-Serbian population had already been expelled'.[39]

UNPROFOR's mandate in Croatia had been to ensure that the UNPAs were de-militarised, and that all persons residing in them were protected from the fear of armed attack. This was to be achieved by the control of access to the UNPAs and the monitoring of local police to help ensure non-discrimination and the protection of human rights. UNPROFOR was also to supervise the withdrawal of the Yugoslavian National Army (JNA) from the whole of Croatia and support humanitarian agencies in the return of displaced persons.[40] From the very beginning, however, the UN was unable to secure the necessary co-operation from either of the parties in order to achieve these aims. Whilst the Croats continued to conduct incursions into UNPA territory in order to seize strategic sites, unhappy at the failure of the UN to disarm the Serbs, the Serbs themselves refused to disarm citing the need for self-defence against the Croatian army's revanchivist actions. Meanwhile, the Croatian government continued to insist that the UNPAs be reincorporated into Croatia, whilst the Serbs insisted that a pre-condition for talks on the future status of the areas was that they be recognised by the Croatian authorities as the State of the Republic of Serbian Krajina (RSK).[41] These problems were exacerbated when the UN monitors (UNMOs) reported that whilst elements of the JNA were withdrawing from the UNPAs as agreed, they were leaving behind arms and equipment for the Serb militias. The formation of the Federal Republic of Yugoslavia, announced by Serbia and Montenegro on 27 April 1992, and the subsequent withdrawal of the JNA from other republics also had the effect of leaving large numbers of well armed troops in Croatia and Bosnia, many keen to join local militias. Responsible for all disarmament, this development left UNPROFOR with a much more militarised situation than it had previously anticipated.

When in June 1992 UNPROFOR's mandate was extended to cover the 'pink zones', which were areas outside of the UNPAs not covered in the original agreement but containing significant numbers of Serbs, and previously occupied by the JNA, the operation's objectives became ever more elusive. With parts of the Serb enclaves in which it had deployed run by local 'gangsters and hoodlums' who were reportedly murdering up to five non-Serbs every week, UNPROFOR was unable to stymie the deterioration in effectiveness of the local police resulting in a situation in which no system of law and order existed in the UNPAs by the end of September.[42]

In Bosnia, the war which had followed its international recognition by the European Community on 6 April 1992, and the UN shortly afterwards, had by late summer of the same year produced such horrific humanitarian consequences that the international community had felt compelled to act. When the Security Council agreed to a plan proposed by Lord Carrington calling for the supervision of heavy weaponry in and around Sarajevo by UN forces in mid-1992, however, the Secretary General complained that not only was this new mandate virtually impossible to execute, but that the Security Council had 'thrust' it upon UNPROFOR without adequate consultation and without the necessary financial or other material commitments. In the Secretary General's opinion the inspection of heavy weapons would have required some 1,100 observers alone, especially as none of the warring parties had declared the locations or quantities of weapons to be supervised.[43] The UN believed this break in communication had been caused by the fact that the Organisation had not been represented at the discussions leading to the Security Council request, and that 'such difficulties could [have] been avoided if the whole peace negotiations were handled by the world organisation.'[44] It was in response to the Secretary General's criticisms of the lack of co-ordination between Lord Carrington and the UN that Britain proposed the London Conference of 26 August 1992.

Without the existence of a durable ceasefire the Secretary General had warned about the consequences which a mandate for the protection of humanitarian supplies might have upon both the peacekeeping operation already under way and on the position of relief organisations operating in the area. The Secretary General, in recognition of UNPROFOR's limited personnel, weapons and logistics, as well as the Security Council's reluctance to become involved in a military operation in Bosnia, advocated an impartial and conciliatory operation, preferring to negotiate for, rather than force through, the delivery of aid. By October 1992, however, with the failure to implement the agreements of the London Conference, the continuing siege of Muslim enclaves, ethnic cleansing, and attacks on aid convoys and relief flights, the UN was forced by public opinion to take a more concerted approach.[45] Therefore, as the next chapter will elucidate, with the Security Council's adoption on 14 September 1992 of Resolution 776 extending UNPROFOR into Bosnia and mandating that it support efforts by the UNHCR to deliver humanitarian relief, and in particular to provide protection, at the UNHCR's request, where and when it considered such protection necessary, together with the adoption of Resolution 781 of 9 October 1992 establishing a 'No-Fly Zone' over Bosnia, the first seeds of UN partiality in the former Yugoslavia were sown.

Somalia

Although, as in Yugoslavia, the greatest obstacles to the delivery of humanitarian aid in Somalia had been the absence of a durable ceasefire, the UN was also to create problems for itself. When the first UN peacekeeping force (UNOSOM I), which included 500 troops for the protection of UN personnel and equipment involved in the delivery of humanitarian aid, attempted to deploy, they were to be frustrated by the refusal of Mohammed Aideed, one of the leaders of the two main factions in Mogadishu, to accept their presence. His change of mind was not due to a capricious nature, but to the fact that his supporters had witnessed a Russian plane with UN markings delivering military hardware to Ali Mohammed, his main rival, in the north of the city. Under the circumstances, the SGSR for Somalia, Mohammed Sahnoun, believed Aideed's decision was totally 'understandable' and criticised his own organisation's 'lack of vigilance'.[46]

With the security situation deteriorating and the aid agencies unable to seek protection from the UN, their only option was to hire small armies of mercenaries to protect relief convoys, the UN itself hiring 10,000 local gunmen from both main factions, to guard the wheat shipments to Mogadishu port. Even when in mid-August 1992 the 500 Pakistani troops were able to deploy, a lack of sufficient weapons and armoury had prevented them from securing either the seaport or airport, both essential pre-requisites for the delivery of humanitarian aid. When the Secretary General requested the deployment of a further 3,000 troops, the UN once again managed to overlook the objections of Aideed by adopting Security Council Resolution 775 which included the proposed establishment of a police force and a food-for-weapons disarmament programme, neither of which he had agreed to.[47] Aideed, therefore, interpreted this resolution as the UN attempting to act against his wishes and the security situation deteriorated correspondingly.

By October 1992, the UN had managed not only to upset one of the two main local leaders in Somalia, but as a result had also failed to deploy the 3,000 troops it felt necessary to deliver humanitarian aid to the Somali populace. The Secretary General, therefore, was faced with a situation in which both the number of starving civilians and the intensity of the conflict were escalating.

Conclusion

Despite the Secretary General's recommendations in *An Agenda for Peace* on how to strengthen and make more efficient the UN's capabilities for peacekeeping, it was apparent by November 1992 that he was facing a losing battle. An already overstretched and under-resourced Organization was now facing an exponential increase in the size and cost of peacekeeping missions, without a commensurate improvement in its finance and manpower. Unable to amend the problems which its previous operations had made apparent, the Organization had already begun to suffer the consequences of the developing chasm between the tasks entrusted to it, and the international community's willingness to provide it with the necessary means to carry them out. With its complex budgetary processes; inefficient procurement procedures; lack of pre-operational planning; and dearth of manpower and finances; all of the operations being conducted during 1992 faced similar problems to those of previous operations, only now they were becoming worse. Compounded in Western Sahara, Yugoslavia, Cambodia and Somalia, by the intransigence of the warring parties, these problems posed a serious threat both to the success of peacekeeping and the credibility of the Organisation itself. And with the decision of Jonas Savimbi in Angola to return to war after elections held there in October 1992, the Organization's attempt to save money by cutting corners had made it look both helpless and ineffectual. As the following chapter will show, the UN's attempt to force warring parties into compliance was to have equally disastrous results.

Suggested Reading

Bailey, S.D., and Daws, S., *The United Nations,* Third edition, London, Barnes and Noble Books, 1995.

Boutros-Ghali, B., *An Agenda for Peace,* United Nations, New York, 1992.

Boutros-Ghali, B., 'Empowering the United Nations', *Foreign Affairs,* vol.2, no.5, 1992.

Durch, W., 'Building on sand: UN peacekeeping in the Western Sahara', *International Security*, vol.17, no.4, Spring 1993.

Gardenker, L., and Baehr, P., *The United Nations in the 1990s,* Second edition, London, Macmillan Press, 1990.

Liu, F.T., *United Nations peacekeeping and the non-use of force*, London, Rienner, 1992.

Roberts, A., and Kingsbury, B., *United Nations, divided world,* Oxford, Clarendon Press, 1993.

Roberts, A., 'The UN and international security', *Survival,* vol.35, no.2, Summer 1993.

Urquhart, B., 'The United Nations in 1992: problems and opportunities', *International Affairs,* vol.68, no.2, 1992.

White, N.D., *Keeping the peace: the United Nations and the maintenance of international peace and security,* Manchester University Press, 1993.

Peacekeeping and the UN

Notes

1. cf.Boutros-Ghali, B., *An agenda for peace*, United Nations, New York, 1992, p.1.

2. cf.Boutros-Ghali, B., 'UN peacekeeping in a new era: a new chance for peace', *World Today*, April 1993, p.68.

3. Roberts, A., 'The UN and international security', *Survival*, vol.35, no.2, Summer 1993, p.4.

4. Boutros-Ghali, B., *An agenda for peace*, op.cit, p.11.

5. Boutros-Ghali, B., 'Empowering the United Nations', *Foreign Affairs,* vol.72, no.5, 1992, p.93.

6. cf.*United Nations document, S/2486*, 14 July 1992.

7. 'Letter dated 27 July 1992 from the Special Representative to the Secretary General concerning the situation in Cambodia', The United Nations and Cambodia 1991-1995, *The United Nations blue book series*, vol.2, 1995, p.206.

8. Durch, W., 'Building on sand: UN peacekeeping in the Western Sahara', *International Security,* vol.17, no.4, Spring 1993, p.168.

9. Stahler-Sholk, R., 'El Salvador negotiates transition: from low intensity conflict to low intensity democracy', *The Journal of inter-American studies and world affairs*, Winter 1944, pp.12-13.

10. Weiss, G. et al., 'The United Nations and changing world politics', Oxford, Westview Press, 1994, p.64.

11. *United Nations document, S/24578*, 21 September 1992.

12. Boutros-Ghali, B., 'Empowering the United Nations', op.cit, p.95.

13. Boutros-Ghali, B., 'UN Peacekeeping in a new era: a new chance for peace', op.cit, p.67.

14. See Durch, W., 'Paying the tab: financial crises' in *The evolution of UN peacekeeping*, ed. Durch, W J., St. Martin's Press, New York, 1993, p.41.

15. *United Nations document S/24858*, 25 November 1992 in Berdal, M., *UN peacekeeping at a crossroads: IFS Information*, no.7, 1993, p.10.

16. The Secretariat must first prepare a mission budget which takes a period of several weeks. The Secretariat then submits this budget to the Advisory Committee on Administrative and Budgetary Questions (ACABQ) for approval. Meanwhile the United Nations cannot contract for equipment or services above a $3 million annual limit for each operation, on the Secretary General's 'unforeseen and extraordinary' spending authority. ACAQB normally takes less than a week to approve a mission budget; once it does the UN can obligate funds up to an annual limit of $10 million per mission. When the budget is finally approved by the General Assembly's 5th Committee, and then by the General Assembly, an assessment letter is sent to member states and then the UN can begin spending up to full mission cost. See *Financing an effective United Nations: a report of the independent advisory group on UN financing*, New York, Ford Foundation, 1993, p.17.

17. Fortna, V G., 'United Nations Angola Verification Mission II' in Durch, W. J., *The evolution of UN peacekeeping*, op.cit., p.395, 398.

18. 'UNclear', The Economist, February 29, 1992.

19. Lewis, P., 'UN sets June deadline in Cambodia', *The International Herald Tribune*, 11 May 1992.

20. cf.*The International Herald Tribune*, 11 May, 1992.

21. Awanohara, S., and Delfs R., 'Travelling salesman', *Far Eastern Economic Review*, 9 April 1992, p.12.

22. Thayer, N., 'Biding their time', *Far Eastern Economic Review*, 27 February 1992, p.27.

23. United Nations Military Operation in Cambodia, May 1992.

24. cf. Schear, J. A., in Findlay, T., 'Cambodia - the legacy and lessons of UNTAC', *SIPRI Research Report no.9*, Oxford University Press, 1995, p.113.

25.   Findlay, T., 'UNTAC-lessons to be learned', *International Peacekeeping*, vol.1, no.1, Jan-Feb 1994 p.7.

26.   Boutros-Ghali, B., *An agenda for peace*, op.cit, p.41.

27.   The Field Administration and Logistics Division within the DPKO develops plans for logistical support of field missions, specifying equipment, supplies and services needed. It participates in technical survey teams and determines mission start-up requirements and, on the basis of contingency planning activities, assembles, maintains and arranges the deployment of missions, equipment and supplies to permit a rapid initial deployment of key mission elements. cf.*Economic and Social Council document, E/AC.51/1995/2*, 17 March 1995.

28.   Findlay, T., *Cambodia: the legacy and lessons of UNTAC*, op.cit, p.117.

29.   cf.Ibid., p.114.

30.   cf. Sanderson, J. M., (Lieutenant General), 'UNTAC: successes and failures', in *International peacekeeping, building on the Cambodian experience*, ed.Smith, H., Australian Defence Studies Centre, Canberra, 1994, p.18.

31.   'Demobilisation after civil wars', *Strategic Survey 1993-94*, Brassey's for the International Institute of International Studies, p.26.

32.   cf.Warner, N., in Findlay, op.cit., p.118.

33.   cf.Ibid., p.115.

34.   cf.Berdal, M., 'Whither UN peacekeeping', *Adelphi Paper 281*, October 1993, Brassey's for the International Institute for Strategic Studies, pp.35-36.

35.   cf.Hiebert, M., 'Draining the swamp', *Far Eastern Economic Review*, 11 June 1992, p.25.

36.   Nye, J., in Gerlach, J. R., 'A UN army for the New World Order', *Orbis*, vol.37, no.2, Spring 1993, p.225 and President Clinton in

Berdal, M., 'Fateful encounter: the US and UN peacekeeping', *Survival*, vol.36, no.1, Spring 1994, p.31.

37. Fetherston, A., Ramsbotham, O., and Woodhouse, T., 'UNPROFOR: some observations from a conflict resolution perspective', *International Peacekeeping*, vol.1, no.2, Summer 1994, p.191.

38. Berdal, M., 'UN peacekeeping in the former Yugoslavia', in ed. Darvel, D., and Hayes, B., *Beyond traditional peacekeeping*, Macmillan Press, 1995, p.229.

39. cf.Fetherston, A., et al, op.cit, p.182.

40. United Nations, 'The United Nations and the situation in the former Yugoslavia', *Reference paper revision 4*, Department of Public Information, p.4.

41. Bair, A., 'What happened in Yugoslavia? Lessons for future peacekeepers', *European Security*, vol.3, no.2, Summer 1994, p.343.

42. Fetherston et al, op.cit, p.183-184.

43. Ibid., p.185. See also Mauther, R., 'Boutros-Ghali attacks EC peace plan', *The Financial Times*, 22 July 1992.

44. cf.Fetherston et al, ibid., p.186.

45. These included an attack on an aid convoy approaching the besieged town of Gorazde in late July 1992; the downing of an Italian aid plane on 3 September 1992 causing the closing for a month of Sarajevo airport. ibid., p.186.

46. cf.Stevenson, J., 'Hope restored in Somalia?' *Foreign Policy*, no.91, Summer 1993, p.145.

47. See 'UN Chief wants 3,500 troops to guard Somalia aid', The Financial Times, 26 August 1992 and *United Nations Document S/RES/775*, 28 August 1992.

Chapter 5
Crisis in UN Peacekeeping
November 1992-1993

Introduction

Although the failure of the international community to prevent a resumption of civil war in Angola had dealt the first serious post-Cold War blow to the confidence of the Organisation, the establishment of the operation in Mozambique in December 1992, followed by the installation of the Clinton Administration in January 1993, helped to rejuvenate the UN. The Organisation had, after all, much to expect from the Presidential candidate who only the previous August had declared that because 'multilateral action [held] promise as never before', that the UN deserved 'full and appropriate contributions from all the major powers'.[1] It was not initially to be disappointed. On taking office the new administration appointed Madaleine Albright as American Ambassador to the UN, but unlike previous appointees gave her a Cabinet seat and made her a member of the National Security Council. It also created the new post of Assistant Secretary for Peacekeeping. With the new prominence awarded to the UN in Washington, it seemed that the funding and resource problems which had hampered its peacekeeping operations might finally be eradicated.

The Clinton administration continued to express the new importance of the UN in its foreign policy throughout the early part of 1993. In March,

Secretary of State Warren Christopher stated that the situations in Somalia and Bosnia had resulted from the international community's failure to react quickly enough to impending crises, and reiterated the administration's belief that 'international peacekeeping, especially by the UN, can and must play a critical role' and that 'capabilities must be enhanced to permit prompt, effective, preventive action'. And in what must have seemed like music to the Secretary General's ears, Christopher also stated that the US had to be 'prepared to pay its fair share' because 'millions invested in peacekeeping now may save hundreds of millions in relief later.'[2]

With the establishment of the operation in Mozambique, the UN had in only five years equalled the number of operations it had created throughout the forty or so years of the Cold War. The nature of peacekeeping in these two eras had changed dramatically, however, with the vast majority of new peacekeeping operations being internal missions. In the optimistically entitled *UN Peacekeeping in a New Era, A New Chance for Peace*, the Secretary General noted in April 1993 how these latest operations were being called to perform a 'growing litany of new responsibilities other than the traditional military aspects of peacekeeping'. In what he described as 'expanded peacekeeping', the Secretary General listed the major demands being made on post-Cold War operations, including the repatriation of refugees; overseeing the conduct of elections; maintaining law and order; promoting political dialogue; assisting with economic reconstruction and rehabilitation; preventive deployment; sanctions on commerce and communications; and providing protection for the delivery of humanitarian assistance in volatile areas.[3] In Somalia this latter role had also caused the UN to break new ground by providing a UN peacekeeping mission with a Chapter VII mandate. So, although the Secretary General was well aware of the inadequacies of the UN in its peacekeeping operations, the future as of summer 1993 must have looked reasonably bright.

Also in the summer of 1993, Adam Roberts warned that it was by no means impossible 'that internal conflicts could drag the UN down'. He cited the resumption of the civil war in Angola as 'an ominous indicator of this type of hazard'.[4] His warning was to be somewhat prophetic. In June, Washington was nearing the completion of an internal review of US support for peacekeeping, which had been ordered by President Clinton the previous February, and which was to have been used as the basis for his maiden speech to the United Nations General Assembly in late September. Initial indications had been that the administration's new policy towards peacekeeping had even included the willingness of the US to accept UN command over American forces, a major shift in policy from the previous Bush administration. With the murder of American soldiers serving in Somalia in August, however, the direction of US involvement in UN peacekeeping was to change dramatically. Rather than elucidating the manner in which the US was to enhance the role of UN peacekeeping in the resolution of conflict, the review (PRD 13) transformed into an illustration of the 'limitations of multilateralism and US involvement' in peacekeeping.[5] In October, following the deaths of even more Americans in Somalia, Congress began a series of measures designed to limit the American contribution to peacekeeping, and even in some cases reduce it.

Within twelve months, therefore, the resolve of the US government to suffer the political consequences of American deaths in peacekeeping operations, in situations of little or no national interest, had been tested and found wanting. As a result the UN was to suffer the humiliation of not only having US financial and political support reduced, but also being accused of contributing to the catastrophe in Somalia through its confused command structures and operational procedures. Although, as the following pages will explain, the American deaths were the fault of no one but the Americans themselves, the crisis in the UN had been truly precipitated.

TABLE 5: Peacekeeping Operations established November 1992-1993

Mission	Brief Explanation
United Nations Operation in Mozambique (ONUMOZ) 1992-94	Verify demobilization and disarmament; withdrawal of foreign troops; assistance in monitoring of elections; coordinate humanitarian assistance
United Nations Operation in Somalia II (UNOSOM II) 1993-95	Ensure maintenance of secure environment for humanitarian relief operations; foster national reconciliation and the rehabilitation of political institutions and economy of Somalia
United Nations Observer Mission (UNOMUR) Uganda-Rwanda 1993-94	Monitor the Rwanda/Uganda border; verify cessation of military assistance to Rwanda

Ongoing Operations

By the end of 1992 the situation in Cambodia had deteriorated even further. The PDK continued to refuse to fulfil any of its commitments under the Paris Accords whilst Vietnamese soldiers remained in the country, and UNTAC could not provide a 'neutral political environment'. UNTAC attempted to reassure the PDK that all foreign forces had left by the 31

October 1991 deadline set by the Accords, by offering to establish a further ten border posts at which PDK representatives could be present. This offer, however, was not taken up by the PDK. The second complaint of the PDK was not quite so easily refuted by UNTAC. A lack of funding and personnel had resulted in UNTAC's failure to 'supervise and control' the five key ministries which the Paris Accords stipulated would be necessary to produce a 'neutral political environment'. Although the PDK's interpretation of a 'neutral political environment' continued to request measures far beyond those which the UN had envisaged, UNTAC could never categorically state that it had fulfilled its own commitments under the Accords.

With the cantonment of forces suspended by November 1992, the Secretary General was faced with the decision of whether or not to continue with the operation. He personally rejected a withdrawal of UNTAC on the grounds that it would be 'unacceptable after so much [had] been achieved and so many hopes raised that Cambodia [would] at last achieve peace and democracy'. He also rejected a suspension of the operation, stating that it 'would require the international community to maintain indefinitely a large and very costly operation, whose recurrent costs are now running at almost $100 million per month'.[6] He therefore took the courageous decision to continue with the operation without the co-operation of the main resistance faction, the PDK, whilst admitting that the elections to be held in May 1993 would 'clearly not be taking place in an environment as disarmed and politically neutral as was envisaged in the Paris Agreements and in the implementation plan'.[7]

On the Iraq-Kuwait border a reinforcement of UNIKOM was to be required as a result of a series of incidents involving the unauthorised intrusion by Iraqis into the Kuwait side of the de-militarised zone (DMZ) in 1993, ostensibly to recover property. The Security Council through Resolution 806 (1993) expanded the mandate of UNIKOM to include the physical action to prevent or redress small-scale violations of the DMZ or Iraq-Kuwait boundary, and authorised an increase in its strength to 3,465.

The issues which had led to the suspension of FMLN demobilisation in El Salvador were resolved in early October 1992 by a solution proposed by the Secretary General. With the dismantling of the FMLN military structures completed by 15 December 1992 the armed conflict was pronounced finished on the same day, and the FMLN was recognised as a legitimate political party seven days later. On 8 January 1993, the government of El Salvador requested the United Nations to observe the elections which were due to be held in March 1994. In response, the Security Council adopted Resolution 832 in February 1993, establishing the Electoral Division of ONUSAL, which represented the second enlargement of the operations mandate. Although the discovery of illegal arms caches belonging to the FMLN in May 1993 threatened to derail the peace process, a renewed commitment by the FMLN allowed the destruction of all weapons and equipment belonging to the party to take place by 18 August.

In Angola, despite the apparent success of the elections held on 29-30 September 1992, the leader of UNITA, Jonas Savimbi, accused the MPLA of fraudulence and threatened to return to war. With 90 percent of the 4.9 million Angolans registered to vote having done so, the official announcement of the result was postponed whilst an investigation into the allegations was carried out. With no evidence of 'significant or systematic' fraud found, the results were officially declared, with the MPLA winning 53.7 percent and UNITA 34.1 percent for the Angolan legislature. In the elections for the Presidency, which were held at the same time, the MPLA leader, dos Santos, won 49.6 percent whilst Savimbi registered 40.1 percent.

Unwilling to enter into the democratic spirit, Savimbi executed his threat, and Angola returned to civil war. However, by November 1992, 80 percent of government troops had demobilised, whilst almost all of UNITA's troops had remobilised. With UNITA's numerical advantage it was able to capture two-thirds of Angolan territory within months of the elections. In such a strong position UNITA was unwilling to negotiate with either the MPLA or the small UN presence which had remained. However, the US recognition of the MPLA as the legitimate government of Angola in May, followed by its lifting of sanctions on the sales of non-lethal military equipment in July, helped the MPLA recoup by the end of the year. With its diplomatic isolation increasing, UNITA once again began to negotiate, although by December 1993 the UN had retained only 43 military observers, 18 police observers and 11 paramedics in the field.[8]

United Nations Operation in Mozambique (ONUMOZ: 1992-1994)

Founded in 1962, the *Frente de Libertacao de Mocambique* (FRELIMO), began its armed struggle against the country's Portuguese colonialists two years later. After eleven years of liberation struggle, the Portuguese finally capitulated in 1975, leaving the country in devastation. In its first five years of government FRELIMO was to find itself caught up in the fight for independence in neighbouring Rhodesia (Zimbabwe), until liberation was achieved in that country in 1979. Once Zimbabwe had achieved independence, Mozambique was to become embroiled in another conflict, this time involving the exiled African National Congress (ANC) and the

South African Armed Forces. By the mid-1980s, in an effort to destabilise the Mozambiquan pro-Marxist government, the South African security forces had transformed the Mozambiquan rebel group *Resistencia Nacional Mocambicana* (RENAMO) into a formidable military organisation. By the time the General Peace Agreements (GPA) were signed between the leaders of FRELIMO and RENAMO in Rome in October 1991, Mozambique had suffered from 16 years of bloody and brutal civil war.

The first real movements towards national reconciliation were to take place in 1988, in juxtaposition with the peace agreements being negotiated in Angola and Namibia. Over the next four years talks were held between the two opposing parties, ending with the signing of the GPA in Rome on 4 August 1992. Three days later the Secretary General informed the Security Council that both parties wished the UN to provide assistance during the peace process, which would include monitoring a ceasefire, demobilisation and the verification of elections. By mid-September the UN had been able to send two survey teams to assess the operation's requirements to monitor elections and for general peacekeeping, the latter of which reported that the UN operation would be faced with a situation including an estimated 3 million internally displaced persons, 1.5 million refugees, millions of unmarked landmines and the possibility of soldiers waiting for demobilisation drifting into banditry. On 16 December 1992, the United Nations Operation in Mozambique was established pursuant to Resolution 797 (1992).[9]

In accordance with the GPA (also known as the Rome Agreement), ONUMOZ was assigned a wide range of tasks, which included *inter alia*: the verification of the maintenance of the ceasefire; the assembly and demobilisation of troops; collection of weapons; verification of military locations; assistance in the formation of a new Mozambiquan Defence Force; monitoring of security along the corridors and main routes; maintenance of police functions in those areas where the Mozambiquan police was unable to establish its presence; monitoring of the activities of the Mozambiquan national police; co-ordination and monitoring of humanitarian assistance operations; implementation of a mine-clearing programme, including the build-up of a Mozambiquan de-mining authority; technical and financial assistance in the electoral process; and the monitoring of the elections to be held on 27-29 October 1993.[10]

However, as soon as it had begun the ONUMOZ operation was to be delayed by the pedantic approach being taken by the parties to the agreement, and the lack of resources and personnel available to the UN. On 7 January 1993, the leader of RENAMO, Alfonso Dhlakama, announced that his forces would not proceed with demobilisation until most of the ONUMOZ forces had deployed. And for their part FRELIMO hampered the deployment of ONUMOZ by drawing out negotiations over a status of forces agreement until 14 May 1993. Both parties also failed to agree on assembly points for their demobilising troops. In June, British Ambassador Richard Ellis, stated that London would not be prepared to carry on 'throwing money down the drain' waiting for both sides to get moving on the matter of demobilisation.[11] With delays in the implementation of the peace agreement accumulating, the SGSR, Aldo Ajello, was left with little option but to renegotiate the time frame for implementation, postponing the date for elections until October 1994.

Preventive Deployment

The deployment of peacekeepers in the Former Yugoslav Republic of Macedonia (FYROM) during 1993 represented a new development in UN peacekeeping. It set a precedent for future peacekeeping missions because the UN deployed the force before hostilities had broken out. Boutros-Ghali, writing in *An Agenda for Peace*, perceived such deployment could take place either in inter-state disputes or intra-state crisis. (See Appendix 5.) In the case of the former, UN peacekeepers could be deployed along both sides of a mutual border in order to discourage hostilities, or where one state feared attack by another, UN peacekeepers could be deployed on its border territory to symbolise the international community's wish to prevent an attack. In the case of intra-state crisis the Secretary General envisaged UN troops alleviating suffering through the delivery of humanitarian aid and assisting the maintenance of security through either military or civilian personnel. Deployment would of course be confined to requests by the 'government or all parties concerned, or with their consent'.[12]

In the former Yugoslavia the UN was anxious not to allow the war to spread into the FYROM. The threat of Serb aggression was beginning to upset the delicate ethnic and religious balance, and any invasion would have risked embroiling neighbouring countries such as Albania, Bulgaria and Greece, all of whom have close cultural and historical ties with the region. If the Serbs had attacked, forcing hundreds of thousands of Muslims to flee in the fear of ethnic cleansing, the consequences could have been horrific. With reports of increasing risks, therefore, the Security Council passed Resolution 795 in December 1992 authorising the Secretary General to establish an UNPROFOR presence in the FYROM.[13]

The UN did not intend the force to be able to resist an armed offensive by the Serbs. Instead, it deployed sufficient troops (700) to symbolise the international community's determination to prevent the war from escalating.

As a 'thin blue line', the peacekeepers in the FYROM represented a trip wire, warning the Serbs that aggression would have serious repercussions. For this reason, all preventive deployments in inter-state disputes need to be planned so that Chapter VII reinforcements can be speedily deployed. In the case of the FYROM, the presence of American troops probably increased Serbian fears of a greater US involvement if they were attacked, adding to the symbolic weight of the force.

Successes

With the mission in Western Sahara still bogged down in fruitless discussions, the only successes in the implementation of negotiated settlements were to come in the operations in Cambodia, El Salvador and Mozambique. Cambodia, as the largest and most ambitious operation of 1991-92 was to experience its greatest success with the organisation of democratic elections in late May 1993. Although the UN had previously monitored and supervised elections in Namibia, Angola, and Nicaragua, Cambodia's was to be the first election that the UN had directly organised from the planning stages, through the writing of the electoral law, to the registration and conduct of the poll.[14] Despite attempts by the Khmer Rouge to upset the elections with the threat of violence, 4,267,192 Cambodian citizens, representing 89.56 percent of all registered voters, turned out to cast their ballots. The Secretary General was able to declare the poll both 'free and fair' on 29 May although he could not say the same for the electoral campaign.[15] This overwhelming success, coming as it did at the culmination of an operation that had for so long teetered on the edge of failure, was a testimony to the courage of both the volunteer electoral workers and Cambodian people, who together braved the threat of violence and intimidation in an attempt to create a safer and more prosperous future.

The elections were not, however, the only success of the Cambodian operation. UNTAC peacefully repatriated 365,000 refugees, and working in conditions in which land mines and the continuation of civil war had severely reduced the amount of land available, still managed to voluntarily locate them in places they could accept.[16] UNTAC also verified the withdrawal of foreign forces, and although the numbers remained relatively low due to its inability to complete the programme, cantoned and disarmed all those forces who had presented themselves to it. Human rights also gained greater recognition through the work of UNTAC's human rights component, and the process for social and economic rehabilitation and restructuring had begun.

On a more sober note, Stephen Solarz, the American Congressman who had first proposed a United Nations role in Cambodia, claimed that UNTAC had achieved the 'minimum' and unspoken aim of the Paris Accords, which in effect was 'to place the Khmer Rouge in isolation'.[17] Although the operation had not brought peace to Cambodia, UNTAC had managed to defuse the international dimension to the conflict, by allowing reconciliation on the matter between the Chinese, Vietnamese and Americans. This had culminated in the reopening of trade links between the three countries. The Khmer Rouge, having lost their principal foreign backer, were left with only the Thai military to lend support. They had failed to legitimise their position by refusing to take part in the election, thereby losing the 8-10 percent of the vote they had been predicted; they had lost control over the thousands of refugees in Thai border camps; and the legitimacy they had previously maintained through their recognition as one of the representative parties at the United Nations, had disappeared. It had even suffered the defection of an estimated 2,000 soldiers during UNTAC's tenure.[18]

In El Salvador, despite setbacks due to the discovery of illegal arms caches belonging to the FMLN and fears in the latter part of 1993 that the assassinations of prominent officials had marked the re-emergence of the infamous 'death squads', ONUSAL had officially opened an election campaign on 20 November 1993. This campaign had been planned to culminate in elections in April/May 1994. The National Public Security Academy, responsible for the training of recruits to the new National Civil Police, celebrated its first anniversary in September 1993 with over two thousand graduates, contributing to the Secretary General's assessment in November 1993 that the implementation of the Accords had 'on the whole progressed well.' Although he remained concerned that at the end of the year 'some very important elements' of the Accords remained only partially implemented', he was sure that through ONUSAL's work 'enormous advances [had] been achieved, advances that it would have been difficult to imagine when the UN first became involved in the effort to make peace in El Salvador four years ago'.[19]

In Mozambique, delays in the cantonment and demobilisation of troops which had threatened to derail the peace process had been overcome, and the assembly of troops began on 30 November 1993. Thirty-five of a planned forty-nine assembly sites had been opened by the end of the year and negotiations were continuing to open the remaining fourteen. A new Electoral Law had been approved by the Mozambiquan National Assembly on 9 December and the Secretary General had in the previous month recommended that the mandate for ONUMOZ be extended to cover the elections which had been rearranged for October 1994.[20]

Successes in the operations in Somalia and Yugoslavia had been limited to the aversion of humanitarian disasters, which although the primary goal of both missions, had subsequently become subordinated by the increased politicisation of their roles. In Somalia, food was at last reaching all parts of the country, and the levels of malnutrition and death from starvation had fallen dramatically. Attempts by UNITAF and UNOSOM II to prevent one of the Somali parties from upsetting the peace negotiations, however, was to redirect attention away from its humanitarian successes towards the failure of the UN to recreate stability and security. In Yugoslavia, despite the creation of safe areas in Bosnia itself, and the continuing negotiations between the parties, no real peace looked imminent. The delivery of humanitarian aid was being constantly hindered by the Bosnian Serbs, and the bombardment of the so-called safe areas had compelled the UN to take Chapter VII military action on three occasions. Even on occasions when UNPROFOR had evacuated Bosnians from areas under attack, the UN had been accused of complicity in 'ethnic cleansing'. Like the Somalian operation, therefore, the successes that UNPROFOR had achieved in the delivery of humanitarian aid had become subordinated by the failure to halt the Bosnian-Serb offensive, and the continuing stories of massacres, ethnic cleansing, rape and torture reported in the international media.

So although the UN had achieved some substantial successes in 1993, especially in Cambodia, El Salvador and Mozambique, its public image was beginning to falter. This was mainly due to the operations in Somalia and Yugoslavia, which under the microscopic scrutiny of the public eye became embroiled in seemingly intractable conflicts. The post-Cold War Security Council consensus, which had heralded so much hope, was looking increasingly fragile on the issue of Chapter VII enforcement action in Bosnia, and the belief that international will could enforce peace was dissipating in Somalia. Thus, 1993 was the year in which the international community recognised the limitations of UN peacekeeping.

Problems

Funding

Although 1993 witnessed the end of the operation in Cambodia, the expansion of the operations in Somalia and Yugoslavia had served only to worsen the UN's funding problems. By the end of January 1994 the UN had accumulated a deficit of more than $2.7 billion dollars in assessed contributions, of which $1.3 billion was owed for the regular budget and $1.4 billion for peacekeeping operations. The greatest debtors at this stage were the US, which owed approximately \$530 million for the regular budget and \$288 million for peacekeeping, and the Russian Federation, which owed \$68 million for the regular budget and \$507 million for peacekeeping.[21] At the same time, the annual cost of peacekeeping had risen to around \$3.2 billion a year, compared with the \$9.4 billion for all the UN operations since 1948. The number of UN troops deployed had also risen to around 70,000.[22]

Matters had begun to reach crisis proportions when the collapse in support for American involvement in peacekeeping operations, precipitated by its experience in Somalia, led in late October 1993 to a compromise bill between the House and Senate cancelling a proposed \$175 million contingency fund to cover immediate peacekeeping costs. At the same time Congress had also decided to withhold 10 percent of its regular contribution to the Organisation, until the Secretary General appointed an Inspector General to eliminate corruption. As well as cancelling the fourth of five special payments planned by the Bush administration to cover existing arrears, Congress also informed President Clinton that the US share of future peacekeeping bills had to be cut from 31.7 percent to 25 percent. This bill was eventually passed, but only after the House had already rejected a rather modest proposal from the Pentagon for a \$10 million fund to help strengthen the UN Situation Centre in New York.[23] Both the House and Senate had already approved fiscal 1994 spending bills in late July 1993, which cut the administration's peacekeeping request by 32 percent, 'effectively killing a proposed peacekeeping contingency fund that would have enabled the US to contribute emergency start-up funds to unforeseen peacekeeping operations' the following year.[24] In order to facilitate the process of financing the start up of operations the General Assembly, pursuant to Resolution 47/217 of 23 December 1992, had established a Peacekeeping Reserve Fund, to become effective from 1 January, 'as a cashflow mechanism to assist in the rapid response of the Organisation to the needs of peacekeeping operations'. However, the failure of the member states to make systematic payments to the accounts of existing peacekeeping operations resulted in the Secretary General borrowing from the resources available in the Reserve Fund to keep them afloat. The Fund had subsequently become insufficient to provide the basic start-up costs for newly established operations. Embarrassingly, the general lack of funds for peacekeeping operations was to result in the Secretary General admitting to the two main parties in Mozambique in October 1993, that '... in the UN now we have problems due to the number of situations all over the world, due to the fact that we have a financial crisis, and we will not be able to provide immediately the police necessary in conformity with the agreement that was concluded in Rome'.[25]

Planning

In 1993 the US Ambassador to the UN, Madaleine Albright, stated that she had been 'surprised' to find that when a peacekeeping operation was launched it started from scratch. She noted a number of problems which had beset peacekeeping, including the absence of contingency planning and prior knowledge about available forces; the lack of centralised command and control capabilities; improvised lift arrangements and a cumbersome and complex procurement system. As Berdal remarked, these comments revealed a curious lack of knowledge about both the nature of UN peacekeeping and, more generally, the extent to which the workings of the UN reflect the international system in which it operates.[26] However, her comments did go to explain why the major powers on the Security Council had continued to expect the UN to cope with ever expanding mandates whilst stubbornly refusing to settle their financial accounts. To those involved in peacekeeping operations, the limitations of the Organisation were not surprising. The Secretary General had stated as early as November 1992 that as the Secretariat was 'already overstretched in managing greatly enlarged peacekeeping commitments' it did not at that time have 'the capacity to command and control an enforcement action of the size and urgency required by the present crisis in Somalia'.[27] It was precisely this realism which had led the Secretary General to seek US intervention through UNITAF. Although attempts had been made to rectify the most serious deficiencies in the DPKO, including a modest expansion of staffing levels, the creation of an embryonic Planning and Co-ordination Cell and the establishment of a Situation Room in New York, major problems still remained. The Situation Room, set up initially to deal with the UNPROFOR and UNOSOM operations, had been extended to cover all UN missions, but it was still not a command centre in the military sense nor the command and control centre an operation such as UNITAF would have required. Neither had these reforms reversed the growing decentralisation of peacekeeping functions within the Secretariat and the consequent diffusion of authority in the management of operations. For Berdal the reforms had been both 'incremental and fragmented' and as such had paid insufficient attention to the requirements of co-ordinating activities between Departments, Divisions and Offices within the Secretariat.[28]

The deficiencies of the UN which Albright listed had already resulted in the UN experiencing difficulties in fulfilling its mandates. In Cambodia,

UNTAC's failure to supervise and control the five key areas of the State of Cambodia (SoC) administration, resulted in an inability to deal effectively with the regime's corruption and intimidation of opposing political figures. In Gareth Evans' view this failure had given at least a 'spurious justification' to the decision of the Khmer Rouge not to comply with the key provisions in the Paris Agreements.[29] The control of the SoC administration had been seen by the PDK as essential to the production of the 'neutral political environment' which the Paris Accords had promised and they had continually cited UNTAC's failure to fulfil this commitment as the reason it was unable to continue with Phase II (cantonment and demobilisation of armed forces). The PDK also accused UNTAC of failing to verify the withdrawal of all foreign forces, although they could not provide any evidence of the Vietnamese troops they believed were still present.

A second area in which UNTAC failed to adequately fulfil its mandate was that of human rights. Through Articles 15 and 16 of the Paris Accords UNTAC had been charged, among other things, with 'fostering an environment in which respect for human rights would be ensured' and preventing a return to the 'policies and practices of the past'. In Findlay's opinion UNTAC's failure to fulfil this mandate was due mainly to its reluctance to deal forcibly with human rights infringements caused mostly by its unwillingness to establish a system of justice to deal with the most egregious crimes.[30] Although UNTAC had never before assumed such an intrusive and authoritative mandate in the area of human rights, in the initial planning stages it had been allocated only ten officers. Although these personnel numbers were subsequently increased, the Human Rights component remained significantly understaffed. In the face of mounting cases of human rights abuses, the UN took a revolutionary step in late 1992 when it appointed its own special prosecutor, Australian barrister Mark Plunkett. However, despite the special prosecutor's office (established in January 1993) issuing warrants for the arrest of known human rights violators, UNTAC lacked even a jail for their incarceration. Although this deficiency was quickly remedied with the procurement of 'detention facilities', other problems still existed. The CIVPOL, unarmed and already lacking credibility, was in no position to arrest armed criminals, and by its own interpretation, the military component had no mandate to exercise force to carry out such duties. With the unwillingness of the SoC judicial system to prosecute SoC members, and the general unreliability of SoC courts to administer justice, UNTAC's mandate was impossible to fulfil.[31] Gareth Evans highlights this inevitability, stating that the '... point is simply that if a peacekeeping operation is given a mandate to guard against human rights violations, but there is no functioning system to bring violators to justice - then not only is the UN force's mandate to that extent unachievable, but its whole operation is likely to have diminished credibility, both locally and internationally.'[32]

Findlay cites the lack of inter-component co-ordination and co-operation as another of the planning failures of UNTAC. As noted in the last chapter, this lack of co-ordination had already hindered the start-up of the operation, with the different components not even holding joint co-ordination meetings until March 1993. Even at the conclusion of the operation, the Force Commander, Lieutenant General Sanderson, admitted that there had never been any 'integrated strategic planning within the UNTAC mission'. The field operation, described as a managerial 'stovepipe', consisted of each component reporting back to its own headquarters in Phnom Penh rather than to UNTAC headquarters. In Sanderson's view this caused 'considerable grief and disharmony' in the operation.[33] As Warner observed, management in the field made it seem 'that the administrative blueprint of previous - and much smaller and less complex - operations [was] simply dusted off and applied to the Cambodia mission'.[34]

Overall, the operation in Cambodia highlighted a number of inadequacies with the UN's planning and administration. In Albright's words '... an elephantine bureaucracy [had] been asked to do gymnastics', and over-exertion had brought the operation close to collapse on a number of occasions.[35] Despite the fact that the Secretary General was forced to admit in May 1993 that 'in the light of the sobering experience of the last thirteen months that the expectations originally entertained for ensuring that the election is free and fair and for the success of national reconciliation were overly optimistic', his brave decision to continue with the operation regardless of the non-co-operation of the PDK, and UNTAC's failure to implement all of its mandate, had allowed the operation to superficially overcome its inherent inadequacies.[36]

With its assembly areas able to accommodate only 30-50 percent of the total number of troops in Mozambique, the UN's planning became unstuck when a massive influx of RENAMO troops led to severe overcrowding. This had led at least one camp to hold twice as many soldiers as intended. The UN also experienced a shortage in the storage capacity for arms in the assembly areas, which by the beginning of 1994 had been far exceeded. Demobilisation of the troops had been delayed due to the refusal of RENAMO to continue with the peace process until it had received financial backing for its political activities from the international community. Ajello, the SGSR for Mozambique, continually refused to continue with the peace process whilst demobilisation was stalled, because he would not allow the same mistake to be made as had been made previously in Angola.

Although UNAVEM II had a mandate only to monitor disarmament in Angola, not conduct it as in Mozambique, elections proceeded whilst it was recognised that UNITA had not disarmed, the major reason cited for Angola's return to civil war.

Personnel and Equipment

The UN's logistics system began to buckle in 1993 under the weight of the massive expansion of peacekeeping in the previous twelve months. At the end of the year an external evaluation study stated that the UN still lacked a logistics system strong enough to support operations as large as UNTAC and UNOSOM. One reason cited for the problems being experienced was the complex nature of the Secretariat's procurement system. An internal assessment produced by UNPROFOR military staff in the summer of 1993 estimated that the process between a battalion commander formally requesting an item from UNPROFOR Headquarters in Zagreb and actually receiving it involved 52 separate steps.[37] The need for a more efficient and less complex procurement system had been evident in other operations. In Cambodia the procurement process for photocopiers had been described as 'farcical' and the need to use cumbersome Secretariat tendering systems had also been cited as the reason for Radio UNTAC falling twelve months behind schedule.[38] In Mozambique, the frustration of the SGSR with the UN's bureaucracy was already showing at the beginning of the year. With so many missions in the field, Ajello believed the administration units in New York had simply become overwhelmed. He could not supply his military observers with vehicles, because '... to get vehicles I have to go through the Contract Committee in New York ... [and] ... That takes months!' In his opinion the various UN budget committees had been designed, rightly, to protect the interests of the world's taxpayers, but added that for the kind of mission ONUMOZ was conducting '... we need different procedures.'[39]

A second reason cited for the logistical problems was the UN's general lack of stock. Two months after UNTAC had deployed the Electoral Component's office automation equipment had still consisted of only one personal computer, and in mid-1993 UNPROFOR's transport section was still short of 465 UN-owned vehicles.

As noted in the previous chapter, the idea of a Standing Force had begun to gain ground mainly due to the frustration the United Nations was experiencing in procuring sufficient numbers of adequately trained personnel. The creation of such a force, however, had never been intended by the founders of the Organisation. As Eric Grove posits, the Charter had always intended forces to be assigned to the Security Council through Special Agreements with member states, allocated to specific operations as required.[40]   Although the Secretary General would no doubt have found a Standing Force helpful, he believed at this time that it 'would be too expensive, wasteful and inappropriate for the Organisation while it was in the process of a vital restructuring exercise aimed at minimising inefficiency and duplication'.[41]   Instead, the Secretary General suggested that force structures for peacekeeping missions could be broken down into standard 'building blocks' of operational capability, such as an infantry battalion, medical company, transport company and observer team.   He envisaged that member states would train and maintain such units, making them available on a stand-by basis for UN operations.[42]   In his opinion, '... if the UN had the elements of a rapid deployment force at its disposal, on a stand-by basis, it would possess an enhanced capacity to deploy while not loading itself down with another layer of bureaucracy.'[43] It was for this purpose that in April 1993, Boutros-Ghali set up a planning team of seven military officers to establish stand-by forces agreements with member states. One of the perceived advantages of possessing a UN Stand-by Force was that personnel could be operationally standardised as well as being taught uniform instructions on such issues as the use of force and how to deal with local non-combatants.   The success of a peacekeeping mission is dependent on the quality of the staff of which it is composed and their good conduct is essential for maintaining public confidence.   In the operations in Cambodia, Somalia, Mozambique and the former Yugoslavia, however, the UN was to face its first serious examples of the lack of discipline within national contingents.

In the Cambodian operation, in which the SGSR Akashi admitted that 'the quality of personnel was not uniformly outstanding' a lack of sensitivity had served to damage the UN's reputation. With peacekeepers earning as much in a day as an average Cambodian earned in a year, the UN was inundated with complaints of sexual harassment, drunkenness and claims that the CIVPOLs behaved as if they were in a conquered country.[44] With a report from a Geneva based charity suggesting that the UN presence had caused an increase in Phnom Penh's prostitution population from 6,000 to 20,000 in less than a year, UN medics were predicting that at least 150 peacekeepers would return home with AIDS. The WHO reported that 75 percent of blood donors in the capital were HIV positive, and a single German field hospital was treating an average of forty cases of venereal disease amongst UN troops every day.   The Khmer Rouge, sensing dissatisfaction with UN behaviour within the indigenous population, attempted to use it as propaganda against UNTAC's real objectives. Akashi, however, defended his troops, stating that '18-year-old hot blooded soldiers' who had been enduring hardships in the field, had a right to a few beers and to chase after 'young beautiful beings of the opposite sex'.[45]

ONUMOZ was also to suffer because of the sexual antics of its force contingents. The Italian 'Albatross' battalion was accused of paying children as young as twelve years for sexual favours, and despite earlier protestations from the Italian Defence Minister that the accusations were 'without foundation', the UN later admitted they were true. Ajello the SGSR, himself an Italian, stated that a 'wrong impression had been created that only one contingent had been involved', little consolation for the UN operation as whole. As a result a number of troops were repatriated and others had their movements restricted.[46]

One of the most serious incidents was to occur in Somalia after the torture and murder of a 16-year-old Somali, Shidane Abukar Arone, at the hands of a Canadian Airborne Regiment after he had broken into their barracks. As a result of subsequent investigations nine Canadians were found guilty of various charges relating to the incident. The graphic details recounted during the first court-martial were described as 'more than a sordid tale of soldiers gone amok'.[47] Eight Belgian soldiers have also subsequently stood trial in front of a court-martial after being accused of homicide and maltreatment during their tour in Somalia.[48]

In the former Yugoslavia shame was to be brought upon the UN by the less than honourable actions of some of the UNPROFOR personnel. Major General Alexander Perelyakin, a Russian serving in Croatia, was sacked in April 1995 for 'severe shortcomings', believed to have involved the clandestine supply of heavy weapons and troops from Serbia to the area around Knin. He was also accused of corruption and black marketeering.[49] Similar accusations were also made of the Ukrainian contingent which had engaged in extensive and illegal bartering activities. 'According to French officers the Ukrainian battalion in Sarajevo [had] been unable to respond quickly to developments on the ground because their UN issued fuel had been sold to civilians'.[50] The Nigerian battalion serving with UNPROFOR was withdrawn after it had become involved in drug dealing. All of these incidents have highlighted the need for UN peacekeeping troops to be highly disciplined during an operation. Failure to be so lessens the local trust in their impartiality and motives, embarrasses national governments, and finally diminishes the public perception of the good work the majority of troop contingents conduct.

Intra-state peacekeeping and cultural diversity

Although the traditional perception of peacekeeping during the Cold War was usually one of UN troops placing themselves on international borders separating belligerent governments, this was in some ways a mis-representation. So, although intra-state peacekeeping is not new to the post-Cold War era, the predominance of such missions is. For example, in the twenty-two peacekeeping missions set up since 1988, only two of them are actually categorized as 'frontier missions' (UNIKOM, UNIIMOG) and as of 1995 only the former of these is still in operation.[51] As noted in chapter 3, although the UN had experience of intra-state peacekeeping during the Cold War, it had never actually been required to negotiate with internal factional groups. And as Sydney Bailey points out, even 'the Charter was drafted on the assumption that disputes arise between states', and included no provision 'by which the Security Council or General Assembly [could] relate to non-state agencies such as liberation movements, communal minorities, or political parties'.[52] The UN, therefore, needed to learn new skills when it began its operations in Namibia (UNTAG) and Angola (UNAVEM II) which required it to negotiate and mediate between the resistance groups SWAPO and UNITA and their respective governments. These skills were also required later in the operations in El Salvador, Cambodia, Somalia and Mozambique.

Negotiating with the internal factions involved in these operations has highlighted an important factor relatively absent from the equivalent State level talks. Unaffected by the expectations of behaviour associated with inter-state diplomacy, internal parties and groups have conducted themselves according to their own cultural traditions. The UN has learnt, therefore, that understanding the cultural attitudes of the people with whom it is dealing in peacekeeping operations is an essential factor affecting their success. As the following examples will show, however, the Organisation, dominated as it is by 'Western' traditions, has not always fully appreciated the cultural context within which it has operated.

Pierre Lizee has argued that the Cambodian factions refused to participate in the conflict resolution procedure of the Paris Accords, not because of UNTAC's failures in deployment or planning, but because their attitude toward conflict itself differed fundamentally from that of the Organisation. Whilst the UN's 'Western' traditions prescribed 'liberal democracy' through the organisation of elections, as the cure for all violent conflict, Cambodian society, dominated by Brahmanism and Buddhism, confined social interactions to small groups of personal relations in which 'well defined status and ranks' and predestined 'fatalistic outlooks' precluded its introduction.[53] Indeed, even the words 'society' and 'consensus' did not exist in the Khmer language until a few years ago.[54]

In Somalia, many believed attempts to broker a peace had failed because of the UN's ignorance of the clan structure of Somali society. For example, by only inviting the fourteen warlords to a peace conference in

Addis Ababa in January 1993, the UN not only legitimized those directly responsible for the ensuing civil war, but by failing to include Somali intellectuals and elders absented perhaps the most important groups from the talks.[55] Clan elders are essential to finding any real reconciliation between the warlords, because only they can settle disputes over issues such as property and grazing rights. The prospects for peace were diminished, therefore, when UNOSOM II attacked a suspected headquarters of Mohammed Aideed's on 12 July 1993 killing more than 50 Somalis and injuring 170, including key religious leaders and clan elders.[56] As Anderson points out, this personalisation of the conflict was never understood by the Somali people, anyway. The traditional clan structure of Somali society dictates that an attack on one member is an attack on all. If one member of a clan is guilty of a crime, the whole clan assumes responsibility. Therefore, when the UN attacked Aideed, it automatically attacked all the members of the Haber-Gedr clan.

The first SGSR in Somalia, Mohammed Sahnoun, also criticised the insensitivity of the UN's bureaucracy to local culture when it announced the deployment of more than 3,000 troops without notifying either the UNOSOM delegation in Mogadishu or the leaders of the neighbouring countries. This announcement had the effect of diminishing the UN's credibility, threatening to undo long worked for local support, because it had also been made 'without consulting the Somali leaders and community elders.'[57] The UN's insensitivity to religious beliefs was also to cause problems in the solidarity of the UNOSOM II force. Uncomfortable at the escalating violence being used by the UN force against what were perceived as fraternal Muslims, contingents from at least three Islamic countries began to relay their orders home before carrying them out.

A successful example of how the local culture of a people involved in a peacekeeping operation was taken account of by the UN was to occur in Mozambique. As an essential element of the agreements signed in Rome, the UN was to provide budding political parties with enough money to contest the forthcoming elections on an equitable basis. At the heart of this commitment was the recognition of the cost required in converting previous paramilitary organisations into democratic political parties. Aldo Ajello, the SGSR in Mozambique, therefore persuaded the UN to set up a $7.5 million trust fund to help in this transformation. However, he subsequently realised that this amount would not be enough to cover all the parties, especially the costs associated with the largest rebel group RENAMO. As Ajello explained of the rebel group's leader, 'Dhlakama is regarded as an African chief ... and he needs to be able to act like one. He needs money to pension off his generals, to distribute largesse'.[58] A request to donate money so that a former terrorist leader could distribute it amongst his friends and allies was, of course, not received with great enthusiasm by the countries concerned, but as recognised by Ajello, the $4 million extra he believed Dhlakama required was 'a small premium to ensure the future stability of Mozambique'.[59] In the opinion of Ajello himself, one of the reasons ONUMOZ had been so successful was that it had not applied a fixed model of operations but had constantly adapted its mandate to the circumstances of the country. Throughout the mission, therefore, the 'specific cultural and political environment was taken into account'.[60]

So, as can be seen from the UN's experience over the past seven years, the UN as a predominantly 'Western' organisation needs to be aware of the cultural idiosyncrasies of the peoples with which its peacekeeping operations work. If the UN fails to take adequate notice of the religious and cultural traditions of local communities, it risks straying from its ultimate objective of finding lasting solutions to regional problems, to attempting the implementation of its own perceived solutions. If these solutions are alien to the culture of the people they are seeking to reconcile, then they can only ultimately end in failure.

Peacekeeping and the provision of Humanitarian Aid

Somalia

With the situation deteriorating, the Secretary General informed the Security Council in November 1992 of five options which the Organisation had in order to create conditions 'for the uninterrupted delivery of relief supplies to the starving people of Somalia.'[61] The first two options were either to carry on with the operation as it was, or to withdraw all UN personnel and leave the remaining aid agencies to fend for themselves. Neither of these options seemed credible given that Aideed's refusal to allow the 3,000 troops to deploy had effectively stalled the operation, and that the Secretary General had personally rebuked a withdrawal, believing the problems in Mogadishu were being caused not by the presence of troops but the lack of them. The final three options all contained elements of force, in varying degrees, as a means to show greater resolve by the UN to deliver aid. The first of these was for the UN to become more forceful in the provision of relief in Mogadishu in the hope that such a show of strength would prevent further attacks on aid convoys by armed bandits and local militias. The fourth and fifth options proposed sanctioning either a force under UN command or a force of a multi-national coalition with a Chapter VII enforcement mandate. As the Secretary General also informed the Security Council that as of that time the UN did not possess the capability to command and control an enforcement operation of the size and complexity of that required in Somalia, the final option seemed the most credible.[62]

Therefore, when President Bush offered 28,000 troops to act as part of a UN force to safeguard food and medical supplies, the Secretary General was quick to accept. In Makinda's opinion this offer was made by a Bush administration embarrassed by the fact that the 'New World Order' its leader had heralded and which was therefore identified with American leadership, was now being characterised by the 'mass starvation of Somali children.' Makinda also believed it helped the Secretary General demonstrate the need for a rapid deployment force, something he had called for throughout his period in office.[63]

In early December 1992 Operation Restore Hope was launched by the US led United Task Force (UNITAF) comprising of 30,000 troops, 28,000 of which were American. Pursuant to Security Council Resolution 794 the force was mandated through Chapter VII of the Charter to use 'all necessary means to establish as soon as possible a secure environment for humanitarian relief operations in Somalia'.[64] Although the mission was to be under US control it appeared that the UN was to be allowed to play a greater role than it had done in the Chapter VII operation in the Gulf nearly two years before. At least on this occasion the US was willing to ensure that both the Secretary General and the Security Council were more closely informed as to the day-to-day running of the mission. However, right from the early days of the UNITAF operation, disagreements between the UN Secretariat and the Bush administration were evident. Whilst President Bush continued to emphasise that the UNITAF operation was 'limited and specific', designed only to 'create security conditions which will permit the feeding of the starving Somali people and allow the transfer of this security function to the UN peacekeeping force', the Secretary General was expressing his desire to see the operation not only disarm all of the Somali factions, but also to defuse all mines in the country, set up a civil administration and begin to train a civil police force.[65] Following increasing numbers of attacks on UNITAF itself and under intense pressure from the UN and NGOs, the operation did conduct some disarmament, although it did so only in urban areas and only a significant time after the majority of weapons, including most of the infamous 'technicals' (trucks with mounted machine-guns), had been evacuated to the countryside.[66]

When UNITAF did eventually turn over the operation to the second United Nations Operation in Somalia (UNOSOM II) on 3 May, claims of an American organised success were hotly disputed. In hindsight, Chester Crocker believes the UNITAF operation was nothing short of a 'dramatic success'.[67] Similar claims by US officials at the time of the handover to

UNOSOM II were, however, treated with scepticism by aid workers and UN officials, who believed they were purposely painting a rosy picture in order to make their withdrawal more palatable. Indeed, by the end of UNITAF's mandate 'the consensus within the aid community' was that it had failed to create anything resembling a 'secure environment for humanitarian relief operations'.[68]   The UNITAF operation was also criticised for wasting a great deal of effort on securing bulk food deliveries when those in most need did not have access to feeding centres. The futility of the operation was also magnified by the fact that the greatest killer at the time was not hunger but disease. As in other relief operations, the importation of large amounts of food had also helped to discourage local economic recovery by undermining efforts to create a self-sufficient food supply. So, when the real needs of Somalia centred around the re-establishment of law and order, economic recovery and the reconstruction of the Somali health care system, UNITAF had concentrated on purely palliative measures. And as for its role in the prevention of starvation, African Rights stated that 'the basic food problem underlying the famine was solved at least one month before the marines had landed'.[69]

It seemed to many, therefore, that when UNOSOM II was handed the reins on 3 May, the US had pressured the UN to take over the operation before it felt ready, and without fulfilling the conditions the UN thought it had promised.[70] Approximately one month later on 5 June, 24 Pakistani peacekeepers were killed in an ambush while inspecting an arms dump belonging to Aideed. In the escalating spiral of violence which followed, UNOSOM II was to embroil itself in an intractable conflict leading to President Clinton's televised 7 October statement that all American troops would be withdrawn by March 1994. So what went wrong with UNOSOM II?

Makinda cites three factors. The first is the gap between the operation's stated objectives and its actual activities. The second is the problems created by UNOSOM II's command and control structure. And the third concerned the divisions among the states which contributed contingents to the force.[71] Established pursuant to SC Resolution 814 of 26 March 1993, UNOSOM II was requested not only 'to assume responsibility for the consolidation, expansion and maintenance of a secure environment throughout Somalia' but also to seek financing for the 'rehabilitation of the political institutions and economy of Somalia'.[72] With its experiments in 'peace-enforcement', however, UNOSOM II was to fail miserably in this regard. And as for solving Somalia's humanitarian problems, Under Secretary General for Humanitarian Affairs, Jan Eliasson, informed an ECOSOC meeting in Geneva in July, that of $166 million the UN had earmarked for humanitarian assistance only 15 percent had been provided, and that the international community was 'spending ten dollars on military protection for every dollar on humanitarian assistance'.[73] It would seem, therefore, that UNOSOM II was in essence self-defeating.

As explained earlier in this chapter, the problems with UNOSOM II's command and control structures were to originate specifically from the hegemony acquired by the US. A pre-requisite of Bush's offer of 28,000 marines in November 1992 had been that they would remain under US command and control. Although UNITAF's mandate had been terminated by May, the US still retained a substantial number of troops and logistics in the UNOSOM II operation.[74] Therefore, when the first casualties occurred on 5 June, and the main peace-enforcement operation began with SC Resolution 837 (6 June 1993), the US, in the interest of its own troops, began to assume ever greater control of the operation. Although the overall commander of UNOSOM II was a Turkish General, Civik Bir, he had been nominated by the US. Not only that, but his deputy, Major General Thomas Montgomery, was American, as was the Secretary General's Special Representative, Admiral Jonathan Howe. So too was the tactical commander of the 1,700 strong American Rapid Deployment Unit, which was responsible for many of the attacks on Aideed's supporters and strongholds. The UNOSOM II headquarters had been initially staffed by about 28 US officers in key positions. Even with the UN's limited role, the US retained the tendency to operate outside the UN chain of command. Berdal cites the events leading up to the catastrophic events of 3 October as evidence of this;

> The decision to use units of the Special forces against a suspected Aideed stronghold was made at the headquarters of the Special Operations Command in Florida and relayed directly to the Special Operations Command deployed in Mogadishu. Admiral Howe, the Special Representative of the Secretary General, was not informed and General Civik Bir, the Force Commander, was only told about the operation just before it was launched.[75]

Sent to apprehend suspected members of Aideed's 'war cabinet', which was meeting at the Olympic Hotel in South Mogadishu, the US Special forces found themselves ensnarled in a battle which left 18 of their number dead, 75 wounded and several score Somali also dead and wounded. Unprepared for the operation, the UN could only hastily dispatch the Nigerian contingent to help rescue them. One US helicopter pilot and one Nigerian peacekeeper were subsequently taken hostage.

Further animosity between the contingents was fuelled by the American refusal to allow other nations to influence the direction of the operation.

The Italians had a request from their Defence Minister for representation in the command structure refused. And the French, with a contingent of 1,700 and a thorough knowledge of the region as an ex-colonial power in neighbouring Djibouti, were also unhappy at not securing representation. US accusations that the problems experienced by UNOSOM II were due to the inability of the UN to conduct such 'enforcement' operations were, therefore, tenuous at least.

John Bolton recalls the 20 January changeover of Washington administrations as the beginning of the Somalia catastrophe. When the Bush administration left office 'humanitarian assistance was regularly flowing to critical areas. Mediation efforts were progressing with all the major factions agreeing to a conference on national reconciliation in mid-March. US forces were already withdrawing, replaced by troops from other nations.'[76] The new Clinton foreign policy of 'assertive multilateralism', however, was to change the direction of the operation towards the 'nation-building' mission of Resolution 814. As Albright stated; 'With this resolution, we will embark on an unprecedented enterprise aimed at nothing less than the restoration of an entire country as a proud, functioning and viable member of the community of nations'.[77] And in early May she expressed confidence and enthusiasm that through this new 'assertive multilateralism' the UN was increasingly ... 'fusing peacekeeping and peace-enforcement with the delivery of humanitarian assistance to civilian populations trapped in the hostilities'.[78] However, by the end of 1993 the Clinton Administration's experience with Somalia had worked to temper its enthusiasm for the new post-Cold War role it had envisaged for the UN. Instead of the optimistic statements of Albright, the Clinton policymakers were attempting to find criteria for future peacekeeping missions which would prevent the US from becoming embroiled in open-ended commitments in operations which did not directly involve its national interest.

In conclusion, it would seem that a number of lessons can be learnt from both the UNITAF and UNOSOM II operations. Although UNITAF did aid the delivery of humanitarian relief, its resources were mostly wasted. Rather than concerning itself with the reconstruction of the Somali infra-structure and conducting a general disarmament, for which there was recognised support, it limited its own role to the delivery of food and medicine. When UNOSOM II took over in May 1993, the UN was no more capable of conducting an 'enforcement' operation than it was when the Secretary General admitted its limitations in November 1992. However, as Berdal notes, it was 'not only disingenuous but also factually inaccurate to assert, as was done in Congress, that Americans had died in Somalia because they were operating under UN command.'[79] As Crocker posits, the 'failure' in Somalia was not a failure of either 'humanitarian or muscular peacekeeping' but a failure to apply them 'steadily and wisely'.[80]   Both UNITAF and UNOSOM II were guilty of that. UNOSOM II, however, lost local support because it had failed to take account of local culture and traditions.   It attempted to isolate one of fourteen warlords and personalise a conflict in a culture which did not understand the concept of individual responsibility. And in its attempts to capture one individual it killed numerous civilians, including important local elders, and turned a whole nation against it.   Whether or not it is better for the international community to accept the disintegration of 'failed states' is a matter for discussion not within the remit of this book. However, despite UNOSOM II's failure, the concept of nation-building should not take the blame for mistakes made by a US administration, a US peacekeeping doctrine, and a UN leadership, all of which failed to take adequate account of the problems posed by involvement in civil conflicts in non-western societies.

Rwanda

The first major involvement of the UN in the conflict in Rwanda was to follow the adoption of Resolution 812 on 12 March 1993. This resolution requested the Secretary General to examine ways in which the ongoing peace process could be strengthened. Consequently, following a request from both the Rwandan government and the rebel Rwandese Patriotic Front (RPF) the Security Council, pursuant to Resolution 846, established the United Nations Observer Mission Uganda-Rwanda (UNOMUR). With its headquarters in Kabale in Uganda, UNOMUR was mandated to monitor the smuggling of weapons and reinforcements for the RPF across the 150 km border between the two countries. However, due to an objection by the RPF, UNOMUR was unable to operate on Rwandan territory. As of 10 December 1993 this mission was composed of 81 military observers, with observations posts stationed at five points along the Ugandan-Rwandan border.   Later the same month UNOMUR was to be integrated into a larger mission established in Rwanda itself.

Following the signing of the Arusha Accord on 4 August 1993 by the nominal Rwandan government and the RPF's political chairman, Alex Kanyarenwe, the UN was to become further involved through the establishment of the United Nations Assistance Mission in Rwanda (UNAMIR). Created to oversee the parties' commitments to provide a basis for power sharing before the holding of democratic elections and the formation of a new national army, Resolution 872 mandated UNAMIR to remain in Rwanda after a ninety day period only if substantial progress had been made on the implementation of the Arusha Accord.[81]

The mandate of UNAMIR included seven main elements. These were for the mission to contribute to the security of Kigali, the capital, within a weapons secure area established by the parties; to monitor the observance of the ceasefire agreement; to assist in mine clearance through training programmes; to investigate non-compliance with the Arusha peace agreement; monitor the process of repatriation of Rwandan refugees; and finally to assist in the co-ordination of investigating incidents regarding the activities of the police and gendarmerie. On 20 December 1993, through the adoption of Resolution 891 the Security Council approved an extension of UNAMIR's mandate for a period of six months, concluding that the mission had played a useful role as a confidence-building measure. In the interests of simplifying administration, Resolution 891 also integrated UNOMUR's activities into the UNAMIR operation.

In its function of helping to co-ordinate the installation of a transitional government, the Secretary General suggested that the mission's mandate be separated into four phases. The first phase was to see the establishment of conditions necessary for the secure installation of a transitional government. This he believed would require approximately 1,400 military personnel. The second phase, expected to last for ninety days, was to see the mission continue its monitoring functions to ensure that the preparations for disengagement, demobilisation and integration were in place. The third phase was to see a reduction in the number of personnel whilst the mission continued to monitor a de-militarised zone and the Ugandan-Rwandan border. And the final phase was to see the reduction of personnel to the minimum possible.

The assassination in late October of the President and a number of Cabinet Ministers in Burundi, however, was to mark the beginnings of increased tensions between the Hutu and Tutsi tribes. Although the coup was to ulitmately fail, it had been instigated by members of the Tutsi tribe, whereas the deceased President had been a Hutu.[82] Although senior military officers in the army, itself Tutsi dominated, had distanced themselves from the coup and had promised to restore democracy in exchange for an amnesty, most of the serious damage had already been inflicted. Following the coup attempt over half a million refugees fled from Burundi into neighbouring Zaire and Tanzania.

The former Yugoslavia

With tensions in the region rising from November 1992, the first major setback for the UN in 1993 was to occur in Croatia, with the Croatian army's offensive against the Krajina Serbs on 22 January. The Croatian government cited the slow progress of negotiations regarding the various economic facilities in and adjacent to the UNPAs and 'pink zones' as the reason for the attacks. The Serbs responded by breaking into a number of UN weapon storage areas and removing arms and heavy weapons.[83] When the Security Council adopted Resolution 802 on 25 January, its demands that the Croatian army withdraw from Serb-held regions were mostly ignored.

In Bosnia, having criticised the Geneva plan (Vance/Owen) for rewarding ethnic cleansing, the US proposed humanitarian air-drops to feed besieged Muslims in Eastern Bosnia. Critics believed, however, that this was 'little more than a well-staged PR exercise for domestic consumption'.[84] Parachuting supplies from high altitude is an inaccurate exercise in the best of conditions, but more importantly the plan did nothing to alleviate the persecution or siege of Muslim communities, a necessary condition for the provision of long term aid. By mid-1993, the Muslim enclaves in Eastern Bosnia had been under siege for over ten months. At the beginning of March, reports indicated that Serbian forces had overrun the town of Cerska and surrounding villages and were threatening the region of Srebrenica.[85] In a highly publicised event, French General Morillon publicly declared his refusal to leave the Srebrenica enclave until aid had arrived. Although an aid convoy did get through on 19 March, subsequent efforts by the UNHCR to evacuate the elderly, young and sick led to a 'stampede of evacuees, some of whom died *en route* to Tuzla'.[86] For his troubles General Morillon was criticised by the Secretary General for having exceeded his mandate.

With the Bosnian Serb refusal to sign the peace plan, and their continuing siege of Srebrenica, the Security Council passed Resolution 819 on 16 April 1993. Demanding an end to Serbian attacks on Srebrenica, the Security Council declared the town and its surrounding areas a 'safe area'.[87] The Council also requested an increased UNPROFOR presence in order to safeguard the population. With the adoption of Resolution 824 on 6 May 1993, the same status was awarded to the towns of Tuzla, Zepa, Gorazde, Bihac and Sarajevo. The Security Council decided that these towns and their surrounding areas should be 'free from armed attacks and from any other hostile acts which endanger the well-being and the safety of their inhabitants'.[88] This accreditation, however, failed to prevent further attacks, with Gorazde being 'bombarded by Bosnian Serb militia for eighteen consecutive days in June' leaving 'half its houses destroyed'.[89] This occurred despite the Security Council's adoption of Resolution 836 on 6 June 1993, authorising UNPROFOR to act in 'self defence, to take the necessary measures, including the use of force, in reply to bombardments against the safe areas by any of the parties or to armed incursion into them or in the event of any deliberate obstruction in or around those areas to the freedom of movement of UNPROFOR or of protected humanitarian convoys.'[90]   Although the Secretary General had informed the Security Council that a force of 34,000 would be required to 'obtain deterrence through strength', the Council adopted Resolution 844 on 18 June, authorising the enlargement of UNPROFOR in the 'safe areas' by only 7,500. This number represented the minimum 'light option' the Secretary General believed was necessary to begin the implementation of its mandate, and as such would be dependent on the consent and co-operation of all the parties.[91]   However, the Secretary General also informed the Security Council around the same time that with the dire condition of the UN peacekeeping budget it was 'highly probable that in the coming months the Organisation [would] not be able to meet its day-to-day obligations.'[92] This may go some way to explaining why as late as February 1994 only 3,500 troops had been deployed in the safe areas, mostly in Sarajevo and Tuzla, with the eastern enclave of Zepa receiving a UN advance party consisting of only ten soldiers.

With the situation throughout the former Yugoslavia deteriorating, the possibility of a UN withdrawal was becoming ever more real. With the Geneva plan effectively dead, the Bosnian government had criticised the UN for freezing Croatian and Serbian gains by stranding tens of thousands of Bosnians in so-called 'safe areas', and for apparently being reconciled to an eventual partition of the Bosnian state between Croatia and Serbia. In July, the UN mediator, Thorvald Stoltenberg, warned the Security Council at a closed door meeting, that there was a real risk that if the downward spiral in fighting continued it would become impossible for the UN to stay in Bosnia.[93] By August 1993 the Serbs had arrived on Mount Igman overlooking Sarajevo and were poised to capture Butmir and Hrasnica, both of which stood at the gates of the capital, Sarajevo. Despite its safe area status it was clear that the Serbs had been faced with little real UN resistance.[94]

Unable to implement the negotiated agreements, UNPROFOR in Croatia had by September 1993 been confined to a 'de facto minimalist position', with one UN report explaining that: 'The role of UNPROFOR in present circumstances is thus to prevent the resumption or escalation of conflict; to provide a breathing space for the continued efforts of peacemakers; and to support the provision of essential humanitarian assistance'.[95] Reporting on developments the Secretary General stated that he had been 'sorely tempted' to recommend the withdrawal of UNPROFOR from Croatia, citing the criticism of the UN by both sides and the dangers and abuse which the force had been exposed to. He refrained from doing so, however, because of the consequences he believed would result from such action.[96] Increasingly agitated at the inability of the UN to re-incorporate the UNPAs under its authority, the Croatian government, on 24 September, informed the Security Council that if the mandate of UNPROFOR was not amended to promote energetic implementation of the relevant resolutions of the Security Council, then it would be forced to request UNPROFOR to leave Croatia by the end of November.

In Bosnia, despite the signing by all three parties of the Joint Declaration on the delivery of humanitarian aid on 18 and 19 November, 'the level of violence, the imposition of bureaucratic procedures hindering the transport of relief goods or the denial of clearance for the passage of UNHCR convoys [had] reduced deliveries of humanitarian assistance to half the amount required'.[97] Following the abduction and mock execution of eleven of its peacekeepers Canada announced it would be reviewing its role in Bosnia and UN mediator Thorvald Stoltenberg noted that a total of sixty-nine ceasefires had been negotiated and broken.[98] Also as 1993 came to a close, the Belgian Commander in Bosnia, Lieutenant General Francis Briquemont, whose position had become untenable after criticising the UN Secretariat for refusing to back a call for air-strikes, announced his resignation on the grounds of exhaustion. In doing so he pointed to a 'widening rift between the UN in New York and peacekeepers on the ground', and when asked what advice he would give to his successor, suggested that he should 'constantly remind those politically responsible about the difficulties in which they put us because there is no coherence in their strategies'. In a sombre indictment of the Security Council's lack of realism with regards to its expectations of what could be achieved on the ground, he added; 'I don't read the Security Council resolutions any more because they don't help me'.[99]

So, by the end of the year the operation in the former Yugoslavia was looking increasingly incredible. The Croatian government's impatience to see the reintegration of the UNPAs under national control, and the Serbs' refusal to disarm within them, was making an all out confrontation inevitable. Although the UN had been able to mediate a Christmas Truce, with the intransigence of both sides it was impossible to see how a mutually acceptable agreement with regards to their future status could be achieved. In Bosnia, the pressure of public opinion had forced the international community to declare six towns as 'safe areas' when it did not have the political will to protect them. With less than half the 'minimum' number of troops the Secretary General had deemed it necessary to provide a credible deterrent to attack actually deployed, the 'widening gap' between the Security Council's declarations and UNPROFOR's ability to implement them was becoming ever more apparent. Although in recognition that a peacekeeping role was not feasible the UNPROFOR operation in Bosnia had begun simply to protect the delivery of humanitarian aid, it had quickly become involved in the state's political problems. This 'mission creep' had, therefore, enmeshed UNPROFOR in the intractable problems of a civil war. And with the delivery of humanitarian aid even more precarious than before, the viability of the operation was being questioned even by the UN itself.

Conclusion

With the installation of the Clinton Administration in January 1993, therefore, the United Nations began the year with renewed optimism. The financial support which had been so obviously lacking from the international community in previous years, at last seemed to be imminent. However, as this chapter has demonstrated, by the end of the year the Organisation's fortunes had turned full circle. Rather than searching for ways in which it could help the UN conduct peacekeeping operations, the US began to elucidate criteria which would limit its involvement. The cause of this change of heart had been the political consequences of its involvement in a peace-enforcement operation in Somalia. Both the US and UN had learnt the lessons of failing to appreciate the effects which the use of force could have on the impartiality of peacekeepers, and the impossibility of regaining that impartiality once it had been lost.

Although the most significant operation in terms of its effect on US policy, Somalia represented only one type of crisis facing the UN in 1993. Following the return to war in Angola, the Organisation's lack of finances and resources, together with the intransigence of the parties, continued to threaten the success of the operations in Cambodia, Yugoslavia, Mozambique and Western Sahara. And although the UNTAC operation eventually concluded with elections in May, the failure to include the PDK meant that the overall success of the mission had been limited. As the end of the year approached, therefore, the optimism of the early months of 1993 had been transformed into the pessimism with which the Organisation was to enter 1994.

Suggested Reading

Berdal, M., 'Whither UN peacekeeping', *Adelphi Paper 281,* October 1993, Brassey's for the International Institute for Strategic Studies.

Boutros-Ghali, B., 'UN peacekeeping in a new era: a new chance for peace', *World Today, April 1993.*

Boutros-Ghali, B., 'Agenda for peace one year later', *Orbis,* vol.37, no.3, Summer 1993.

Chopra, J., 'Breaking the stalemate in Western Sahara', *International Peacekeeping,* vol.1, no.3, Autumn 1994.

Diehl, P. F., *International peacekeeping,* Baltimore and London, The Johns Hopkins University Press, 1994.

Doyle, M., *UN peacekeeping in Cambodia: UNTAC's civil mandate,* International Peace Academy, Occasional Paper Series, Lynne Rienner, London, 1995.

Findlay, T., 'Cambodia: the legacy and the lessons of UNTAC', *SIPRI Report,* no.9, Oxford University Press, 1995.

Findlay, T., 'UNTAC-lessons to be learned', *International Peacekeeping,* vol.1, no.1, January/February 1994.

Gerlach, J. R., 'A UN army for the New World Order', *Orbis,* Spring 1993.

Howe, J.T., 'Somalia: learning the right lessons', *The Washington Quarterly,* vol.18, no.3, Summer 1995.

Roberts, A., 'The crisis in UN peacekeeping', *Survival,* vol.26, no.3, Autumn 1994.

Smith, H., *International peacekeeping, building on the Cambodian experience,* Canberra, Australian Defence Studies Centre, 1994.

Stevenson, J., 'Hope restored in Somalia?', *Foreign Policy,* no.91, Summer 1993.

Notes

1.   cf.Gerlach, J, R., 'A UN army for the New World Order', *Orbis*, vol.37, no.2, Spring 1993, p.244.

2.   cf.Ibid.

3.   cf.Boutros-Ghali, B., 'UN peacekeeping in a new era. A new chance for peace', *World Today*, April 1993, p.67 and 'An agenda for peace, one year later', *Orbis*, vol.37, no.3, 1993, p.328.

4.   cf.Roberts, A., 'The UN and international security', *Survival*, vol.35, no.2, Summer 1993, p.10.

5.   cf.See Berdal, M., 'Fateful encounter: the United States and UN peacekeeping', *Survival*, vol.36, no.1, Spring 1994, p.33-35.

6.   *United Nations document, S/24800*, 15 November 1992.

7.   *United Nations document, S/25719*, 3 May 1993.

8.   Vortna, V, P., 'Success and failure in Southern Africa: peacekeeping in Namibia and Angola' in ed. Daniel and Hayes, *Beyond traditional peacekeeping*, Macmillan Press, 1995, pp.290-292.

9.   See Hume, C., 'Ending Mozambique's war', US Institute of Peace Process, Washington D.C., pp.118, 130, 131, 141-142.

10.   See Kurzidem, T., 'ONUMOZ - How to make a successful peacekeeping operation', *International peacekeeping*, vol.1, no.4, September-November 1994, p.133.

11.   cf.Isaacs, D., 'Mozambique told to speed peace process', *Daily Telegraph*, 10 June 1993.

12.   cf.Boutros-Ghali, B., *An agenda for peace,* United Nations, 1992, p.16.

13.   Boutros-Ghali, B., *Agenda for peace one year later*, op.cit, p.324.

14. Doyle, M., and Suntharalingham, N., 'The UN in Cambodia, lessons for complex peacekeeping', *International Peacekeeping*, vol.1, no.2, Summer 1994, p.124.

15. *United Nations document S/25913*, 10 June 1993.

16. Doyle, M., and Suntharalingham, N., op.cit, p.124.

17. cf.Solarz, S., in Findlay, 'Cambodia: the legacy and lessons of UNTAC', *SIPRI Research Report*, no.9, Oxford University Press, 1995, p.105.

18. Idem.

19. cf.*United Nations document S/26790*, 23 November 1993.

20. *United Nations documents S/1994/89*, 28 January 1994, *S/26666*, 1 November 1993.

21. Kostakos, G., 'UN reform: the post-Cold War Organisation', in *The United Nations in the New World Order*, ed. Bourantonis, D., and Wiener, J., Macmillan, London, 1995, p.70.

22. Elliot, L., 'Debts fetter world's police force', *The Guardian*, 13 May 1994.

23. See Berdal, M., op.cit, p.34.

24. cf.Puchala, D.J., 'Outsiders, insiders and UN reform', *Washington Quarterly*, vol.17, no.4, 1994, p.168.

25. cf.*United Nations document, SG/SM/5133*, 20 October 1993.

26. Berdal, M., op.cit, p.33.

27. cf.Roberts, A., 'The UN and international security', *Survival*, vol.35, no.2, Summer 1993, p.6.

28. See Berdal, M., *UN peacekeeping at the crossroads*, IFS Information, no.7, 1993, pp.6-7.

29. cf.Evans, G., 'Peacekeeping in Cambodia, lessons learned', *NATO Review,* no.4, vol.42, August 1994, pp.26.

30.   Findlay, op.cit, p.106.

31.   Doyle, M., *UN peacekeeping in Cambodia: UNTAC's civil mandate*, International Peace Academy, Occasional Paper Series, Lynne Rienner, London, 1995. pp.46-47.

32.   cf.Evans, G., Nato Review, op.cit, p.27.

33.   cf.Findlay, op.cit, p.124.

34.   cf.Idem.

35.   cf.Findlay, T., 'UNTAC-lessons to be learned', *International Peacekeeping*, no.1, January-February 1994, p.7.

36.   cf.*United Nations document, S/25719*, 3 May 1993, p.140.

37.   Berdal, M., 'Whither UN Peacekeeping', *Adelphi Paper,* no.281, October 1993, Brassey's for the International Institute for Strategic Studies, p.36.

38.   Findlay, 'Cambodia, the legacy and lessons of UNTAC', op.cit, p.123.

39.   cf.Bridgland, F., 'Shoestring peace about to snap', *The Telegraph*, 21 February 1993.

40.   Grove, E., 'UN armed forces and the Military Staff Committee: a look back', *International Security*, vol.17, no.4, Spring 1993, p.177.

41.   cf.Boutros-Ghali, 'UN peacekeeping in a new era: a new chance for peace', op.cit, p.69.

42.   Roberts A., op.cit, p.17.

43.   cf.Boutros-Ghali, 'UN peacekeeping in a new era: a new chance for peace, op.cit, p.69.

44.   Klintworth, G., 'United Nations: a poor job in Cambodia', *International Herald Tribune,* 2 February 1993.

45.   cf.Harris, F., 'AIDS legacy taints UN's success in Cambodia', *The Daily Telegraph,* 8 November 1993 and Pringle, J., 'Sex and

inflation end the UN honeymoon in Cambodia', *The Times,* 26 November 1992.

46.	cf.'UN troops in Africa paid for child sex', *The International Herald Tribune,* 26 February 1994.

47.	cf.Holland, J., 'Canadian court martial resulting from participation in the UNITAF mission in Somalia', *International Peacekeeping,* vol.1, no.4, September-November 1994, p.131-132.

48.	'Chronicle of events', *International Peacekeeping*, vol.2, no.1, 131 December 1994, p.18.

49.	Fox, R., 'UN sacks pro-Serb-Russian general', *The Daily Telegraph*, 12 April 1995.

50.	cf.Berdal, M., 'Whither UN Peacekeeping', op.cit, p.47.

51.	The acronyms stand for UNIKOM: United Nations Iraq-Kuwait Observer Mission and UNIIMOG: United Nations Iran-Iraq Military Observer Group.

52.	cf.Bailey, S., quoted in Cooper, R., and Berdal, M., 'Outside intervention in ethnic conflicts', *Survival*, vol.35, no.1, Spring 1993, p.139.

53.	cf.Lizee, P., 'Peacekeeping, peace-building and the challenge of conflict resolution in Cambodia', in *Peacekeeping and the challenge of conflict resolution,* ed., David Charters, Canada, University of New Brunswick, 1994, pp.135-148.

54.	Findlay, 'Cambodia, the legacy and lessons of UNTAC', op.cit, pg.110.

55.	Ozanne, Julian, 'UN struggles for a role in Somalia', *The Financial Times*, 4 January 1993.

56.	Berdal, M., 'Fateful encounter: the United States and UN peacekeeping', op.cit, p.42.

57.	cf.See Sahnoun, S., *Somalia: the missed opportunities*, Washington D.C., United States Institute of Peace Press, 1994, pp.38-39.

58.   cf.Crawford, L., 'Mozambique's fragile peace process risks too-easy derailment', *The Financial Times*, 25 January 1994.

59.   cf.Idem.

60.   cf.Kurdizem, T., op.cit, p.133.

61.   cf.Bolton, J, R., 'Wrong turn in Somalia', *Foreign Affairs,* vol.73, no.1, January/February 1994, p.59.

62.   *United Nations document, S/24859,* 24 November 1992 and Thakur, R., 'From peacekeeping to peace-enforcement: the United Nations operation in Somalia', *The Journal of Modern African Studies,* vol.32, no.3, p.394, and idem.

63.   cf.Makinda, S.M., 'Somalia: from humanitarian intervention to military offensive?' *World today*, October 1993, vol.49, no.10, p.185.

64.   cf.*Security Council document, S/RES/794,* 3 December 1992.

65.   cf.Bolton, J, R., op.cit, p.60-61.

66.   Farrell, T., 'Explaining the failure of the UN intervention in Somalia', Paper presented at the *British International Studies Association Conference,* York, 1994, p.3.

67.   cf.Crocker, C., 'The lessons of Somalia', *Foreign Affairs*, vol.74, no.3, May/June 1995, p.4.

68.   Farrell, T., op.cit, p.2.

69.   cf.Ibid., pp.4-5.

70.   'Give the UN the Power it needs', *International Herald Tribune*, 7 October 1994.

71.   Makinda, M., op.cit, p.184.

72.   cf.Idem., and Sicherman, H., 'Winning the peace', *Orbis*, vol.38, no.4, Fall 1994, p.527.

73.   cf.Ibid., p.185.

74. The US had contributed 4,600 (including 2,900 logisitics elements) to the UNOSOM II operation. Idem. Only this logistics component was to actually be under UN 'operational control'. See Berdal, 'Fateful Encounter: the United States and UN peacekeeping', op.cit, p.40.

75. cf.Berdal, Ibid., p.41.

76. cf.Bolton, J, R., op.cit, p.61.

77. cf.Ibid., p.62.

78. Berdal, M., 'Fateful encounter: the United States and UN peacekeeping', op.cit, p.44.

79. cf.Ibid., p.40.

80. cf.Crocker, op.cit, p.5.

81. *Security Council document, S/RES/872*, 5 October 1993.

82. 'Burundi in the grip of machete war', *The Independent*, 25 October 1993.

83. United Nations, *The UN and the situation in the Former Yugoslavia*, Reference Paper, Revision 4, Department of Public Information, p.4.

84. cf.Lee, B., 'UNPROFOR's mandate to protect', *Balkan war report: bulletin of the Institute for War and Peace Reporting*, no.18, February/March 1993, p.1.

85. 'Security Council condemn continuing military attacks in Eastern Bosnia by serb military units, calls for increased presence of UNPROFOR', *United Nations Document*, SC/5564, 3 March 1993.

86. cf.Fetherston, A., Ramsbotham, O., Woodhouse, T., 'UNPROFOR: some observations from a conflict resolution perspective', *International Peacekeeping*, vol.1, no.2, Summer 1994, p.188.

87. *Security Council document, S/RES/819*, 16 April 1993.

88. cf.*Security Council document, S/RES/824*, 6 May 1993.

89. cf.Fetherston et al, op.cit, p.188.

90. cf.*Security Council document, S/RES/836*, 4 June 1993.

91. *Security Council document, S/RES/842*, 18 June 1993. Also see 'Ex-Yugoslavia: proposals by Boutros-Ghali for implementation of Resolution 836 - New London Conference', *Atlantic News*, no.2535, 16 June 1993, p.2 and *The UN and the situation in the former Yugoslavia*, op.cit, p.15.

92. cf.*The UN and the situation in the former Yugoslavia*, Ibid., p.16.

93. Pringle, P., 'West snubs UN plea for action', *The Independent,* 1 May 1994.

94. Burns, J, F., 'UN Force is doing no peacekeeping', *The International Herald tribune*, 22 July 1993.

95. cf.Fetherston, et al, op.cit, p.184.

96. *The UN and the Situation in the former Yugoslavia*, op.cit, p.17.

97. cf.Ibid., p.19.

98. Fetherston et al, op.cit, pp.188-189.

99. cf.Idem.

Chapter 6
The Retrenchment of Peacekeeping 1994-1995

Introduction

Testifying before the House Appropriations Subcommittee on Foreign Operations on May 5 1994, US Ambassador to the UN, Madaleine Albright, stated that peacekeeping lent 'global legitimacy to efforts to mediate disputes, demobilise armed factions, arrange ceasefires and provide emergency relief. It reduces the likelihood of unwelcome interventions by regional powers. And it ensures a sharing of the costs and risks of maintaining world order'.[1] As such, this assessment of the importance of peacekeeping was reminiscent of the optimistic language which the Clinton Administration had used twelve months earlier. However, the attitude of the US towards the role of the UN in its foreign policy had changed dramatically in the intervening period. In what it described as a more 'balanced view' the Clinton Administration began to look upon the UN as more of a 'contributor to', than the 'centrepiece of', its national security policy, stating that its new policy was 'not intended to expand UN peacekeeping, but to help fix it'.[2]

The cornerstone of this new policy was to be Presidential Decision Directive 25 (PDD25 - Reforming Multilateral Peace Operations) released in May 1994. PDD25 sought to reassess US support for new and

continuing peacekeeping operations in six areas. The first of these
addressed the issue of US participation in peacekeeping operations. Before
the US would participate in any UN operation it would first ask a number
of questions. These included whether participation would advance US
national interest; whether there existed a threat to international peace and
security; if the operation had clear objectives and whether its scope was
clearly defined; whether an endpoint to participation could be identified;
and whether a ceasefire existed or if peace-enforcement might be required.
In essence, for the US to participate, the consequences of inaction had to
be unacceptable. Second, was the issue of the command and control of
American troops. Although PDD25 stated that the President would
consider, on a case by case basis, the possibility of placing appropriate US
forces under the operational control of a competent UN commander, it
reiterated that the President would never relinquish command and authority
over the nation's forces. It also stressed that the greater the contribution
of US personnel, the less likely it would be that it would agree to have a
UN commander exercise operational control over its forces. The reason
for the Administration's hesitancy to place its forces under UN operational
control obviously emanated from the political consequences from the deaths
of US soldiers in the latter part of 1993. As already explained, although
officially under UN control, the US forces assigned to UNOSOM II had
actually remained under the effective control of US command. Only the
US logistics division of the UNOSOM II operation had actually operated
under UN control. PDD25, therefore, seemed only to clarify what had
remained US policy.

A third area covered by PDD25 was the US dissatisfaction with the
disproportionate share of the UN's costs which it had been asked to carry.
At the end of the Cold War the US assessment had been set at 28 percent,
but due to various reasons, including the break up of the former Soviet
Union, this had risen to 31.7 percent by 1991. Although the US itself had
recognised only an assessment level of 30.4 percent, PDD25 sought to
reduce that level to only 25 percent. The final three areas addressed by
PDD25 covered the reform of UN management of peacekeeping operations,
the improvement of US management of its own forces deployed in UN
operations, and the co-operation required between the Executive, Congress
and the American public.

In her testimony to the House Appropriations Subcommittee in May 1994,
Albright commented that the new policy had already begun to make a
difference. The US had insisted that expansions of the operations in
Angola and Liberia be dependent on the progress of peace negotiations;
that the additional cost incurred by the increase in the numbers of police
monitors for ONUMOZ be offset by a reduction in the number of military

troops; and that 'sunset' clauses be introduced into resolutions authorising or extending peacekeeping operations 'so that the burden of proof will rest on those who favour extension rather than termination'. She noted that operations proposed for Burundi, Sudan, Nagorno-Karabakh, Tajikistan, Afghanistan and Sierra Leone, had already been refused on the criteria established by PDD25.[3]

This new frugality was also beginning to pervade the corridors of the UN itself. Noting that the number of peacekeeping operations being conducted by the Organisation had risen from 5 in 1988 to 16 in 1994, and that in the same time period the number of personnel deployed had risen from 9,000 to 60,000, the Secretary General stated in March 1995 that 'the number of UN operations, the scale of the operations, [and] the money spent on operations, [could not] keep growing indefinitely. The limits [were] being reached'.[4] This exponential increase was essentially rooted in the nature of the latest peacekeeping operations. Rather than separating belligerent states, as it had traditionally done during the Cold War, the UN was increasingly being called to deal with conflicts not between states, but within them. As Boutros-Ghali explained; 'Everyday, the Organisation must confront civil wars, secessions, partitions, ethnic clashes and tribal warfare'. Thus, he concluded, the UN was once again being 'forced to adapt to the violent evolution of the world.'[5] Of the 16 operations being conducted in mid-1995, over two-thirds of them were related to internal conflict, in which the aim of the UN was 'no longer to contain a situation pending a political settlement', but to 'seek to restore, or even build peace'.[6] With the cost of peacekeeping in 1995 estimated to be approximately \$3.1 billion, the Secretary General had begun to take a number of steps in order to reduce expenditure. The first of these was to streamline and restructure the UN departments dealing with peacekeeping. The second was to seek to reduce, or end, operations which were no longer cost effective, such as UNOSOM II, which at its height was costing \$3 million a day with little if any progress being made in the resolution of the conflict. Boutros-Ghali also ordered the operation in Cyprus (UNFICYP), which had entered its third decade, to be 'scaled down considerably'. Termination of UNFICYP was unacceptable, however, due to its continuing importance in preventing a resumption of conflict.

However, by the end of the year the true effect of the new US policy was being felt in the crisis in Rwanda. In May 1994, the US had refused to allow the dispatch of a UN force to Rwanda arguing that it would overstretch the resources of the Organisation. Meanwhile hundreds of thousands of innocent civilians died as the result of mass starvation and systematic murder. Even when the US did eventually become involved in the provision of humanitarian aid, one relief worker commented that 'the

Americans' came in full of plans and promises to put everything right, and as soon as they came in, they started talking about getting out'.[7] Following their lead over sixty states failed to provide a single positive response to a request by the Secretary General to contribute troops to a UN force for the country in mid-1994.

TABLE 6: Peacekeeping Operations established 1994

Mission	Brief Explanation
United Nations Confidence Restoration Operation (UNCRO) 1994-present United Nations Protection Force (UNPROFOR) 1992-present United Nations Preventive Deployment Force (UNPREDEP) 1994-present	UNPROFOR reconfigurated in March 1994 into three separate operations; UNCRO to create conditions for a negotiated settlement consistent with the territorial integrity of Croatia; UNPROFOR to continue with its existing mandate in Bosnia; UNPREDEP to prevent expansion of conflict into FYROM
United Nations Assistance Mission in Rwanda (UNAMIR) 1994-present	Contribute to the security of Kigali; monitor ceasefire and compliance with Arusha Peace Agreements; monitor repatriation of refugees
United Nations Verification Mission in Angola (UNAVEM III) 1995-present	To assist in the implementation of the Lusaka Protocol by providing good offices and mediation; verify and monitor the electoral process; verify and monitor neutrality of Angolan National Police

Ongoing operations

On visiting the Western Sahara in late November 1994, the Secretary General stressed that the 'continued involvement of the UN would depend on the demonstrated political will of the parties' to resolve their outstanding differences.[8] Although the lack of convergence with regards to the eligibility criteria for voter registration was still blocking substantial progress in the operation, the Secretary General was still optimistic that by 31 March enough progress would have been made on voter identification for the transitional period to begin on 1 June 1995 (known in operational terms as D-Day). By this time, it was hoped, all combatants would have been confined to designated locations, prisoners-of-war would have been exchanged, and amnesties would be proclaimed for political prisoners, detainees and refugees. This would be followed by a reduction in the number of Moroccan forces present in the territory and the suspension of all laws or measures that could obstruct the conduct of a free and fair referendum. This second phase was to be completed by mid-August 1995 (D-Day + 11 weeks). Finally, the identification and registration of voters could be completed by the end of September (D-Day + 17 weeks). This latter date would coincide with the start of the referendum campaign in time for the referendum to take place in October 1995.

By the end of August 1994, however, the identification and registration of voter applications had progressed slowly, and by mid-1995 a UN mission sent to the Western Sahara to try and provide an impetus to the MINURSO operation noted that POLISARIO had become concerned about the Mission's ability to ensure fairness in the process. The Mission stated that the two tribal leaders who were present at identification centres in order to identify individuals as Western Saharan tended to disagree on about 60 percent of cases. This problem had potentially catastrophic consequences for the registration process, given that only 20 percent of those individuals presenting themselves had actually been around at the time of the Spanish census in 1974, and that 80 percent of all applicants were said to be without adequate documentation.[9] Observers from the Organisation of African Unity (OAU) had told the mission that in their view 'although a January [1996] deadline for the referendum might not be realistic, it would be unthinkable to talk about MINURSO's withdrawal at the present stage'.[10] The OAU observers also urged the Security Council to become more forceful in its approach to eliciting the consent of the parties to abide by their original agreements, and that the Council should entrust MINURSO to take over the identification process completely. For its part the Mission concluded that the 'continuing suspicion and lack of trust' between the two parties had resulted in 'technical problems that could have been resolved easily had there been goodwill' becoming 'politicised and blown out of proportion, with each party blaming the other for lack of progress'.[11]

Although the UN had maintained a humanitarian and political presence in Angola, the prospects for peace were to diminish over the early part of 1994, as the intensification of the war led to only a small part of the country being accessible for humanitarian work.[12] By the end of the year, however, the negotiations which had begun in the latter half of 1993 were to conclude in another agreement, the Lusaka Protocol, on 20 November 1994. Although the ceasefire was to begin 48 hours after the Protocol was signed, by 24 November in true Angolan style, reports of renewed clashes were accompanied by accusations of blame being made by each side. Despite these initial difficulties the SGSR in Angola, Alioune Blondin

Beye, was able to inform the Secretary General that the ceasefire had on the whole been maintained.[13] On 8 February 1995, the Security Council *inter alia* authorised the establishment of the United Nations Angolan Verification Mission III with an initial mandate until 8 August.[14] By August 1995, however, little progress had been made on the implementation of the Lusaka Protocol. Discussions related to the disarmament of UNITA's 75,000 troops, the confinement to barracks of the government's security forces, and the formation of an integrated 70,000 strong national army, remained the most substantial impediments to the operation's progress. By this time fewer than half the expected 7,500 UN troops had arrived and efforts to deal with the removal of millions of landmines were lagging months behind schedule. In a move to form a government of national unity, Angola's parliament created the posts of two Vice Presidents, one of which was to be offered to the UNITA leader Jonas Savimbi. It insisted, however, that Savimbi could not take up the offer until his troops had been disarmed.[15]

On 29 September 1994, in his periodic report on the operations of UNIKOM, the Secretary General noted that the mission had 'continued to exercise a high degree of vigilance and through its patrols and liaison activities has contributed to the calm which has prevailed along the Iraq-Kuwait border'. He therefore recommended that UNIKOM's mandate be maintained.

Having overcome the majority of the problems which had caused a near twelve month delay in the implementation of its mandate, ONUMOZ began to supervise the assembly of government and resistance troops in their respective cantonment sites from November 1993. However, an agreement to begin demobilisation could not be reached until March of the following year. Exacerbated by overcrowding and inadequate supplies, this further delay served only to increase already heightened tensions amongst assembled troops, leading to numerous violent protests throughout the early months of 1994. And despite the demobilisation process having been substantially concluded by the end of August, it was apparent to all concerned that both parties had maintained substantial manpower and weaponry outside the UN disarmament process. Estimations of the number of troops withheld ranged as high as 2,000 for RENAMO and 4,000 for government forces. Worries of a failure similar to that which had occurred in Angola in late 1992 re-emerged, therefore, when the leader of RENAMO, Alfonso Dhlakhama, officially withdrew from the elections one day before voting began. However, unlike Jonas Savimbi, Dhlakama succumbed to international pressure and returned to the democratic process and a new president was sworn into office in late December 1994.

In Somalia, the American contingent of UNOSOM II had departed by the end of March 1994 and was to be quickly followed by contingents from thirteen other nations. This left behind a force of approximately 20,000 mainly Indian and Pakistani troops, who complained that the equipment and resources they subsequently inherited were completely inadequate. Complaining that the helicopters which the US had leased to the UN were outmoded and that the surveillance aircraft used by the US had not been made available to the remaining troops, Pakistan's Foreign Minister, Asif Ali, asked whether 'Pakistani personnel's lives [were] cheaper than those that came from the West?'.[16] With little progress being made towards national reconciliation, the Secretary General recommended in October 1994 that the mandate for UNOSOM II be extended to 31 March 1995 in order to prepare for a safe and orderly withdrawal of the remaining troops. He did, however, state a willingness to continue the operation after that date, but only if sufficient progress had been made in negotiations to reach an agreement on the establishment of a transitional government.[17] With no such agreement imminent, the Security Council decided on 3 November 1994 to terminate the mandate of UNOSOM II by 31 March 1995.

With little let up in the factional fighting, the UN troops abandoned their headquarters in the capital, Mogadishu, on 1 February and retreated to the airport to await evacuation. Twenty-six days later 2,500 American and 500 Italian marines landed in operation 'United Shield' in order to provide a safe withdrawal for the approximately 2,500 UN troops still present in the country. Under-Secretary General for Peacekeeping, Kofi Annan, stated that the decision to leave Somalia had been deliberate and painful, but that given the number of crises around the world, the Security Council felt compelled to let the protagonists know that there was a limit to the international community's patience and resources.[18]

In March 1994, the Head of ONUSAL, Enrique Ter Horst, warned that the peace process in the country was still incomplete with only two months of the operation's mandate remaining. Whilst encouraging the parties to accelerate the implementation of outstanding elements of the Accords, the Secretary General recommended the establishment of a small team of observers, known as the UN Mission in El Salvador (MINUSAL), to ensure their compliance.[19] However, in the opinion of the El Salvadorian Minister of Co-ordination of Economic and Social Development, Ramon Gonzales Giner, these remaining problems were insignificant in relation to what had been achieved. For as Giner stated, in 'El Salvador the peace plan [had] been so successful that it would be unfair to talk about pros and cons. The very few difficulties we have run into are hardly worth mentioning compared with the enormous success' of the operation.[20] With relatively little media attention focused on the first UN peacekeeping success of 1995, at least one analyst believed the departure of ONUSAL in April could be celebrated as a 'quiet victory'.[21]

Successes

Although subsequently dwarfed either in terms of expense or media attention by the operations in Somalia, Yugoslavia and Rwanda, the greatest successes for the UN in 1994 were to come in El Salvador and Mozambique. In El Salvador, approximately 1,000 military personnel, 170 international civilian staff and 187 local staff helped over a period of three years to bring an end to one of Central America's bloodiest civil wars. At the request of both contending parties, (the FMLN and government) the Secretary General had been able to send a preliminary mission to the country in March 1991, even before hostilities had stopped and whilst negotiations for a comprehensive settlement were continuing.   This presence, although small, acted as a confidence building measure between the parties.   It also meant that 'without precedent in the history of UN peacekeeping and peacemaking missions, the ONUSAL [became] the first mission to accomplish its tasks of verification and observation of respect for human rights and international humanitarian law during an internal conflict'. [22]

Three years later, in March 1994, the first post-conflict elections were held in El Salvador for the Presidency, Vice-Presidency, the Legislative Assembly and Municipal Councils and for the representatives to the Central American Parliament. In his report of 11 May 1994, the Secretary General declared that the 'elections [had been] held under generally acceptable conditions, without any major acts of violence, although serious flaws regarding organisation and transparency were detected. These were not, however, deemed to have had an effect on the final outcome.'[23]

ONUSAL, officially launched on 26 July 1991, had been initially composed only of a Human Rights Division, established in May 1991 pursuant to SC Resolution 693. On deployment, this Division became responsible for monitoring and verifying a general respect for human rights within El Salvador. In January 1992 (SC Resolution 729) ONUSAL's first expansion was to encompass the creation of both the Military and Police Divisions, the former created to oversee the agreed ceasefire and other military aspects, including the demobilisation and reintegration of former government and guerilla troops (the agreements stipulated the disarmament of all FMLN guerillas as well as the reduction of the national army to half its present size), and the latter to supervise the maintenance of public order by the already existing National Police (PN) during a transition period culminating with the creation of the new National Civil Police (PNC). The final expansion of ONUSAL in February 1993 (SC Resolution 832) was to see the creation of the Electoral Division, to monitor free and fair elections, through the supervision of electoral enrolment and elections. Together they allowed ONUSAL to serve '... as a trusted mediator in a place where trust was in short supply.'[24] Speaking proudly of what the UN had achieved in El Salvador, the Secretary General stated that not only had it succeeded in negotiating an end to the confrontation, but had '... participated in the demobilisation of the combatants ... established a new civilian police ... reformed the judicial and electoral system ... encouraged the promotion of human rights by establishing new institutions ... [and] introduced an extraordinarily ambitious economic programme, promoting such goals as land reform and land redistribution'. In short, the UN had turned a war-ravaged country into a state that could now plan and implement its own economic and social development.

In Mozambique, ONUMOZ monitored and verified the first ever democratic elections in Mozambiquan history in October 1994. Although the whole process had come close to derailment when the leader of the former rebel group RENAMO, Alfonso Dhlakama, officially withdrew from the elections only a day before voting began, diplomatic persuasion by the SGSR Aldo Ajello and representatives of interested nations prevented the cancellation of the elections. With RENAMO's reinstatement, an extra day's voting was added to account for lost time, and the elections for the Presidency and Legislative Assembly were held simultaneously on 27-29 October. Following over 17 years of civil war, 7,244 polling stations received greater than three million votes for the Presidency and nearly four million for the Legislative Assembly.[25] The new President, Joaquim Chissano, became the first democratic leader of Mozambique when he was sworn into office in December 1994.

ONUMOZ, besides providing essential logistical support to the electoral process, cantoned, demobilised and helped re-integrate approximately 80,000 of the forces of the nominal Mozambiquan government and rebel groups. It also assisted in the formation of a new joint army of 12,000 troops. ONUMOZ was also entrusted with the co-ordination and monitoring of all humanitarian assistance programmes, and its civilian police (CIVPOL) observed police activity, (although only in government held territory), investigated complaints relating to human rights violations and was actively involved in the monitoring of the electoral process. The mission also helped repatriate 4.3 million displaced persons, provided relief supplies, and restored essential services, including the school system, health care system and water supply in rural areas.[26]

In his final report on ONUMOZ, in December 1994, the Secretary General described the mission as a 'remarkable achievement', the success of which he attributed to several factors. The first was the strong commitment to peace and reconciliation of the Mozambiquan people and their leaders. He also noted the importance of the 'political pragmatism' of the General Peace Agreement, the 'clarity' of the ONUMOZ mandate, and the constant support of the Security Council. Finally he recognised the international community's 'significant political, financial and technical support of the peace process.' In essence the Secretary General believed the ONUMOZ operation was '... an example of what can be achieved through the UN when all forces join together in one common endeavour towards a common goal'.[27]

Problems

Funding

Few good omens for the state of UN finances emerged in 1994. With the introduction in May of US Presidential Decision Directive 25, stringent new measures were to be applied to assess future US funding of new and continuing peacekeeping operations. With Washington unhappy with its relatively large financial burden (whilst the US paid for just over a third of all peacekeeping operations, China, with an expanding economy and a permanent seat on the Security Council was paying for just 0.8 percent), PDD25 also sought to reduce the US contribution from some 32 percent to the 25 percent it will pay for the period 1995-97.[28] The US Ambassador to the UN, Madaleine Albright, made numerous statements throughout 1994-95 clarifying the new US policy for peacekeeping funding. As she stated in July of 1995, with the 'current budgetary climate, neither [the US] nor the UN can continue to pour resources into operations for which we can see no end ... Each time we vote to create or extend a peacekeeping operation, we must consider whether that use of resources is justified or whether the limited funds available should be spent elsewhere'.[29]

Yet a full year before Albright made this statement the crisis in UN peacekeeping funding had become so severe that the Secretary General had reported the need for several austerity measures to be introduced in an attempt to limit future spending. Besides asking all peacekeeping operations to reduce, or postpone, expenditure to the maximum extent possible, he also requested the UN Secretariat and peacekeeping operations centre to delay procurement and recruitment spending, except in 'the most essential cases'. Requiring a minimum of $200 million per month to maintain the operations ongoing in July 1994, and a further $100 million per month to reimburse troop-contributing countries, the Secretary General reported that the funds for Somalia and Mozambique had run out completely, and that the operations in El Salvador, Lebanon, Iraq and the former Yugoslavia were also in a 'precarious situation'.[30] Despite these measures, ten months later, in May 1995, the UN was still owed $2.89 billion: $1.02 billion for the regular budget and $1.87 billion for peacekeeping. With the US itself owing $527 million and $650 million for the regular and peacekeeping budgets respectively, Albright's observations regarding the UN's lack of finances did not include an acknowledgment of America's own role in its precipitation.

With the optimism of previous years eroding, member states were finding even less reason to be prompt and up to date with their contributions. Despite being required to pay their instalments within thirty days of receiving an assessment, the UN had found that it was recouping only 45 percent of contributions in the first three months and only 68 percent after one hundred and eighty days.[31] As the Secretary General himself noted, although member states continued to blame these poor payment records on the fact that they receive assessments at various times during a budget cycle and cannot therefore prepare for them properly, they also remained in arrears for longstanding peacekeeping commitments. He suggested that member states help increase the UN Peacekeeping Reserve Fund, or establish their own peacekeeping reserves for unforeseen peacekeeping commitments as a way to ameliorate this problem.[32] The Secretary General also criticised the capricious manner in which the Security Council tended to create mandates without ensuring the means to carry them out, stating that he was 'particularly concerned that a peacekeeping operation is frequently established, its budget approved, perhaps even troops contributed to it, but the necessary financial means withheld for long periods of time. Yet, this is what takes place routinely.'[33]

By September 1995 the UN's financial situation had still not improved. Despite measures implemented to cut spending, including a freeze on new recruitment, the Organisation was still owed $3.7 billion for both the regular and peacekeeping budgets. In fact, due to the funds in the regular budget running out in mid-August, the Secretary General had no option but to raid the peacekeeping budget just to keep the Organisation afloat. Reimbursements for peacekeeping costs to eighty UN member states were suspended.

Planning

Although it would be difficult to look upon the operations in El Salvador
and Mozambique as anything but highly successful, both suffered from
problems which affected the implementation of their mandates.   In El
Salvador, the failure to implement areas of the peace accords covering land
distribution, judicial reform, the reintegration of demobilised fighters and
the prevention of former security forces from joining the new police force,
had led the Secretary General to seek an extension of the UN presence. A
small team was set up to verify the implementation of these remaining
elements of ONUSAL's mandate. This team, known as the UN Mission
in El Salvador (MINUSAL), was expected to complete the majority of its
work by the end of October 1995.[34]

The failure of ONUSAL to complete some of the elements of its mandate
on time was due mainly to the opposing sides of the conflict having what
Richard Stahler-Sholk described as 'different kinds of democracy in
mind'.[35]   In the case of the nominal government, its lack of enthusiasm
for a transition to true democracy caused it to continually obstruct the
implementation of certain aspects of the agreements.   One of the worst
affected was the area of human rights.   For example, within days of the
publication of a report by the International Truth Commission, a body
created to investigate the overall problem of human rights, the ruling
ARENA party pushed a 'sweeping, and apparently unconstitutional,
amnesty law' through parliament. This served to prevent any investigation
or determination of guilt for previous human rights violations, and together
with other omissions in the implementation of human rights agreements
'seemed to maintain and perpetuate' past practices, such as the use of death
squads for politically motivated assassinations.

A similar situation was to occur in the formation of the new national
police (PNC). The objective of the peace agreements had been to separate
internal security from the military, screen the new police force from
previous human rights abusers, and increase training to include human
rights education.   However, the government attempted to postpone the
planned phasing out of the old National Police as long as possible, and
exacerbated the problem by also trying to circumvent ONUSAL's
supervision in order to transfer military personnel into the new PNC.[36]
Although the peace agreements had stipulated that 60 percent of the
composition of the PNC was to be made up by civilians who had not taken
part in the armed conflict and the remaining 40 percent divided equally
from past members of the old National Police and FMLN, ONUSAL
reported that the incorporation of former military units, a pattern of
favouritism for promoting members of security forces and the government's

opposition towards allowing the UN to check the human rights records of personnel transferred from the military, had all 'run counter to the letter and spirit of the Peace Accords'. In May 1994 the Secretary General called for these imbalances to be urgently addressed to prevent any further militarisation of the new PNC and at least one Human Rights group believed it posed a 'potentially permanent problem'.[37]

The Secretary General described the problems facing the re-integration of demobilised soldiers in his report of 23 November 1993. In this report he noted three failings which had hampered the process. The first was the lack of a 'global strategy' in the formulation programmes which had subsequently affected their design and planning. Secondly he noted that the training programmes did not start at the same time and were not synchronised with the dates of demobilisation, with the result that some beneficiaries registered in programmes because of economic need rather that as a vocation. Finally, the Secretary General pointed to the lack of overall planning which had allowed the same mistakes to be repeated in the different programmes. With unemployment running at 60 percent in mid-1995, the reintegration of demobilised fighters was still experiencing delays eighteen months after the Secretary General's report. A main cause of this was the government's inertia in implementing its promises over the redistribution of land. Despite the recognition that inequality in land ownership was a central factor in the polarisation of Salvadorian society, approximately 38 percent of former fighters and rural people were still waiting for land three years after the peace process had begun.[38]

The intransigence of the parties was also to affect the implementation of judicial reforms and the general process of elections. Ignoring recommendations from the Truth Commission that the Supreme Court resign, political wrangling among the parties was to hold up judicial reforms until after the elections. And a relatively low turnout for the elections themselves (only 45 percent on 24 April) was subsequently blamed on the Supreme Electoral Tribunal's (TSE) rejection of applications for obtaining voting cards; its failure to provide them to more than a quarter of a million people prior to the vote; and the UN's estimation that as many as 100,000 Salvadorians were turned away from the polls during round one of the elections due to a general confusion or an inability to find their names on the registration lists.

As touched upon earlier, none of these problems could be placed at the door of the UN mission in El Salvador. As in all the operations which preceded it, and all those which have followed, the success of a peacekeeping mission is completely dependent on the co-operation of the parties to the agreements. This is especially the case with operations like ONUSAL which are required only to verify, supervise and monitor the implementation of agreements agreed to by other parties. In cases such as those elucidated above, where at least one of the parties fails to abide by previous commitments, there is little the UN can do to force them to co-operate. What it can do, however, is to refuse to proceed with other elements of its mandate when certain aspects remain incomplete. This has the effect of threatening the removal of international legitimacy from the proceedings. In this case, such action could have taken the form of refusing to monitor and verify elections whilst the new PNC remained controversial, or the land and judicial reforms had not been implemented. Pressure on the UN to gain a 'success' in peacekeeping operations can, however, work to the detriment of the true objectives of the peace accords. For some at least it seemed that the UN had developed an institutional interest in promoting a benign view of the elections because any bad publicity would have reflected unfavourably on the UN operation. This was particularly the case given the UN's previously bad experiences in Angola and Somalia. Stahler-Sholk notes that ONUSAL became increasingly frustrated over the fact that their critical reports targeting defects in the electoral process were being watered down, or simply ignored, before summaries were sent to New York. And that some UN observers had felt that as the term of the SGSR for El Salvador, Augusto Ramirez Ocampo, came to an end, he became less aggressive in pushing the government toward compliance owing to his personal interest in concluding the operation with a 'success'.[39] With the UN appearing less and less concerned with ensuring full compliance, at least one disgruntled UN official felt that the UN wanted simply '... to get out of the place as soon as possible with its victory intact'.[40]

Like the operation in El Salvador, ONUMOZ was also to suffer from a lack of co-operation from the parties to the Rome Agreement. In his report of April 1994 the Secretary General stated that the 'political will of the parties, whilst appreciated, is unfortunately not always translated into the political steps that must be accomplished to ensure the implementation of the peace process.'[41] Especially worrying to the Secretary General at this time were the delays not only in the assembly of government troops, but also in the demobilisation of the rebel group RENAMO and in the training of the new national army (FADM).[42]

The delay in the cantonment and demobilisation of former fighters had for a long time threatened to upset the peace process in Mozambique. Demobilisation did not actually begin until March 1994, more than a year after it had been initially planned and less than eight months before the elections were due. In July of the same year, discontent with the slowness of the process had led thousands of assembled troops to rampage through the streets, seizing hostages, looting shops and in some cases threatening

UN officials. Reporting that there had been twenty such protests between January and April, the Secretary General blamed them mostly on the failure of the Maputo government to pay its soldiers' expected wages, and the unrealistic promises concerning possible benefits made to demobilising RENAMO soldiers. These problems had been exacerbated at some assembly sites by severe overcrowding which had resulted in shortages of food and inadequate lodging facilities.

Having spent most of their lives in combat, few Mozambiquan soldiers wished to continue. A UN poll in late 1994 showed that only 2.1 percent of cantonned fighters wished to stay in the armed forces, whilst 97.9 percent wanted to be demobilised.[43] As the SGSR, Aldo Ajello stated, '... the two parties have to face the fact that their people feel free for the first time to say what they want, and they don't want the army - the military option is over'.[44] Although this was a good sign as far as free choice was concerned, it had, however, caused severe problems for the formation of the 30,000 strong new national army (FADM) envisaged in the Rome Accords. Faced with insufficient numbers and a lack of adequate training facilities, the parties to the Accords agreed to continue the process after the elections and reiterated their commitment to compose it only of volunteers.[45] By October 1994 only approximately 10,000 soldiers had been enlisted.

Together with the experiences of the UN in the cantonment, demobilisation and reintegration of former fighters in Nicaragua, El Salvador, Cambodia and Angola, Mozambique provides many lessons for future UN missions. All of the aforementioned operations experienced similar problems in the process of de-militarisation. Although the intransigence of the Khmer Rouge prevented Phase II (cantonment, disarmament and demobilisation) of UNTAC's mandate from being completed, the operation still experienced problems as it approached the rice season with thousands of Phnom Penh troops in assembly areas waiting for demobilisation. In Angola, without any investigative powers UNAVEM II's uneven quality of personnel, insufficient tactical mobility and lack of advanced search and track systems, conspired to make its objectives completely unattainable.[46] Although both the UNTAC and UNAVEM II operations ended with democratic elections, the failure to remove the gun from Cambodian and Angolan politics has meant that neither peace nor democracy developed in either country. In Nicaragua, ONUCA's mandate was expanded after a request from the Contra rebels to be demobilised inside Nicaragua itself, rather than in the neighbouring countries within which it had been based. ONUCA provided security within the Contra assembly areas, monitored the withdrawal of government troops from the surrounding areas and received and destroyed each demobilising fighter's personal weaponry. Although delays did occur in the demobilisation process, the establishment of 'development areas' for demobilised soldiers and their families, together with the establishment of a police force for security, helped to overcome the greatest problems. ONUCA also maintained observers in areas with large numbers of demobilised Contra fighters to encourage a sense of security and confidence amongst the population.

As General Sir David Ramsbotham commented, surrendering a Kalashnikov for $50 does not in itself amount to disarming. It is essential that demobilised soldiers be put to work for the good of their country.[47] Proper reintegration of demobilised soldiers into civilian life can only take place within a wider process of confidence-building or 'national reconciliation', and as a long term process should not be subordinated to an inflexible schedule of implementation. These lessons were taught by the Angolan debacle, and were successfully heeded by the SGSR, Aldo Ajello, in Mozambique. However, both Nicaragua and Mozambique exhibited the dangers which dissatisfied soldiers can pose to the peace process as a whole. Once the troops are assembled, the UN needs to be assured that the finances and reintegration programmes which will prevent the former fighters from rioting or resorting to banditry are both sufficient and in place. This, however, was not the case in Mozambique. When the Secretary General reported that 20,000 more government and RENAMO soldiers than expected had presented themselves for demobilisation and that the budget for the Reintegration Support Scheme had subsequently increased to $31.9 million, he also reported that only $27.6 million had been pledged and as of November 1994 only $8.9 million had been received.[48] A similar situation had also developed for the financing and training of the new national army. The credibility of the Organisation will always be on the line when it is an axiom that only with adequate resources can the UN hope to facilitate a viable transformation from internal conflict to peaceful democracy.

As in the ONUCA and UNTAC operations, the missions in Mozambique and El Salvador had, as part of the de-militarisation agreements, also been requested to locate, collect and in some cases destroy weapons and ammunition belonging to the warring factions. In all these operations the UN lacked the personnel, tactical mobility, advanced technologies and investigative powers that would have allowed it to locate and destroy arms caches and ammunition dumps which had not been declared. In El Salvador the inability of ONUSAL to take an inventory of FMLN weapons after the discovery of large arms caches meant that the operation eventually requested the FMLN itself to provide a complete inventory of its arms and ammunition.[49] In Mozambique, the SGSR Aldo Ajello, had accepted that 'huge stocks' of arms and ammunition which should have been surrendered lay hidden throughout the country.[50] In September 1994 more than 1,000 RENAMO soldiers were discovered at secret bases, after the August 30 deadline which had been set for their registration. RENAMO also refused to hand over the sophisticated communication equipment with which it had organised its military campaign.[51] And on one occasion in October 1994, when UN teams went to check three arms dumps under RENAMO control, they were given the wrong co-ordinates for one cache, the local leader could not find the second, and the commander in charge failed to turn up at the third. Asked whether RENAMO still had a military capacity as the elections approached, Ajello admitted that it had, but said that RENAMO's 'declaration' of the missing troops and equipment pointed to good faith.[52] With the RENAMO leader's pledge that he would not return to civil war regardless of the election results, and Ajello's confidence that his promise was good, the existence of these weapons might not threaten the post-election peace. However, as the previous Angolan operations have shown, UNAVEM III may not be able to rely on the good faith of the parties quite so easily.

Personnel and Equipment

Although the Secretariat had introduced a number of reforms by 1994, the continuing lack of centralised and integrated planning mechanisms at UN headquarters in New York meant that it was still practically impossible for the Organisation to anticipate logistical requirements in the field. The result was a continuation of the dislocation and delay in the deployment of material and personnel which had caused so many problems for past operations. For example, despite the obvious lessons of the tardy and late deployment of UNTAC, ONUMOZ was still not deployed until ten months after the ceasefire.

The Secretariat's procurement system continued to cause problems. An internal study dated March 1994 found that since 1990 professional staff levels at the Field Missions Procurement Section in the DPKO had remained constant, whilst the total procurement dollar volume had increased by 872 percent. It therefore concluded that the Secretariat could no longer accommodate or service the rapid growth in procurement and contracting activities without a very substantial infusion of staff resources and a change in the organisational structure.[53] In the same month the UN's 'antiquated' procurement regulations had generated such acute logistical difficulties in Mozambique that the entire demobilisation of government and RENAMO troops had been threatened.[54] And at the beginning of 1995, General Lewis Mackenzie reported that the 'overstretched and inefficient' supply system had left some peacekeepers in Bosnia without even appropriate accommodation. Around the same time a UN Commission warned in its report that 'inexperienced, untrained or unwanted staff' in the procurement office had resulted in a 'breeding ground for malpractice, waste and possibly fraud'. Accusing the UN of 'wasting and losing millions of dollars' the document called for a streamlined bureaucracy, increased training, greater use of technology, increased use of competitive bidding and the establishment of an impartial complaints bureau.[55]

As mentioned in the previous chapter, the Secretary General had authorised a planning team in April 1993 to establish standby-forces agreements with member states. By the end of June 1994 this team had reported that 21 member states had confirmed a willingness to provide standby-forces, raising a potential 30,000 troops.[56] By May 1995 the number of committed states had reached 41.[57] As well as troops, the UN Stand-by Arrangements System (UNSAS) also consists of data bases on available services and equipment which states are also willing to supply. By creating this system the planning team has 'established a more formalised and specific procedure', than the previously traditional method based on an exchange of letters between the Secretary General and contributing countries.[58] To complement this the Secretariat has also compiled a roster of qualified civilian staff and revised its staff rules to enable it to 'identify, recruit, deploy and withdraw rapidly and efficiently' civilian staff for UN peacekeeping missions. By the end of 1994 this roster contained over 5,000 names.[59]

However, there still remained regional imbalances in the geographical distribution of troop contributing countries. Only five of the states which had committed themselves by May 1995 were from Africa. One month later, the Organisation for African Unity (OAU) agreed to place their troops on stand-by for peacekeeping operations in Africa under UN auspices.[60] Despite this welcome contribution, the limitations of the stand-by system had also been exhibited in the months preceding. Due to the fact that all forces remain under national control, at least until they are donated, and that they are donated only on a case-by-case basis, the UN has found that the UNSAS will not always solve its manpower problems. When the Security Council extended the mandate of the UNAMIR in May 1994, after 19 countries had committed themselves to the UNSAS, not one of these, nor any others for that matter, agreed to contribute forces. Also, at the beginning of the following year, despite the deteriorating security situation in Rwanda, or more to the point because of it, the UN failed to receive a single positive response from the sixty member states requested to form a multinational force to protect Rwandan refugees in Zairean camps. The Secretary General also admitted that although he had stressed that 'with four hundred paratroopers, [the] genocide could have been stopped', he had failed to persuade 35 African Heads of State to intervene in the Rwandan crisis.[61] The UNSAS had, therefore, hardly fulfilled the Secretary General's dreams of a 'Rapid Reaction Force' which would be able to intervene in situations like Rwanda to prevent potential escalations of violence.[62]

It is also unclear just how effective the UNSAS will be at alleviating the problems posed by the lack of standard training, inter-operability, and the need for specialised personnel to be deployed for specific operations. Such problems have been manifest in all the UN's peacekeeping missions, but especially so in the multi-dimensional operations of recent years. A full year after the UNSAS team had begun its work, when Kofi Annan, the Under-Secretary General for Peacekeeping, confirmed that approximately 3,000 troops would be dispatched to aid the refugee relief effort in Rwanda, the senior military advisor in the field, General Maurice Baril, warned that the situation may be made worse by the lack of training received by incoming troops, the African nation's lack of equipment, and by problems in matching equipment from other countries. Also, in June 1995 a UN official in Angola disclosed that most of the 220 police officers in his charge did not speak Portuguese.[63] The Uruguayan police sub-commander, Jose Manuel Pereira, stated that his problem was 'that I have only 16 Portuguese speaking Brazilian officers and another five from Guinea-Bissau. But for the most part my men are native English speakers and completely inept at communicating with local police and civilians in Angola'.[64]

With neither the international community nor the Secretary General wishing to establish a UN standing army, the UNSAS is the only credible alternative. It has, however, inherent inadequacies. Contributing countries are only required to list units which they are prepared to make available to UN operations. As the Rwandan case has shown, they are not required to make any formal commitments to actually deploy them when requested. And when countries like the US refuse even to earmark specific military units upon which the UN can call, the Organisation's task is made even harder. By its very nature, the UNSAS can do nothing to help increase the training and technological endowment of national troop contingents. Created mainly to help provide the technical and specialist units and troops required by the UN's multi-dimensional peacekeeping and humanitarian operations, and also to help reduce the amount of time needed to prepare troops for deployment, the UNSAS has so far failed to deliver on both counts. As witnessed in the latest Angolan operation the former has seemingly suffered through a lack of organisation. So far the international community's inertia has put paid to the latter.

Use of Force

With the end of the Cold War and the new consensus within the Security Council it seemed to many that the policy of 'self-defence' for peacekeepers, although appropriate to the situation in which it developed, was no longer applicable to the post-Cold War world. This belief was strengthened after the successful execution of the first ever Chapter VII enforcement action in the Gulf, in 1990-91. And with the heralding of a 'New World Order' by President Bush, it seemed little could stand in the way of a united Security Council. It did not come as a surprise, therefore, that when the Security Council requested the Secretary General in January 1991 to report on ways that UN peacekeeping may be strengthened in the future, Boutros-Ghali's replying document, *An Agenda for Peace*, included a suggestion for 'peace enforcement units', which he envisaged might enforce a ceasefire where one was not already present.[65]

Whether the UN had thought through the implications of such a use of force, however, was questionable. One of the earliest warnings was to come from Brian Urquart, a former Under-Secretary General, who stated in 1990 that 'before changing the existing rules on the use of force in peacekeeping or moving towards enforcement, it is important to consider the implications, practical, military, legal, political and even psychological and the likely responses of those most directly concerned in peacekeeping operations, the parties to the conflict and the troop contributing countries.'[66] As its experiences over the proceeding five years have testified, all of the considerations Urquart alluded to have featured in the problems which the Organisation has faced in the use of force. Unfortunately, as the following pages will elucidate, in failing to heed Urquart's warning the UN has chosen to learn the lessons of the use of force the hard way.

Cambodia

The first post-Cold War operation in which the use of enforcement action was seriously considered was Cambodia. As the SGSR, Yashushi Akashi, noted, however, unlike the operations in Bosnia and Somalia, UNTAC at no stage had a mandate referring to a Chapter VII enforcement action.[67] The Cambodian parties had, nevertheless, mandated UNTAC through the

Paris Accords with 'all means necessary to ensure the implementation of this agreement', allowing room at least for an interpretation in favour of enforcement action.[68] The SGSR and the Military Commander, Lieutenant General Sanderson preferred, however, to use negotiation rather than coercive action to maintain co-operation for the implementation of their mandate. Therefore, when Sanderson's French deputy, General Loridon, proposed in the early stages of the operation that the Khmer Rouge should be forced to comply with the prior commitments, 'even if it cost the lives of two hundred soldiers, including himself', he was speedily replaced.[69]

It is possible, however, that combined with the slow deployment of UNTAC military personnel, a lack of forceful resolve may have hampered the proceeding implementation of UNTAC's mandate. Cambodia, through its cultural heritage and historical experiences, had developed a society ruled by force, rather than law. It is probable, therefore, that ordinary Cambodians expected the provisions of the Paris Accords to be policed by an effective military force. As Chopra states 'When armed representatives of the world's most powerful nations finally arrived with such lack of impact, the [Khmer Rouge] were tempted to challenge their authority. And once their expectations of coercive, or at least effective, policing had been removed, they realised they could not be forced to comply with the terms of the Agreements'.[70] This feeling was re-enforced when at an incident on the road to Pailin in the Spring of 1992, SGSR Akashi and Lieutenant General Sanderson, were stopped at a makeshift roadblock by Khmer Rouge soldiers. Despite the fact that only a few soldiers and a bamboo pole barred their path, the entourage preferred to negotiate and finally turn back, rather than force their way through. Although this was recognised as part of the strategy applied by Akashi and Sanderson to the whole operation, many critics at the time accused the UN of a lack of resolve and of having a 'spineless abhorrence for forceful measures'.[71] Yet what might have been the consequences of forcing their way through and continuing with what would have amounted to an enforcement operation? If neither the government of Lon Nol in the 1970s, or the whole of the Vietnamese army during the 1980s, were able to defeat the Khmer Rouge, what chances would UNTAC have faced in succeeding where its predecessors had failed? John Mackinlay noted that it would have been 'almost impossible' for a cobbled together multilateral peacekeeping army like UNTAC to conduct a full-scale counter-insurgency campaign, which such an operation would have required. Segali and Berdal were equally sceptical, stating that an effective enforcement operation was beyond the means of UNTAC due to its '... lack of interoperability of equipment, absence of close air support, dearth of adequate tactical communications and tracking equipment and the effective absence of logistical support'.[72]

Other factors also existed to prevent UNTAC from expanding its mandate in the direction of enforcement. For one, the troop contributing countries were in no hurry to see the safety of their personnel endangered any further than they were already. In fact the Japanese contingent, due mostly to their country's pacifist constitution, could not even become involved in a conflict to help other UNTAC troops when they had come under fire. Subsequent anxiousness about how much protection such a contingent could provide, General Sanderson blamed for adding 'to the insecurity of other military units and civilian components'.[73] It is unlikely also that China, as a past supporter of the Khmer Rouge, would have been willing to allow the UN to continue with a military operation designed to remove them from the political equation altogether. As severing Chinese support for the Khmer Rouge was one of its primary goals, the UN would have achieved nothing if the operation had faltered on a Chinese withdrawal.

Somalia

All of the fears which had plagued UNTAC's decision not to enact enforcement measures in Cambodia were to manifest themselves in the first Chapter VII enforcement operation directed by the Secretary General, in Somalia. With the increased powers provided to UNOSOM II through Resolution 837, the UN operation lost its impartiality as it attempted to find and arrest the warlord Mohammed Farah Aideed. Adopted one day after the ambush and murder of 26 Pakistani peacekeepers as they inspected an arms dump owned by Aideed on 5 June 1993, Resolution 837 condemned the killings, authorised 'the arrest, prosecution and trial' of those responsible and called for a 'comprehensive programme for disarmament'.[74] In the ensuing months, UNOSOM II was to become embroiled in a conflict which by the end of 1993 had effectively ended the operation.

The decision to avenge the death of the Pakistani peacekeepers had been supported by Major General Lewis Mackenzie, who argued that unlike Bosnia '... Somalia was a relatively easy military problem. The point about the credibility of the UN in the emerging new world disorder had to be made somewhere, and Somalia was the right place to make it.'[75] Experience, however, was to prove the Major General wrong. The first measure taken was to bomb arms dumps suspected of belonging to Aideed, which resulted in the deaths of 20 Somalis. Increased tension in the hours after the raids also led to the killing of unknown numbers of Somalis by

Pakistani peacekeepers, who interpreted their demonstrations as hostile. Further attacks on Aideed's positions led to conflicting reports between the International Red Cross and the UN on how many Somali casualties had occurred. In one attack the ICRC claimed 54 Somali deaths, whilst the UN had insisted that there were only 17. Apparent confusion also led to the misrepresentation of other events. On one occasion the UN continued to deny the involvement of one of its gunships, a full twelve hours after television footage had been broadcast proving its implication.[76]

With the increasing numbers of Somali deaths the UN was finding that it was losing public support. By targeting Aideed, who represented just one of a total of fourteen warlords, the UN had declared war on the Haber Gedr subclan of which he was leader. With the Somali population turning against outside interference, the personal security of foreigners became precarious. Rushing to capture the immediate after-effects of a UN raid, two journalists were murdered by Somali crowds in Mogadishu in July.

Even the problems of conducting military operations in urban areas were beginning to seriously worry the UN troops. As a commander of one of the American 10th Divisions battalions stated, it '... is the worst kind of warfare because it is insidious. You are surrounded by the enemy. You are surrounded by the friendlies. You are surrounded by the innocent and the guilty.'[77] Other perils of urban combat had led the 10th Mountain troops to profit from the 'experience of US Army Rangers in modifying the traditional means of clearing a room - a heavy firepower method called 'spray and slay' - with a more delicate approach called 'instinctive fire', designed to minimise ricochets.[78] However, the increasing use of force by the US troops began to cause serious unease amongst many of the other UN contingents. Italy condemned the spiralling violence and asked the UN to suspend combat operations in an attempt to reduce tensions. And a number of contingents from Islamic countries, including Morocco, Pakistan and Saudi Arabia, began to refer their orders back to their national governments before executing them.

By September 1993 the recently installed Clinton administration was beginning to experience growing domestic unease with its role in Somalia. US resolve was finally broken following the catastrophic events of the 3 October. On their 6th mission to capture top members of Aideed's 'war cabinet' US Rangers became involved in a firefight which resulted in the deaths of 18 US soldiers, 78 injuries and the abduction of a US helicopter pilot and a Nigerian peacekeeper. Compounding unrest over the high number killed 'televised images of chanting Somalis dragging a US soldier's body through the streets and pictures of a distressed helicopter pilot held hostage' resulted in the immediate collapse of 'domestic support for the Somali operation', resulting in the subsequent announcement by the

US administration of a complete withdrawal by March 1994.[79]   As an early draft of a paper on British peacekeeping doctrine stated:

> The multinational force in Beirut and, more recently, UNOSOM II have demonstrated what seems likely to happen in theatre if a peacekeeping force crosses the impartiality divide from peacekeeping to peace-enforcement.   If perceived to be taking sides, the force loses its legitimacy and credibility as a trustworthy third party, thereby prejudicing its security.   The force's resources will then become ever more devoted to its need to protect itself ... Such a situation will almost certainly result in the loss of popular support, a loss of control and uncontrolled escalation upwards in the ambient level of violence which will heighten political tension and foreclose opportunities for resolving conflict.   To cross the impartiality divide is also to cross a Rubicon. Once on the other side, there is very little chance of getting back and the only way out is likely to be by leaving the theatre.[80]

Yugoslavia

The discussion on peace-enforcement in the former Yugoslavia has taken place on two levels.   The first has concerned the credibility of a large enforcement mandate, similar to that witnessed in Somalia.   The probability that the international community might commit itself to such an operation was never very high.   Estimates for the number of troops that might have been required ran as high as 500,000, and even then there was still no guarantee of success.   Awash with sophisticated weaponry and manpower, even a highly trained UN combat force would probably have suffered substantial fatalities.   And as the UNOSOM II operation showed, even the most powerful governments are unwilling to ignore the adverse public opinion generated by such events.   Even in the unlikely event that the UN had been able to enforce a peace, the parties would have been no nearer a peaceful solution.   The complications associated with attempting a peace-enforcement operation were elucidated by British Foreign Minister Douglas Hurd in a speech to the diplomatic and Commonwealth Writer's Association, when he stated, 'We should not pretend more than we can achieve.   Neither marines, nor parachutists, nor new-fashioned blue-helmets can fight their way to peace among people mingled together village by village ... It is easier to sketch a military operation in theory than to launch it in practice - and easier to launch it than to see how it can be successfully completed.'[81]

The second level of discussion has concerned the introduction of enforcement measures into a humanitarian operation. As in Somalia one of the problems in Yugoslavia was that humanitarian aid was being prevented from reaching its destination by small groups of paramilitaries. Although UNPROFOR would have been quite capable of forcefully breaking through the first, or second, or even third of these impromptu road blocks, resistance would have increased at every point and could have eventually escalated into a full confrontation. In this scenario, the delivery of humanitarian aid, which had essentially been the first priority of the operation, would have ceased altogether. For this reason, the UN maintained the strategy of negotiating at every checkpoint, regardless of the frustration, in order that at least some of the aid would get through.

However, continued reports of human rights violations and the siege of Muslim communities by the Bosnian Serbs forced the international community to adopt a more coercive approach. The first and politically easiest Chapter VII enforcement action was to be the introduction of Resolution 752 of 30 May 1992, which imposed mandatory sanctions against Serbia for its failure to abide by the terms of earlier resolutions requesting the withdrawal of the former Yugoslav army from Bosnia. With stockpiled supplies, and the existence of porous borders with its neighbours, sanctions were unlikely to have any great effect on the conflict in Bosnia. The Security Council did try and improve matters with the adoption of Resolution 787 on 16 November 1992, which dispatched NATO warships to the Adriatic and empowered them to halt shipping, inspect cargoes and destination documents, powers which Resolution 752 had not endowed. These sanctions were to be used later as the negative element of a carrot and stick strategy designed to seek acceptance of proposed peace plans. However, the precarious political position of Boris Yeltsin ensured that on almost all occasions the threat of a conservative backlash in Moscow lessened Russian enthusiasm in the Security Council for further sanctions.[82]

The second move towards enforcement was initiated in 1993 with the introduction of a 'no-fly zone' over Bosnia. With the continued violation of agreed ceasefires, and with the US claiming that Serbian warplanes had been using the UN air corridor as cover for raids, the French argued for the introduction of a UN ban on all military flights. The idea of a 'no-fly zone' had first been endorsed at the London Conference in August 1992, and all the warring parties were understood to have agreed to its establishment. Although the suggestion had gained general UN support, certain states remained reluctant to commit themselves to enforcing such a ban. Russia was unsure about the political consequences in the unhappy event that NATO planes may eventually be required to shoot down planes belonging to a long time ally. For this reason, the Security Council, through Resolution 781, established a ban on all non-UNPROFOR and non-humanitarian military flights in the airspace of Bosnia-Herzegovina, but with compliance to be simply monitored, rather than enforced. Willingness to enforce the ban was not demonstrated until the adoption of Resolution 816 on 31 March 1993. The timing of this Resolution was significant in that its implementation did not occur until after a crucial Russian referendum involving Boris Yeltsin on 25 April.[83] The first violent confrontation over the 'no-fly zone' was not to take place until an incident on 28 February 1994, nearly a year after its establishment, when US F-16s under NATO command shot down four Bosnian Serb Galeb ground attack aircraft shortly after they had attacked towns held mainly by Bosnian government forces.

The third chapter in the story of peace-enforcement in the former Yugoslavia surrounded the establishment of 'safe havens', in the same manner as those established by the international coalition after the Gulf War of 1990-91. The first declared 'safe haven' was to be the city of Srebrenica which had been coming under Serb attack for some time. Resolution 819 of 16 April 1993 demanded an end to the attacks, declared Srebrenica and its surrounding areas a 'safe area' and requested the enlargement of UNPROFOR to safeguard the population. Other cities were designated with the same status after the adoption of Resolution 824 on 6 May 1993, which stated that the international community was;

> ... determined to ensure peace and stability throughout the country, most immediately in the towns of Sarajevo, Tuzla, Zepa, Gorazde, Bihac, as well as Srebrenica ...' and was '... Convinced that the threatened towns and their surroundings should be designated as safe areas, free from armed attacks and from any other hostile acts which endanger the well-being and the safety of their inhabitants.[84]

Designation itself, however, was not sufficient to prevent further attacks, with a Serb attack on Gorazde occurring immediately after Resolution 824 was adopted. Options on how to react to Serb aggression were outlined by the Pentagon, which provided four possible alternatives.[85] The first option, entitled the 'Operational Air Strike', advocated a direct attack on Serb heavy weapon installations, whilst the second, the 'Message Air Strike', suggested an attack on other installations of primary importance, such as ammunition dumps, bridges, electricity grids and oil refineries. Although both options involved attack from high altitude in order to avert anti-aircraft weaponry, the second option was more likely to be successful due to the nature of its static and easily identifiable targets. This latter option would, however, incur a greater risk of civilian casualties. The third option proposed was a cessation of the arms embargo, a move most of the Security Council believed would serve only to escalate the conflict to include other countries in the region. And the final option was to use ground forces to enforce a peace, an incredible alternative for the reasons cited earlier.

With assaults on the 'safe areas' continuing, and with the UN's credibility on the line, the Security Council adopted Resolution 836 on 6 June 1993, enlarging the mandate of UNPROFOR so that it could more effectively deter attacks. Paragraph 9 of this Resolution authorised UNPROFOR when acting in self-defence '... to take the necessary measures, including the use of force, in reply to bombardments against the safe areas by any of the parties or to armed incursion into them or in the event of any deliberate obstruction in or around those areas to the freedom of movement of UNPROFOR or of protected humanitarian convoys.'[86]

Interpretations of Resolution 836 were to differ, however, with the Europeans wishing it to provide a mandate to protect civilians within the safe areas and the Americans restricting its interpretation to the protection of UNPROFOR personnel. Within a month of the adoption of Resolution 836 NATO members had reached a compromise which committed them to providing air support for the protection of the 'safe areas', but in concurrence with the Americans, reiterated that they would only do so to protect UN forces. The Serbs, realising the inherent difficulty in distinguishing between the safety of UN personnel and civilians in these areas, attempted by attacking Zetra, a French base in Sarajevo, to prevent the French from dispersing within the city and thereby upholding its 'safe area' status. On this occasion the UN failed to apply the force that Resolution 836 had allowed, but the event did provide the international community with a reason to create a NATO airforce, stationed in Northern Italy, to provide air cover in the event of a reoccurrence. When, therefore, a mortar attack on a Sarajevan market place on 5 February 1994 killed 68 people, international public outrage prompted the Secretary General to issue both the threat of air strikes and a deadline for the besieging forces to pull back their guns. The warnings issued stated that all heavy weapons had to be withdrawn from a circular area surrounding Sarajevo with a radius of 20 km. Any weapons left within this area were to be placed under UN control. The Secretary General, previously opposed to the use of air strikes, began to perceive them as a means to restore credibility to a faltering UN operation.[87]

At the request of the UN, NATO used its air power several nine times in response either to Serb aggression or to their refusal to comply with exclusion zone demands. On the 10 and 11 April close air support was provided to UNPROFOR near Gorazde. This was to be the first time the Serbs were to retaliate through placing restrictions on UNPROFOR personnel and capturing key points around the 'safe area'. On 5 August NATO jets were once again called in to attack Serb heavy weapons in the exclusion zone surrounding Sarajevo and on 22 September attacked a Serb tank near the same city after a French personnel carrier had been attacked. Both 21 and 23 November were to see NATO attacks against the Udbina airfield in Croatia and Serb surface-to-air missile sites in Western Bosnia and in Krajina, after the Serbs had used them to attack the Bihac 'safe area' and threaten NATO aircraft. The Serbs retaliated by taking more than 400 UN personnel hostage, whose release was not secured until 13 December. Following further attacks on Sarajevo in May 1995, NATO planes attacked an ammunition dump and other targets near the Serb headquarters in Pale on 25 and 26 May. On 11 July, in an attempt to provide protection to the Dutch battalion whose safety had been threatened by the Serb offensive on Srebrenica, NATO conducted air strikes on Serb tanks south of the city. However, whether intended to or not, they failed to prevent the fall of the 'safe area' the same day. On 30-31 August and 1 September 1995, NATO aircraft executed air strikes against Serb targets following the death of 37 civilians and the wounding of a further 80 or more in a Sarajevan market place by a Serb mortar. These strikes were halted to allow the Serbs to withdraw from the 20 km exclusion zone around Sarajevo, but when the Serbs failed to comply, were resumed on 5 September. Over the next nine days NATO conducted a total of around 3,400 sorties, 750 of which were against ground targets, including ammunition and armament manufacturing and repair facilities. The US also launched 13 Tomahawk cruise missiles on the night of 10 September, the first time such weapons had been used in any peace-enforcement operation.[88] Together, the nine days of strikes represent the largest bombing mission which NATO has conducted throughout the Yugoslav conflict.

Despite the number of occasions on which they have been called, there has been little consensus between the Europeans, the US and Russia on the use of air strikes and the introduction of peace-enforcement measures in general. The Europeans, with the greatest number of troops on the ground, have always preferred the more cautious approach in the hope of gaining Serb acquiescence for UN objectives. The US on the other hand, with no troops deployed except for those in FYROM, have expressed less patience with the Serbs, preferring force. This friction reached a high point at the end of 1994 with the Serb assault on the Bihac 'safe area' in North-western Bosnia. With the US exerting increasing pressure for NATO to act, the French Defence Minister, Francois Leotard, explained to the Alliance's most powerful member that; 'You can't stop a house-to-house infantry advance with air strikes'. Critical of the US taking the moral high-ground when it continued to refuse to place troops on the ground, Leotard, continued; 'We have told our American friends from the outset that there are limits to the uses of air power. We are seeing these limits today in Bihac'.

Even more difficult to overcome has been the difference in perspective between the NATO countries and Russia. Although there are doubts about the closeness of the Russian-Serb allegiance, the former has continually expressed reservations about the conduct of the UN and NATO in their peace-enforcement actions. For the most part this has been due to the fact that all of the enforcement actions have been directed against the Serbs, but it has also been caused by the Russian impression that they are not always consulted properly, or even that their opinion is ignored, when the decision to act is taken. The first real indication of the Russian insistence not to be sidelined in the conflict came in February 1994 after the UN requested NATO to implement a 20 km 'exclusion zone' around Sarajevo. So sensitive was the prospect of NATO air strikes that the Russians hastily concocted a deal with the Serbs, independently of the UN, thereby averting the need to enact NATO threats. However, when enforcement action was finally taken Russian protestations were quick to follow. After the bombing of the Ubdina airfield in Croatia, in response to the Serb attack on Bihac in November 1994, Russian Foreign Minister Andrei Kozyrev went as far as to question the legitimacy of NATO's actions, stating: 'We are concerned whether the scale and character of these NATO strikes were in full conformity with the UN Security Council's Resolution'.[89] As described earlier, the western nations had done much to temper the introduction of enforcement measures against the Serbs in order not to damage the political popularity of President Yeltsin at home. However, inaction against violations of UN Resolutions was beginning to reap its own detrimental political consequences for Western leaders, especially President Clinton. Although President Yeltsin will face democratic elections in December 1995, his American counterpart will do the same in November 1996. So, despite the Russian Foreign Ministry statement in May, following the bombing of Serbian targets near Pale, that; 'One cannot seek a just solution to the Bosnian conflict by bombing the positions of just one side', the UN and NATO continued to take an increasingly tougher stance with the Serbs.[90] This policy was to bring ever more vitriolic condemnation from Russia. Whilst in a statement letter in September 1995 Foreign Minister Kozyrev declared that his government saw 'no logic except the logic of repression, behind NATO's [enforcement] actions', President Yeltsin asserted that Russia would 'have to consider thoroughly [its] strategy including [its] relations with the North Atlantic Alliance'.[91]

This appeared to represent the first time that President Yeltsin had warned publicly that the use of force in the former Yugoslavia might effect the entire scope of Russian-Western relations.[92] However, even this warning did not prevent both further NATO air strikes, nor the launching of 13 Tomahawk missiles by the US, before NATO action ended on 14 September.

A further potential schism which has developed during the use of force in the former Yugoslavia has taken place between NATO and the UN. Although all NATO action was necessarily at the behest of the UN, there have been times when NATO has seemingly been concerned more with its own *raison d'etre* and credibility rather than the concerns of UN peacekeeping objectives. This dichotomy of interests has on occasions led to friction between the military strategists at NATO and the civilian authorities at the UN. Irritated by UN restrictions on its operations, which at times it believed made it look both 'ineffectual and foolish', NATO on 7 October 1994 proposed three changes to the rules governing air strikes. While it apparently had no dispute with the UN peacekeepers requesting it to conduct strikes at a level proportionate to violations, NATO wanted a more rapid response. It also wanted an end to the practice of warning of impending strikes and a choice of at least four targets.[93] The UN, however, was determined not to leave the choice, either of intensity or of target, to NATO. In the words of the Secretary General, '... the existence of separate commands for the forces on the ground and those in the air heightens the risk that actions undertaken by the latter could have unforeseeable consequences for the former. This is why the "dual key" procedure developed between UNPROFOR and NATO is so vital'.[94]

The Loss of Consent

So, as the Secretary General noted in his supplement to *An Agenda for Peace*, the loss of consent witnessed in recent UN peacekeeping operations can be attributed to three factors. The first is the manner in which the UN has attempted to pressure parties to achieve national reconciliation before they are ready to do so. The second is the role of the UN in the protection of humanitarian operations. And the third: the protection of civilian populations in 'safe areas'.[95] By refusing to attempt any of these, the SGSR and Force Commander in the Cambodian operation took the decision not to exceed their Chapter VI mandate, although some believed that a more determined and slightly more forceful approach could have reaped greater benefits. In Somalia, the UN saw the effect which a loss of consent, and subsequent use of force can have on an operation. Attempting to capture and arrest the leader of one of the warring parties caused the UNOSOM II force to lose its impartiality. Once this had occurred the operation began on a slippery slope, losing popular local support as it became embroiled in a conflict it had come to end; losing its internal solidarity as national contingents bickered over an acceptable level of violence; and eventually losing Great Power support as nations felt the subsequent loss of life unacceptable. In the former Yugoslavia, the UN conducted a difficult balancing trick, initially introducing Chapter VII enforcement measures whilst failing to act upon them so as not to lose Russian support on the Security Council. As public pressure has mounted for a more forceful approach, the reality of divided Great Power loyalty has become apparent. UNPROFOR, therefore, has at times suffered from a lack of credibility, as warnings from the UN of Chapter VII military action have evaporated in the heat of political realities. When on the other hand NATO has reacted, Russia has retorted with damning indictments, threatening the future cessation of Russian co-operation.

For the UN itself, the main lesson of peace-enforcement has been the realisation of its own inadequacies. In the words of Chester Crocker the UN's attempt at a 'peace-enforcement' operation in Somalia '... shows that it cannot manage complex political-military operations when its own structure is an undisciplined and often chaotic set of rival fiefdoms that resist unified command and control in the field at both the military and civilian levels'.[96] This lesson has not been lost on the Secretary General himself, who stated of the Organisation in May 1995, that '... nothing is more dangerous for a peace-keeping operation than to ask it to use force when its existing composition, armament, logistical support and deployment deny it the capacity to do so.'[97]

Peacekeeping and the provision of Humanitarian Aid

The former Yugoslavia

The first half of 1994 was to see a reduction in the overall intensity of the conflict in Bosnia and a corresponding improvement in the delivery of humanitarian aid. This was mainly the result of two developments. The first was the establishment of a heavy weapons exclusion zone around the capital, Sarajevo, and the second was the agreement reached between the respective armies of Croatia and Bosnia on a general ceasefire. The heavy weapons exclusion zone around Sarajevo was to result from the UN reaction to a mortar attack on a Sarajevan market place which took place on 5 February, killing sixty-eight civilians and wounding nearly two hundred. Having declared the city a 'safe area' through Resolution 824 (1993), the international community felt compelled to act as public opinion raged at the continuing Serb atrocities. Although the source of the mortar was never conclusively proven, the credibility of the UNPROFOR operation began to rest on the ability of the UN to end the siege of Bosnia's historic capital. At the request of the Secretary General, on 9 February, NATO issued a ten day deadline for all heavy weapons within a 20 km radius of the city to be withdrawn or placed under UN control. Any that were not withdrawn or placed under UN control, it was warned, would subsequently be subjected to air attack by NATO forces. The Secretary General, previously opposed to the use of air strikes due to the possible recriminations which the forces on the ground might encounter, was now beginning to view them as 'a means of restoring credibility to a faltering UN operation'.[98] However, before the deadline had expired the Russian special envoy to former Yugoslavia, Vitaly Churkin, announced that separate talks in Pale had resulted in an agreement to replace Serbs in the exclusion zone with some 800 Russian peacekeepers. With Russian discontentment at the emerging role of NATO, this announcement was at the very least a 'reminder of Russia's determination not to be sidelined by western initiatives and its willingness to take unilateral action to assure that end'.[99]

The other significant development in Bosnia which had occurred at the beginning of March was the agreement reached between the Bosnian government and Croatian forces after the fighting for Mostar. Spurred on mainly by US efforts, the two sides negotiated a settlement which envisaged a 'federation' consisting of territory controlled by both sides within Bosnia, linked to Croatia in a 'loose confederation'.

Although the threat of air strikes had been sufficient to end the siege of Sarajevo, they were not to do the same for the more Eastern enclave of Gorazde. The city sits astride a main highway connecting Serbia with the Adriatic and Montenegro. When the Serb forces stepped up their bombardment of the city throughout March and April, threatening the safety of UN observers as well as civilians, the UN Force Commander in Bosnia, Lieutenant General Sir Michael Rose, called for NATO air strikes on 10 and 11 April. Despite the air strikes, the first of their kind in UN history, the Serbs continued their offensive, although at a lower intensity. Matters were to come to a head after the Serbs downed a British Harrier aircraft providing close air support to UN observers on 15 April. Three days later the Secretary General requested NATO to authorise strikes against artillery, mortar positions or tanks attacking civilians in Gorazde, Tuzla, Zepa, Bihac and Srebrenica. Such permission had already been granted for Sarajevo on 22 April when the North Atlantic Council had authorised air strikes against Serb forces which had not withdrawn at least 3 km from the city by 24 April, and within 20 km by the 27 April. The NAC also agreed on similar action if any of the other four 'safe areas' were to subsequently come under attack. The Serbian forces withdrew, beating the final deadline by 12 hours.

On the diplomatic level a 'Contact Group' was established on 26 April in an attempt to inject new momentum into the stalled negotiations. Composed of the US, Russia, France, Germany and the UK, the Group proposed a 51-49 percent split of Bosnian territory between a Croat-Muslim federation and the Bosnian Serbs respectively. Despite offering the Bosnian government a more extensive and viable portion of land than any previous proposal, it failed to please any of the opposing parties, except perhaps the Croats. Whilst the Bosnian government described it as 'seriously flawed' for rewarding the Serbs with territory they had ethnically cleansed, the Serbs demanded that they be given the enclaves of Gorazde, Zepa and Srebrenica as well as half the Bosnian capital Sarajevo. They also insisted on a widening of the Posovina corridor linking Serbia proper to Serb territories in Northern Bosnia and that they also be allowed to form a confederation with the rump Yugoslavia. General Rose described the plan as 'unrealistic, ill-conceived and unfair' to the Serbs, who were being offered only 49 percent of Bosnia when they already occupied 70 percent.[100] The Bosnian Serb leader Karadzic believed the plan to be unacceptable because it sought to divide the territory held by the Serbs into four dislocated parts, denied them the bulk of economic resources, obliged them to give up too many cities, and failed to provide them with access to the sea. The Muslims, under pressure from the West, and despite their own reservations, accepted the plan on 17 July, although the Serbs, threatened with increased sanctions and diplomatic isolation to do the same, rejected the plan two days later. Realising the consequences which Serbia would suffer from increased sanctions, its President, Slobodon Milosevic, described Karadzic's rejection of the plan as 'senseless and absurd' and accused his former ally of being driven by 'mad political ambitions and greed' rather than the greater interest of Serbdom.[101] The continuing intransigence of the Pale leadership on these issues had by August of the same year broken Milosevic's patience. Facing increasing economic hardship from the imposition of sanctions, he accepted the deployment of 135 UN observers on Serbia's border in return for a lifting of international embargoes on civilian air traffic, cultural and sporting links.[102] Although the border has remained somewhat porous, the reduced rate of essential supplies, such as oil, has had a significant effect on the Bosnian Serb warfighting capability. On 11 August, President Clinton set down a deadline of 15 October for the Bosnian Serbs to accept the Contact Group's proposal, threatening to lift the arms embargo on the Muslims if they did not. Although the other members of the Group, fearing a subsequent escalation of the fighting, managed to persuade the President not to carry out his threat, Congress has continued to assert pressure on the administration to do so.[103]

While the UN was attempting to redefine its role in Bosnia, President Tudjman was plotting to end its involvement in Croatia. Under the agreement signed in March 1994 the forces of both sides had separated by at least two kilometres along more than 1,600 km of front line, allowing the UN to establish hundreds of observation posts in the 'no-man's land' in between. Believing that this situation was engendering Serbian hopes that the confrontation line would soon become a national border, on 12 January President Tudjman insisted that the 12,000 UN troops stationed in Croatia be provided with a new mandate or be withdrawn at the end of their present mandate on 31 March 1995.[104]   On 22 March the Secretary General reported that the 'failure of the parties to commence serious political negotiations had brought them to the brink of a major war', and that a reduced UN force in Croatia under a new mandate was the only feasible means to prevent its occurrence.[105]   On 31 March, therefore, the Security Council adopted three resolutions restructuring UNPROFOR into three separate but interlinked operations. The first was the operation in Croatia which pursuant to Resolution 981 (1995) was to be subsequently called the UN Confidence Restoration Operation (UNCRO). This new mission was designed to be an interim arrangement which would hopefully create the conditions to facilitate a negotiated settlement consistent with the territorial integrity of the Republic of Croatia and which would guarantee the security and rights of all the communities within it. Resolution 982 (1995) renewed UNPROFOR's mandate in Bosnia until 30 November 1995, and Resolution 983 (1995) renamed the UNPROFOR operation in the former Yugoslavian Republic of Macedonia which was forthwith to be known as the UN Preventive Deployment Force (UNPREDEP).[106]

Also in the latter half of March, Bosnian government forces conducted an offensive near the northern town of Tuzla which was too large to be interpreted as simply a ceasefire violation. In retaliation the Serbs once again began to shell the UN designated 'safe areas', with Sarajevo witnessing its heaviest shelling since the exclusion zone was created in February of the previous year.[107]   Although NATO subsequently threatened air strikes they were not carried out. In early May the UN rejected Bosnian government requests for NATO strikes blaming the Muslims themselves for starting the fighting. When on May 7, after a Serbian mortar attack killed eleven people in Sarajevo, the UN military commander in Bosnia, Lieutenant General Smith, requested NATO air strikes on Serb positions, it was vetoed by the SGSR in Yugoslavia, Yashushi Akashi. When the UN and NATO did finally act, bombing an ammunition depot near the Serbian headquarters in Pale, the Russians criticised the action by accusing the UN of incorrectly apportioning blame when it was impossible to 'seek a just solution to the Bosnian conflict by bombing the positions of just one side'.[108] In order to ward off further NATO strikes the Serbs once again took a number of UN personnel hostage, chained some of them to potential targets, and removed heavy weapons from the UN collection points. By the end of May the Serbs were holding approximately 400 UN hostages, a statistic which forced Alain Juppe to admit in hindsight that as far as NATO air strikes went, '... we'd be better off without any more now that we've seen what they cause'.[109]

In a move to quell public outrage at the hostage taking and to give the impression that the international community was adopting a much harder line with the Serbs, the UN announced in mid-June that a 10,000 strong Rapid Reaction Force (RRF) was soon to be deployed in Bosnia. Its role in the UNPROFOR operation, however, had not been properly clarified. Rather than releasing all the hostages, therefore, the Serbs preferred to keep some as political leverage against a general strengthening of the UN mandate and specifically against the potential role of the RRF. This forced the UN to capitulate to Serb demands, releasing four Serbian detainees in Sarajevo and abandoning the last weapons collection points around the capital, in order to allow the final 26 hostages to be released on 18 June.[110] The failure of the UN to protect the safe areas was to have dire consequences for the inhabitants of the more eastern Muslim enclaves.

Ostensibly in response to Muslim attacks on surrounding Serb villages, the Bosnian Serbs launched a major offensive against the Srebrenica safe area on 9 July. Despite NATO air strikes two days later, providing protection for the Dutch battalion still stationed in the enclave, Srebrenica fell to the Serbs the same day. On the following day the Serbs began to ethnically cleanse the city, expelling all Muslim women and children, but detaining the men. With reports of gross human rights violations, thousands of Muslim men are as yet still unaccounted for. Also on 12 July, the Serbs began an assault on the Zepa safe area, which fell within a matter of a few days. In the latter half of July the Bosnian Serbs, together with the forces of Fikret Abdic, launched a combined assault on the Bihac safe area in North-western Bosnia. Determined not to let Bihac fall to the Serbs, the government of Croatia signed the Split Declaration with the Bosnian government, which made provision for a joint defence against Serb aggression. This combined defence was ultimately successful, although one of the more significant contributing factors was to occur in Croatia.

At the beginning of May the Croatian forces launched an offensive against the Serbian enclave of Western Slavonia, one of three UNPAs designated by the UN in 1991. The Serbs had responded to this attack by launching missiles at the Croatian capital Zagreb, which eventually earned threats from the US when one of them landed very close to US installations.[111] These missile attacks, however, failed to prevent the UNPA's eventual downfall. Without any significant movement in negotiations and with tensions rising, both sides began to amass troops on the front line surrounding Krajina in late July. The day after a meeting on 3 August failed to emerge with an agreement, the Croatian army launched a major offensive into the Krajina UNPA. In a letter to the President of the Security Council the Croatian Foreign Minister, Pavel Granic, explained his government's actions as necessary due to the 'failure to implement the mandate of UNCRO which has been proven totally ineffective' and the 'policy of appeasement of the international community towards the Belgrade government, the sponsor of the occupation of the parts of Croatia and Bosnia and Herzegovina'.[112] The resulting fall of Krajina and the surrender of the forces of Abdic released the pressure on Bihac and helped bring the Serbian offensive on the safe area to an end.

Although the fate of the Bihac safe area had been secured, the future of the last remaining eastern enclave of Gorazde remained precarious. Despite the statement made by the International Meeting on Bosnia, held in London on 21 July, that 'any attack on Gorazde will be met with a substantial decisive response, including the use of air power', the international community's actions in August indicated that the UN's resolve was less than definite. With the fall of Srebrenica and Zepa, Gorazde stood on its own as the last enclave in Eastern Bosnia. Surrounded by Serbian occupied land, to many, including at least one UN commander, the enclave was indefensible.[113] It also represented a stumbling block against Serb acceptance of the Contact Group peace plan. When a third of the UN contingent in Gorazde began to withdraw on 23 August, therefore, to many it seemed that the UN had resigned the enclave to the same fate as its predecessors. *Medecins Sans Frontieres* called the withdrawal a 'blatant contradiction of the various international commitments protecting the enclave'.[114] However, when a mortar attack on 28 August killed 37 and wounded over 80 in a market place in Sarajevo, the UN and NATO responded with air strikes against targets near Tuzla, Gorazde, Zepa and the hills overlooking Mostar. The new RRF was also called into action. With the shuttle diplomacy of the US Assistant Secretary of State Richard Holbrooke, an announcement of talks in Geneva was made as the air strikes came to an end on 1 September. Holbrooke maintained, however, that although the air strikes had strengthened the negotiator's position, NATO did not intend to 'bomb [the Serbs] into the process' because the 'process didn't require the bombing'.[115] For Holbrooke the number one issue at the time was the Contact Group map which had proposed a 51-49 percent split between the Muslim-Croat federation and the Bosnian Serbs. As he stated of their respective positions, '... everyone has agreed to the 51-49 percent split, but everyone's idea of 51-49 is different'.[116]

When the Serbs failed to comply with the 'safe area' conditions NATO air strikes were resumed on 5 September and despite Russian protestations continued for the following nine days. Taking advantage of the damage inflicted upon the Serbs' command and communications system by NATO, the Muslim and Croat forces launched a renewed offensive in North-west Bosnia. This combined assault, although politically embarrassing for the UN and NATO, caused the largest defeats of the Bosnian Serb army since the beginning of the conflict. It also, therefore, produced beneficial results for the prospects of a peace settlement. With the collapse of the Krajina Serbs in Croatia, the resurgence of the Bosnian army and the damage inflicted by NATO, psychologically and militarily the Bosnian Serbs had been left in a much weakened position. The amount of land occupied by the Serbs had dropped by the end of the Muslim-Croat offensive in mid-September from 70 percent to 50 percent, nearer the amount of Bosnia they had been offered by the Contact Group proposal. And with the agreement reached between the Serbian President and Richard Holbrooke at the beginning of the month, Bosnian Serb acceptance of the latest peace talks was inevitable. In fact, it has been proposed that this agreement, and not the NATO bombing, was the most prominent reason for the Bosnian Serbs' recent change of track over the Holbrooke plan.[117]

What have been the lessons of the UNPROFOR operation? For one, the UNPROFOR operation in Bosnia has perhaps been the best example of the hazards of 'mission-creep'. As mentioned earlier in this chapter, the Secretary General has noted the loss of impartiality which can occur when the UN takes on the tasks of providing protection to humanitarian aid delivery and to civilians living in 'safe areas'. When a city is under siege, the termination of essential supplies is as important an offensive weapon as the use of mortars. When the UN is charged with ensuring that the deliveries take place it is inevitable that the Organisation is perceived to have become partial. If the UN attempts to use force to ensure delivery, it risks an escalation of violence which could eventually lead to the UN becoming a party to the conflict itself.

The issue of the 'safe areas' has been equally as contentious. Although the Secretary General advised the Security Council that a force of 34,000 would be required to provide an adequate deterrence to Serb attack, the Council preferred the 'light option' of 7,600, but even then failed to deploy more than 4,000. And as the experience of NATO testified, the use of air-power to deter ground attacks on civilian areas is inherently flawed. The 'protection' of these safe areas also threatened the UN's impartiality in two ways. The first was through the use of air strikes on Serb positions. With the introduction of air defence systems by the Serbs, any use of air power needs to take into account the prior need to suppress these systems. 'Such pre-emptive military action, while undeniably necessary to ensure the safety of the NATO aircraft, is inevitably considered by the Bosnian Serbs as a hostile act and can therefore take UNPROFOR beyond the limits of a peacekeeping operation and quickly make it a party to the conflict'.[118] The second cause of a loss of impartiality was the failure of the UN to de-militarise the 'safe areas' in both Bosnia and the UNPAs in Croatia. The history of UNPROFOR tells a story, therefore, not of operational inadequacy, but of an Organisation acting within a remit provided to it by an international community which did not wish to become involved any further than it already was.

Rwanda

On 6 January 1994 the Security Council adopted Resolution 893; 'Welcoming ... the joint statement made by the parties in Kinihira on 10 December 1993 concerning the implementation of the Arusha Peace Agreement and, in particular, the prompt establishment of a broad-based transitional government'.[119]   The 5 January 1995 target date for the establishment of this transitional government, however, failed to be met. Supported by the National Revolutionary Movement (MRND) and the extremist Hutu party, the *Coalition pour la Defense de la Republique* (CDR), President Habyarimana refused to step down from office. Rather than initiating a two-year phase during which UNAMIR would guide the new political administration through the problems of nation-building, the Security Council could, therefore, only extend the mandate of UNAMIR until July 1994 in the belief that it had at least contributed to the country's stability. By the beginning of April only the institution of the Presidency had been set up, and the resulting political impasse was beginning to cause increased tension and insecurity. While the mortality rates in refugee camps had fallen, a disease epidemic had also developed, requiring UNAMIR to increase its security support for humanitarian assistance.

    Disaster was to strike on 6 April 1994 with the deaths of both the Rwandan President Habyarimana and the Burundi President, Cyprien Ntaryamira. Shot down as their plane approached Kigali airport, the incident sparked a massacre by members of the Hutu tribe which within two days had claimed the lives of the Rwandan Premier Agathe Uwilingiyimana and eleven UN Belgian soldiers.[120] By 8 April an interim government had been established, but not of the kind envisaged by the UN. Instead, this administration was composed of only Hutu extremists, who then began a bloody campaign which within a week had been responsible for the deaths of over 15,000 Rwandans, most of whom were believed to be Tutsis. Despite the closure of Kigali airport, in a re-enactment of the events in the Congo thirty-four years before, Belgian troops landed on 10 April, ostensibly to evacuate European nationals. With the loss of order, NGOs such as *Medecins sans Frontiers* and Oxfam announced that they had no option but to pull their staff out, whilst Belgium and France both insisted that they had no mandate to restore order and were simply concerned with the safe evacuation of foreign nationals.[121] By the end of April, estimations of the number of civilians murdered ran as high as 200,000, the majority of which were Tutsi. However, the majority of the 250,000 refugees which had poured into neighbouring countries were Hutu, who feared reprisals from the advancing RPF led by Major General Paul Kagame.[122]

With the implementation of the Arusha Accord no longer viable and the inadequate protection for UN troops, Belgian Foreign Minister Willy Claes announced the planned withdrawal of the Belgian contingent stating that it would be 'senseless' to continue operations in such conditions. Informing the Security Council that without the Belgian troops, or adequate replacements, the whole operation would be unworkable, the Secretary General requested the Commander of the 2,500 strong UN force, General Romeo Dellaire, to make plans for a complete withdrawal.

Under criticism from the NGOs for abandoning the country, the Secretary General presented three future options to the Security Council. The first option envisaged a massive reinforcement of UNAMIR to enable the operation both to force the nominal Rwandan government and RPF into a ceasefire and to ensure the delivery of humanitarian aid. Such a force would also help to contain the conflict within the country's borders. The second option proposed a small force stationed in Kigali in order to act as an intermediary between the parties. This option would require only a relatively small number of observers and an infantry battalion for protection. The final option was a complete withdrawal. Despite the Secretary General's warning of the consequences this last option would have on Rwandan lives, it was initially preferred by the US. Only the persuasion of the US Ambassador to the UN, Madaleine Albright, helped change the US position, but only as far as to support the second option. With all of the other western nations equally hesitant to become involved, the Security Council adopted Resolution 912 on 21 April 1994, changing

UNAMIR's mandate to act as an intermediary force with some 270 personnel. With the international community unwilling to provide any alternative, Resolution 912 could only reiterate the need for the full implementation of the Arusha Accord.[123]

Although unwilling to become involved on the ground, criticism of the US position had caused it to offer 'financial and logistical support' to encourage African countries to organise a peace enforcement operation. However, leaders of the African nations were in no hurry to become involved themselves, especially as the western nations had refused before them. Meanwhile the UN described the exodus of refugees as the 'largest and fastest ever seen' as the RPF advanced further into Rwanda.[124] In his report of 31 May 1994 the Secretary General presented the findings of a special mission he had sent to Rwanda. The mission had reported that a significant number of the country's seven million inhabitants had been killed (estimates ranged between 250,000 and 500,000). Together with conformation that the areas controlled by the interim government had witnessed systematic massacres, the RPF was also condemned for its human rights abuses.[125]

Facing mounting public criticism for its indifferent attitude towards the conflict, the international community and UN attempted to save face by announcing plans for the establishment of a new Rwandan operation. UNAMIR II was to support and provide safe conditions for displaced persons and other groups in Rwanda, provide security assistance to humanitarian organisations and patrol and monitor protected areas along the Rwandan border. The UN also hoped that it would be able to negotiate with the parties to recognise Kigali airport as a 'neutral zone' under the exclusive control of the UN mission. Given its estimated size of around 5,500 troops, it was not envisaged that the UNAMIR II force would be involved in any form of peace-enforcement operation, although action in self defence, including against elements preventing the UN from implementing its mandate was encouraged. The Secretary General proposed that UNAMIR II execute its mandate over three phases. During Phase I, expected to last for seven days, a Ghanaian battalion of 800 troops would be deployed in order to secure Kigali airport and other key sites in the city where displaced persons had sought UN protection. Phase II was to see the deployment of two more battalions, all of the force headquarters and the signal squadron. These troops were to secure areas of high security concern and provide protection to the majority of displaced persons. In the final phase, the remaining force, including the support battalion and two more infantry battalions would deploy. These forces would establish the logistics and engineer advance bases in key areas around the country.[126]

On 17 May the Security Council approved the Secretary General's proposals, adopting Resolution 918. In addition, acting under Chapter VII of the UN Charter the Resolution also imposed a mandatory arms embargo on Rwanda. However, despite the Security Council's adoption of Resolution 918, and the obvious need for the UN force in Rwanda, the Secretary General was to experience grave difficulty in finding a sufficient number of troops with which to compose the force. Initially only Ghana, Ethiopia and Senegal offered troops, and even then only 800 each. However, the US still refused to authorise the immediate dispatch of the force, declaring that it was essential not to allow the UN to become overstretched. Meanwhile the massacres in Rwanda continued unabated.

It was not until the beginning of June, with the announcement by a number of African states of their willingness to contribute troops, that the UN was eventually given the go ahead by the US administration for the force's deployment. Taking account of the delay, the Security Council adopted Resolution 925 on 8 June reconfiguring the mandate of UNAMIR II. Extending its mandate until December 1994, the Resolution stipulated that the two battalions which had been expected to deploy during Phase II, were now to be deployed earlier, during Phase I. The primary task of all three phases, however, would remain only to contribute to the protection of displaced persons and the delivery of humanitarian aid and would not include either separating the warring parties or enforcement measures.[127] However, in a letter to the President of the Security Council, the Secretary General reported that as of 18 June UNAMIR II still consisted of only 503 troops. Even the number of troops allocated for Phase I had not been deployed. Although he was able to predict that Phase I would be completed by the end of the first week in July, he was unable to do the same for Phase II, although it had been 'intended to be synchronised with the first phase'.[128] This was essentially due to the absence of firm commitments amongst UN members.

The failure of the international community to provide the resources necessary to fulfil the UN's commitments under Resolutions 918 and 925 caused the Secretary General to suggest that the Security Council consider an offer by the French government. Subject to Security Council approval the French had offered to make troops available as part of a Chapter VII multi-national operation, under which UNAMIR II could continue to operate to the greatest extent permitted by the resources made available. Initially the French proposal received a mute response, particularly from the Europeans. Belgium, still smarting from the loss of ten soldiers earlier in the crisis, refused to make any more available and the British and Dutch offered 50 trucks and a field hospital respectively, but no troops.[129] Even the Rwandans themselves were unreceptive to the prospect of French interference. Although the French Foreign Minister Alain Juppe, continued to stress that the operation would only protect civilians and not attempt to separate the belligerents by force, France's continuing connections with the Kigali government caused the RPF leader, Paul Kagame, to vow that a French force would be resisted.[130]

With the French insisting that the mission would be purely humanitarian, the US supporting the idea of setting up enclaves to protect refugees, and the lack of any credible alternative, the Secretary General gave his personal approval to the plan.   Consequently, on 22 June 1994, the Security Council, acting under Chapter VII of the UN Charter authorised the member states to establish a 'temporary multinational operation aimed at contributing to the security and protection of displaced persons, refugees and civilians at risk in Rwanda'.[131]   Formalised in Resolution 929, the Security Council limited the operation to two months, enough time it believed for the UN to secure the 5,500 troops it required.[132]

Entitled 'Operation Turquoise', the French and Senagalese troops were provided with logistical support from the Europeans and US.   Once deployed they found the RPF on the brink of capturing the capital city, with the fighting spreading south towards Burundi. As the RPF advanced the humanitarian situation worsened, as increasing numbers of refugees fled in fear of their lives. Through a letter to the Secretary General the French government sought approval to 'organise, on the basis of Security Council Resolutions 925 (1994) and 929 (1994), a safe humanitarian zone where the population would be protected from the fighting ...'[133] This proposal was initially blocked by the RPF who accused the French of setting up roadblocks with militiamen who had been responsible for past human rights abuses, and of seeking to protect the regime responsible within their 'safe zone'.[134]   Fears of a RPF confrontation with the French force, however, were unfounded, although a substantial amount of pressure was released after the fall of Kigali, the capital, and Butare, the second largest city, on 4 July. Ten days later the RPF captured the last government stronghold in Gisenyi. The RPF now controlled all Rwandan territory except the French 'safe zone' in the south-west.[135]

When the French announced their intention to withdraw the UN was faced with an estimated two million refugees in a 'safe zone' and an operation unable to fulfil its mandate. Claiming that France had 'made the international community recognise' its responsibilities by carrying out its planned mission of putting an end to massacres of civilians by paramilitary groups and soldiers of the deposed Hutu dominated government, President Mitterrand refused to extend the operation's mandate. Forced to speed up the deployment of UNAMIR II, by mid-August the 1,200 strong French contingent in the safe zone was being replaced by Ghanaians and Ethiopian troops under UN command.

With the Rwandan government becoming impatient at the slow progress being made with the repatriation of the refugees, it declared in June 1995 that the UN force had become 'costly, useless and undisciplined and that it [had] caused tensions with the local population'.[136] In his report of 4 June, the Secretary General noted that the RPF had continued to deny UNAMIR access to parts of the country, had searched and seized its vehicles and other equipment, and had even participated in anti-UNAMIR demonstrations. In recognition that the host government no longer needed nor wanted the UN on its territory, the Security Council voted to cut the UNAMIR II force by half. From the present force of 5,600, only 2,330 were to be left within three months and 1,800 in four. UN military observers and civilian police (whose main activity was the training of a new integrated national police force as mandated under SC Resolution 965 (1994)), however, were to remain at the current level of 320 and 65 respectively.

The Rwandan operation had, therefore, displayed the international community's new cynicism towards involvement in peacekeeping and humanitarian intervention. For two months in April-June 1994, whilst the Secretary General searched for troops with which to compose a force, the US refused even to authorise a UN deployment. Meanwhile, a major humanitarian disaster developed. Even when the US finally accepted the need for the UN to become involved, the Secretary General was thwarted in his attempts to find sufficient troops. The sight of hundreds of thousands of refugees fleeing the escalating violence, and reports of massacres throughout the country, were no longer enough to ensure UN action. The Secretary General, therefore, was left with little option but to accept a French offer to establish a Chapter VII operation, whilst he frantically worked to persuade reluctant states to help him fulfil the commitments they themselves had made under Resolutions 918 and 925. And even when in July 1994 the US did finally become involved in the provision of humanitarian relief, it was evident that it intended to do as little as possible in order to ensure that it could conduct a quick and uncomplicated exit. If the catastrophe in Somalia had dealt a deadly blow to the proposed creation of a 'New World Order', then Rwanda was to be the place it finally died.

Conclusion

With the release of its new policy for peacekeeping in May 1994, the Clinton Administration had confirmed the Organisation's worst fears.

Already buckling under the weight of financial pressure, the US was to cut its share of funding to only 25 percent. It had also reassessed its policy of troop contributions and practically eradicated all chance of US troops serving under UN command. With the estimated cost of peacekeeping for 1995 at \$3.1 billion, and with over 73,000 troops required in the field, such news served a critical blow to the future effectiveness of the Organisation. Perhaps the most serious development in the new US policy, however, was the criteria to be applied to new and continuing peacekeeping operations. Although ostensibly designed to make the UN's funding more cost effective, in the case of Rwanda it had done little more than frustrate the deployment of a UN force which could have prevented the massacres of thousands of innocent civilians.

For the UN, therefore, the years of 1994-95 were to witness a retrenchment of peacekeeping. Although the operations in Mozambique and El Salvador had supplied the Organisation with much needed successes, they could not revive the confidence of the Organisation, nor improve the international community's perception of peacekeeping. Far more prominent in the public eye were the failures of the UN in Somalia and Rwanda, and its continuing impotence in the former Yugoslavia. And with the operations in Western Sahara and Angola still suffering from the intransigence of the parties, no new peacekeeping successes looked imminent. The Organisation's lack of finances, together with the new stringent criteria to be applied by the Security Council, also made the establishment of any major new operations extremely unlikely.

Suggested Reading

Alden, C., and Simpson, M., 'Mozambique: a delicate peace' *The Journal of Modern African Studies*, vol.31, no.1, 1993.

Biermann, W., 'Old UN peacekeeping principles and new conflicts: some ideas to reduce the troubles of post-Cold War peace missions', *European Security*, vol.4, no.1, Spring 1995.

Cooper, R., and Berdal M., 'Outside intervention in ethnic conflicts', *Survival*, vol.35, no.1, Spring 1993.

Duke, S., 'The United Nations and intra-state conflict', *International Peacemaking*, vol.1, no.4, Winter 1994.

Evans, G., *Co-operating for peace*, Victoria, Allen & Unwin, 1993.

Kennedy, P., and Russett, B., 'Reforming the United Nations', *Foreign Affairs*, vol.74, no.5, September/October 1995.

Ratner, S. R., *The new UN peacekeeping*, New York, St. Martin's Press, 1995.

Roberts, A., 'From San Francisco to Sarajevo: the UN and the use of force', *Survival*, vol.37, no.4, Winter 1995.

Roberts, A., Kingsbury, B., and Childers, E., 'The United Nations and armed intervention', *Oxford International Review*, Spring 1995.

Weiss, T.G., 'The United Nations and civil wars', *The Washington Quarterly*, vol.17, no.4, Autumn 1994.

Wendt, D., 'The peacemakers: lessons of conflict resolution for the post-Cold War world', *Washington Quarterly*, vol.17, no.3, Summer 1994.

Notes

1. cf.'Albright says UN Peacekeeping reduces the risks in crises', *Official Text*, May 9 1994, p.1.

2. Ibid., pp.1-2.

3. cf.Ibid., p.3.

4. Boutros-Ghali, B., 'Secretary General calls for burden sharing in peacekeeping', *United Nations Document, SG/SM/5589*, 22 March 1995.

5. cf.*United Nations press release, SG/SM/95/147*, p.2. 3 July 1995.

6. cf.Idem.

7. cf. Smith, J. R.,'US to leave Rwanda with several jobs still undone', *The International Herald Tribune*, 6 September 1994.

8. cf.*United Nations document, S/1994/1420*, 14 December 1994.

9. *United Nations document, S/1995/498*, 21 June 1995.

10. cf.Idem.

11. cf.Idem.

12. *United Nations document, S/1994/740 Add. 1*, 29 June 1994.

13. *United Nations document, S/1994/1395*, 8 December 1994.

14. *United Nations document, S/1995/588*, 17 July 1995.

15. Maier, K., 'Summit fails to clear obstacles to Angola peace', *The Independent*, 2 August 1995.

16. 'cf.Pakistan criticises US Somalia gear', *The International Herald Tribune*, 14 March 1994.

17. 'Chronicle of events', *International Peacekeeping*, vol.1, no.4, September-November 1994, p.124.

18. 'Chronicle of events', *International Peacekeeping*, vol.2, no.2/3, February-May 1995, p.56.

19. *United Nations document S/1995/407*, 18 May 1995.

20. cf.*International Peacekeeping News*, ed., Jones, R., Woodhouse, T., and Ramsbotham, O., Department of Peace Studies, University of Bradford, 22 June 1995.

21. cf.'A United Nations success', *The International Herald Tribune*, 6-7 May 1995.

22. cf.Flores, T., 'ONUSAL, a precedent for future UN missions?', *International Peacekeeping*, vol.2, no.1, December-January 1995, p.5.

23. cf.*United Nations document, S/1994/561*, 11 May 1994.

24. cf.'A United Nations Success', *The International Herald Tribune*, op.cit.

25. See Beresford, D., 'Final lap for UN's man in Maputo', *The Guardian*, 26 October 1994, and 'Berseford, D., 'Frelimo hails win', *The Guardian*, 21 November 1994 and *United Nations document S/1994/1449*, 23 December 1994.

26. See Kurzidem, T., 'ONUMOZ, How to make a successful UN peacekeeping operation', *International Peacekeeping*, vol.1, no.4, September-November 1994, pp.132-134 and *United Nations document S/1994/1449*, 23 December 1994. When ONUMOZ was established 80 percent of primary schools in Mozambique were either closed or destroyed and the availability of other social services was minimal. With the help of the UN High Commission for Refugees (UNHCR) and several non-governmental organisations (NGO's) ONUMOZ helped build more than 700 primary schools and 250 health facilities in rural areas.

27. cf.*United Nations document S/1994/1449*, 23 December 1994.

28. Robinson, S., 'Pounds 9.4 million cannot buy UN a happy birthday', *Daily Telegraph*, 26 June 1995, and Sicherman, H., 'Winning the peace', *Orbis*, vol.38, no.4, Fall 1994, p.529.

29.   cf.*International Peacekeeping News*, ed., by Jones, R., et al, op.cit, 19 July 1995.

30.   *International Peacekeeping News*, ed., by Jones, R., et al, op.cit, 20 July 1994.

31.   Boutros-Ghali, B., 'Improving the capacity of the UN for peacekeeping', *Military Technology*, December 1994, p.78. The figure for the contributions paid in the first three months has been estimated as low as 36 percent, see Ogata, S. and Volcker, P., et al, *Financing an effective United Nations: a report of the independent advisory group on UN financing*, New York, Ford Foundation, 1993, p.17.

32.   Boutros-Ghali, B., 'Improving the capacity of the UN for peacekeeping', ibid., p.74.

33.   cf.Ibid., p.82.

34.   *United Nations document, S/1995/407*, 18 May 1995.

35.   cf.Stahler-Sholk, R., 'El Salvador's negotiated transition: from low intensity conflict to low-intensity democracy', *Journal of Inter-American Studies and World Affairs*, Winter 1994, p.9.

36.   Ibid., p.16.

37.   Idem. Also see Flores, T., op.cit, p.7; *United Nations Document, S/1994/561*, 11 May 1994 and Gunson, P., 'Death squads still cast shadow over El Salvador', *The Guardian*, 2 June 1994. A Report by Human Rights Watch published in March 1994 stated that 'the contamination of the new police force with existing police units notorious for abuse poses a serious and potentially permananent problem'.

38.   *International Peacekeeping News*, ed., by Jones, R., et al, 6 July 1995.

39.   See Stahler-Sholk, R., op.cit, p.42.

40.   cf.Gunson, P., op.cit.

41.   cf.*United Nations document, S/1994/511*, 28 April 1994.

42. Idem.

43. Hamlyn, M., 'Poll raises Mozambiquan fears', *The Times*, 21 October 1994.

44. cf.Brittain, V., 'Looting troops spread unease', *The Guardian*, 1 August 1994.

45. *United Nations document, S/1994/1449*, 23 December 1994. This agreement was made on 25 July 1994.

46. Berdal, M., 'Whither UN Peacekeeping?', *Adelphi Paper 281*, October 1993, Brassey's for the International Institute of Strategic Studies, p.20.

47. General Sir David Ramsbotham, 'UN peacekeeping: the art of the possible', *ISIS Briefing no.44*, October 1994, p.6.

48. *United Nations document, S/1994/1449*, 23 December 1994.

49. Berdal, M., 'Whither UN peacekeeping?', op.cit. pp.19-20.

50. Brittain, V., 'Rebel group strangles quarter of Mozambique', *The Guardian*, 3 August 1994.

51. Brittain, V., 'Fears of war cloud poll', *The Guardian*, 23 September 1994. RENAMO has, however, claimed that the communication equipment is necessary for its continuing organisation as a political party.

52. Beresford, D.,'Mozambiquan rebels make peace pledge', *The Guardian*, 27 October 1994.

53. *Economic and Social Council document, E/AC.51/1995/2*, 17 March 1995.

54. *Strategic Survey*, Brassey's for the International Institute of Strategic Studies, 1993-94, p.30.

55. *International Peacekeeping News*, ed., by Jones, R., et al, 1 January, 1995.

56. 'Peacekeeping operations', *The Military Balance 1994-95*, Brassey's, p.268. These states were: Argentina, Bulgaria, Canada, Chad, Czech Republic, Denmark, Finland, Guatemala, Hungary, Jordan, The Netherlands, Norway, Poland, Senegal, Spain, Sri Lanka, Syria, Turkey, Ukraine, United Kingdom, and Uruguay.

57. Kurzidem, T., 'Stand-by arrangements - A way out of the crisis in UN peacekeeping?', *International Peacekeeping*, vol.2, no.1, December-January 1995, p.8.

58. Ibid., p.9.

59. cf.'Improving the capacity of the UN for peacekeeping', Report of the Secretary General, *Military Technology*, December 1994, p.78.

60. *International Peacekeeping News*, ed., by Jones, R., 28 June 1995.

61. cf.*International Peacekeeping News*, ed., by Jones, R., 26 December 1994 and 12 January 1995.

62. The Secretary General reiterated his call for a Rapid Reaction Force in his supplement to *An Agenda for Peace*, stating that such a force might comprise of battalion sized units from a number of countries. These, he envisaged, would be trained to the same standards, use the same operating procedures, be equipped with integrated communications equipment and take part in joint exercises at regular intervals. They would be stationed in their home countries but maintained at a high state of readiness. 'Supplement to the agenda for peace', *International Peacekeeping*, vol.2, no.1, December-January 1995, p.23.

63. *International Peacekeeping News*, ed., by Jones, R., 28 July 1994.

64. cf.*International Peacekeeping News*, ed., by Jones, R., et al, 8 June 1995.

65. See Boutros-Ghali, B., *An Agenda for Peace*, United Nations, New York, 1992, pp.26-27.

66. cf.Urquhart, B., 'Beyond the sheriff's posse', *Survival*, vol.32, no.3, May/June 1990, p.203.

67.   Akashi, Y., 'The challenge of peacekeeping in Cambodia', *International Peacekeeping*, vol.1, no.2, Summer 1994, p.212.

68.   Comprehensive Political Settlement for Cambodia, 23 October 1991.

69.   Chanda, N., 'UN divisions', *Far Eastern Econonic Review*, 23 July 1992, p.9.

70.   cf.Chopra et al, in Findlay, 'Cambodia - the legacy and lessons of UNTAC', *SIPRI research report no.9*, Oxford University Press, 1995, p.129.

71.   cf.Akashi, Y., quoted in Findlay, ibid., p.129.

72.   cf.Ibid, pp.131-132.

73.   cf.Ibid., p.133.

74.   cf.*Security Council document, S/RES/837*, 6 June 1993.

75.   cf.Thakur, R., 'From peacekeeping to peace-enforcement: the United Nations operation in Somalia', *Journal of Modern African Studies*, vol.32, no.3, 1994, p.396.

76.   Ibid., p.400.

77.   cf.Mazarr, M., 'The military dilemmas of humanitarian intervention', *Security Dialogue*, vol.24, no.2, 1993, p.158.

78.   Berdal, M., 'Fateful encounter: the United States and UN peacekeeping', *Survival*, vol.36, no.1, Spring 1994, p.42.

79.   Patman, R., 'The UN operation in Somalia', 1995, pp.107-108 quoted in Adibe, C., *Managing arms in peace processes: Somalia*, UNIDIR Disarmament and Conflict Resolution Project, 1995, p.98.

80.   cf.Lt. Col. Charles Dobbie, in Berdal, M., ibid., p.44.

81.   cf.Hurd, D., in Evans, M., 'UK reluctant to use troops in Bosnia', *The Times*, 3 June 1992.

82.   This was the case with Resolution 824 which, on the request of Yeltsin, had its adoption postponed until after a referendum was held on 24 April 1993.

83. Davies, P. W., 'Fate of Srebrenica spurs call for Serbia blockade', *The Independent*, 17 April 1993. Also see Bone, J., 'UN delays Belgrade sanction as no-fly zone takes effect', *The Times*, 13 April 1993. The United Nations adopted Resolution 820 on 17 April 1993 but the sanctions did not come into effect until April 26. *Security Council document, S/RES/820*, 17 April 1993.

84. cf.*Security Council document, S/RES/824*, 6 May 1993.

85. Ricks, T., 'US Joint Chiefs of Staff oppose air strikes against the Serbs', *The Wall Street Journal Europe*, 28 April 1993.

86. cf.*United Nations document S/RES/836*, 6 June 1993.

87. Marshall, A., et al '10-day deadline for Serbs', *The Independent*, 10 February 1994.

88. See *United Nations document S/1995/444*, 30 May 1995 in *International Peacekeeping*, vol.2, no.2/3, February-May 1995, p.66 and Evans, M.,'Build-up to biggest bombing mission' *The Times*, 31 August 1995. Daly, E.,'Sarajevo resounds again to the sounds of jets', *The Independent*, 6 September 1995. Bellamy, C.,'NATO launches cruise missile raid on Serbs', *The Independent*, 11 September 1995. Bellamy, C.,'How NATO paralysed serb command', *The Independent*, 17 September 1995.

89. cf.'Serb air base destroyed in massive NATO attack', *The International Herald Tribune*, 22 November 1994.

90. cf.'NATO jets bomb Serb arms depot near Sarajevo', *The International Herald Tribune*, 26 May 1995.

91. cf.Sheridan, M.,'Kosyrev questions logic of air attacks', *The Independent*, 6 September 1995.

92. Barber, T.,'Angry Yeltsin berates NATO', *The Independent*, 8 September 1995.

93. 'UN turns again to war in Bosnia', *The International Herald Tribune*, 17 October 1994.

94. cf.*United Nations document, S/1995/444*, 30 May 1995.

95. 'Agenda for peace supplement', *International Peacekeeping News*, ed., by Jones, R., op.cit, 6 January 1995.

96. cf.Crocker, C., 'The lessons of Somalia', *Foreign Affairs*, vol.74, no.3, p.5.

97. cf.*United Nations document, S/1995/444*, 30 May 1995, op.cit.

98. cf.Bone, J., 'UN Chief will not use veto', *The Times*, 11 February 1994.

99. cf.'The Balkan Battlefields', *Strategic Survey*, Brassey's for the International Institute of Strategic Studies, 1994/95, p.95.

100. Cohen, R., 'Map blocks a Bosnian peace', *The International Herald Tribune*, 8 November 1994.

101. See cf.'The Balkan battlefields', *Strategic Survey*, op.cit, p.98 and *The UN and the situation in the former Yugoslavia*, United Nations, Department of Public Information, Reference Paper Revision 4, p.30.

102. 'The Balkan battlefields', *Strategic Survey*, op.cit, p.98. The lifting of these sanctions took place pursuant to Resolution 943 of 23 September 1994.

103. Ibid., p.100.

104. Pomfret, J., 'If UN troops go, can Croatia avoid war with Serbs', *The International Herald Tribune*, 21 February 1995. See also 'Three separate operations created on 31 March' *UN Chronicle*, June 1995, pp.23-25.

105. cf.'The UN and the situation in the former Yugoslavia', op.cit, p.37.

106. Ibid., p.44.

107. See Cohen, R., 'UN reports strategic gain for Bosnia', *The International Herald Tribune*, 24 March 1995. 'UN Threatens Serbs with NATO Strikes for hitting havens', *The International Herald Tribune*, 28 March 1995. 'Serbs shell Sarajevo', *The International Herald Tribune*, 11 April 1995.

108. cf.'New fighting in Sarajevo, hell is starting again', *The International Herald Tribune*, 17 May 1995. Lewis, A., 'NATO support for the UN Protection Force in Bosnia', *The International Herald Tribune*, 20-21 May 1995. Cohen, R.,'NATO jets bomb Serb arms depot near Sarajevo', *The International Herald Tribune*, 26 May 1995.

109. cf.'Eight observers left shackled as potential NATO targets', *The International Herald Tribune*, 27-28 May 1995. Cohen, R., 'Crisis in Bosnia deepens as Serbs add to hostages', *The International Herald Tribune*, 29 May 1995.

110. Cohen, R.,'Serbs to keep hostages to deter new UN force', *The International Herald Tribune*, 13 June 1995. Crossette, B., 'US stalls UN action on Bosnian forces', *The International Herald Tribune*, 15 June 1995.

111. 'Serbs shell Zagreb with cluster bombs casualties put at 126', *The International Herald Tribune*, 3 May 1995. 'US risks grow in Balkan quagmire', *The International Herald Tribune*, 15 April 1995.

112. cf.*Information notes on the former Yugoslavia*, no.8, August 1995, Office of the Special Envoy for the former Yugoslavia, p.i.

113. Helm, S., 'Zagreb likely to be winner under US plan', *The Independent*, 22 August 1995. One UN commander was quoted as saying 'Nobody in their right minds can believe that Gorazde can remain as a Muslim enclave. It is indefensible'.

114. cf.Cornnell, R., 'Clinton rebuilds his Yugoslav team', *The Independent*, 22 August 1995.

115. cf.Vulliamy, E., 'Air strikes crack Serbs' resistance to US deal', *The Guardian*, 1 September 1995.

116. cf.Barber, T., 'Dispute over maps delays US peace deal', *The Independent*, 2 September 1995.

117. Frankland, M., 'Bombs leave Slobodon sitting pretty', *The Observer*, 3 September 1995. Daly, E., 'Fear makes Sarajevo support plan', *The Independent*, 6 October 1995.

118. cf.*United Nations document, S/1995/444*, 30 May 1995 in *International Peacekeeping*, vol.2, no.2/3, February-May 1995, p.64.

119. cf.*Security Council document, S/RES/893*, 6 January 1994.

120. Crawford, L., 'Rwanda PM and UN team die in rampage', *The Financial Times*, 8 April 1994.

121. Landale, J., and Carthaigh, S. M., 'Belgian troops defy Rwandan blockade to land in Kigali', *The Times*, 11 April 1994.

122. Hammer, J., 'Escape from hell', *Newsweek*, 16 May 1994, p.9.

123. *Security Council document S/RES/912*, 21 April 1994. Pringle, P., 'West snubs UN plea for action', *The Independent*, 1 May 1994.

124. Of the majority of African states only South Africa actually had the capabilty to intervene directly. Nigeria was still paying the financial price of having embroiled itself in the conflict in Liberia and Tanzania was in the middle of radical economic reform. Tanzania and Uganda were also unlikely to intervene considering most of the Rwandan refugees were now settled on their territory. See cf.Binyon, M., 'America offers to finance African force for Rwanda', *The Times*, 2 May 1994.

125. *Security Council document, S/1994/640*, 31 May 1994.

126. *Security Council document, S/1994/565*, 13 May 1994.

127. *Security Council document, S/RES/925*, 8 June 1994.

128. cf.*Security Council document, S/1994/728*, 20 June 1994.

129. Drozdiak, W., 'Paris finds no backing on Rwanda force', *The International Herald Tribune*, 18 June 1994.

130. Lambert, S., and Dowden, R., 'French plan for Rwanda gets cool reception', *The Independent*, 18 June 1994.

131. cf.*Security Council press release, SC/5864*, 22 June 1994.

132. Idem.

133. cf.*Security Council document, S/1994/798*, 6 July 1994.

134. Kiley, S., and Bremner, C., 'Rwandan rebels condemn plan for exclusion from French safe zone', *The Times*, 6 July 1994.

135. McGreal, C., 'Regime faces collapse in Rwanda', *The Guardian*, 9 July 1994.

136. cf.Wren, C., 'UN votes to cut its Rwanda force by half', *The International Herald Tribune*, 12 June 1995.

Conclusion

This book has attempted to introduce the reader to the concept of peacekeeping through an analysis of its evolution over fifty years of practice. Unforeseen when the Charter was finalised in San Francisco in 1945, peacekeeping arose principally as a means to prevent the two superpowers becoming embroiled in localised disputes, which could have escalated into global conflict. Seen for this reason as a method of preventive diplomacy, peacekeeping developed its own set of principles and operational norms which enabled UN forces to be perceived as both non-coercive and neutral. With the operation in the Congo (1960-64) being the only notable exception, these principles and norms were maintained throughout the Cold War, generally as a result of the sensitivity of the superpowers to the UN taking on any more responsibility than was absolutely necessary. The 279 Security Council vetoes used before mid-1990 stand as testimony to the deep mistrust which prevailed throughout this tense period.

When the Cold War began to thaw in the latter half of the 1980s however, the superpowers began to disengage, seeking peace dividends wherever they could be found. In their wake, they left behind unstable states which, devoid of the financial and military support they had previously taken for granted, found that independence was far from the harbinger of peace and prosperity they had expected it to be. Both superpowers had supported repressive governments or resistance factions in the name of national security, and the civil wars which ensued were without doubt the most violent conflicts of the Cold War. The expectation of the international community that these conflicts would dry up along with the financial and military support of the superpowers was to be sadly misguided. Contrary to expectations, the international community found that the retreat of superpower hegemony simply uncovered a Pandora's box of cultural, ethnic, tribal, religious and nationalistic disagreements, which were all too ready to fill the vacuum left behind, and possessed a life force of their own. With the fog of Cold War antagonism lifting, public attention focused on the ability of the major international powers to resolve these conflicts, which through war and famine were claiming hundreds of thousands of victims every year. With a consensus never before attained, the international community turned to the UN, not only to oversee the withdrawal of the superpowers themselves, but to attempt ever increasingly ambitious methods of bringing seemingly intractable conflicts to a peaceful resolution. The UN, it seemed, was back in business.

It is, perhaps, misleading to talk of the evolution of peacekeeping in the post-Cold War era. As former Under-Secretary General Marrack Goulding has remarked, the word 'evolution' generally implies a comparatively leisurely process within which change is slow and incremental. This, however, would not suffice as an account of the manner in which changes have been introduced to the orthodox concept of peacekeeping in the past seven years. As chapters 3, 4 and 5, have testified, peacekeeping has gone through what Goulding more appropriately has called a 'forced evolution'. During the period 1988-91, which this book has entitled the 'Rebirth' of peacekeeping, the UN after over a decade of relative quiescence had established ten new operations, only three less than in the whole of the Cold War. By the end of 1992 this number had risen to thirteen and by mid 1995 had reached eighteen. (See Appendix 7.) However, the post-Cold War operations had not only exceeded their predecessors numerically. They had also witnessed a massive expansion in the size and complexity of their mandates. This expansion caused some analysts, including the UN itself, to talk of a 'second generation' of peacekeeping. Such claims, however, have been hotly disputed. Alan James, for one, believes the term to be a misnomer.[1] Although operations such as UNTAG, UNTAC, ONUSAL and ONUMOZ, had all displayed aspirations of peacebuilding to an extent which their Cold War predecessors had not, none of them had operated outside the principles and operational norms which had developed during the Cold War. Even the predominantly internal focus of the new post-Cold War missions, James believes, does not constitute a 'second generation' title. Such a distinction would be wrong because even the peacekeeping operations of the Cold War era had displayed 'something in the nature of a numerical balance between an internal and border focus'. The multi-faceted nature of the new operations, however, does distinguish them from their predecessors. So, although not worthy of a new category of peacekeeping operation, the Secretary-General's description of these operations as 'expanded peacekeeping' does seem appropriate.[2]

The use of force in post-Cold War peacekeeping operations also created a call for a 'second generation' category. With the establishment of UNOSOM II with its Chapter VII 'nation-building' mandate, the UN and international community believed that force could be used to compel an internal faction to comply with their previous agreements or to achieve peacekeeping objectives. As described in chapter 5, however, the operation in Somalia taught the lessons which the introduction of enforcement measures can have on a peacekeeping operation. Rather than there existing a continuum upon which military contingents can slide from consent based peacekeeping to coercive peace-enforcement and back again, Somalia demonstrated that impartiality, once lost, is practically impossible to regain. And in the former Yugoslavia, the difficulties of introducing enforcement measures whilst attempting to maintain a consent based peacekeeping operation on the ground, have been more than apparent. In line with the new army doctrines of the US and UK on peacekeeping (entitled *FM 100-23: Peace Operations* and *Wider Peacekeeping*, respectively), therefore, James believes that operations conducting enforcement measures cannot be classed as 'peacekeeping' operations, because they no longer comply with the essential tenets of peacekeeping; consent and impartiality. 'In principle, therefore, if an operation's *modus operandi* goes beyond behaviour which is characteristic of peacekeeping, it cannot be a form of the latter, such as a second generation of it.'[3]

So, as this book has attempted to show, the evolution of peacekeeping in both the Cold War and post-Cold War eras has been remarkably similar. Born in the late 1940s in response to the constraints applied to UN action by the antagonism of the superpowers, peacekeeping experienced a 'rebirth' in the late 1980s as the Cold War died. Both eras then experienced a period of expansion as the number and size of operations increased, eventually ending with a reassessment of the role of peacekeeping in the resolution of violent conflict. As the international community celebrated fifty years of the United Nations, it is perhaps ironic, that 'as far as peacekeeping is concerned, we are back to 1964 - the year the UN ended the ONUC mission'.[4] Then, as now, peacekeeping is suffering the after-effects of the UN having exceeded the traditional tenets of peacekeeping in its efforts to bring peace to 'failed states'.

What, therefore, does the future hold for UN peacekeeping? As chapters 3-6 have explained, the Organisation has had to operate without the finance, material and manpower which it so obviously required to fulfil its mandates properly. With the international community showing even more scepticism about the effectiveness of UN peacekeeping than it had only a few years ago, the future does not look bright. Operations like those on-going in Western Sahara and Angola will require substantial investments in finance and manpower if they are to bring sucesses like those in Mozambique and El Salvador. The US, however, by reducing its contributions and declaring its restrictions on the donation of troops to UN missions, seems to have set the precedent for the foreseeable future.

Notes

1. James, A., 'Is there a second generation of peacekeeping?' *International Peacekeeping,* vol.1, no.4, September-November 1994, p.11.

2. See chapter 5 of this book.

3. See James, op.cit, p.112.

4. Daniel, D., and Hayes, B., 'Problems and progress: the future of UN peacekeeping', in Daniel and Hayes, *Beyond traditional peacekeeping*, London, Macmillan, 1995, p.303.

Appendices

Appendix 1 - UN Charter - Chapter VI: Pacific Settlement of Disputes

Article 33

1. The parties to any dispute, the continuance of which is likely to endanger the maintenance of international peace and security, shall, first of all, seek a solution by negotiation, enquiry, mediation, conciliation, arbitration, judicial settlement, resort to regional agencies or arrangements, or other peaceful means of their own choice.

2. The Security Council shall, when it deems necessary, call upon the parties to settle their dispute by such means.

Article 34

The Security Council may investigate any dispute, or any situation which might lead to international friction or give rise to a dispute, in order to determine whether the continuance of the dispute or situation is likely to endanger the maintenance of international peace and security.

Article 35

1. Any Member of the United Nations may bring any dispute, or any situation of the nature referred to in Article 34, to the attention of the Security Council or of the General Assembly.

2. A state which is not a Member of the United Nations may bring to the attention of the Security Council or of the General Assembly any dispute to which it is a party if it accepts in advance, for the purposes of the dispute, the obligations of pacific settlement provided in the present Charter.

3. The proceedings of the General Assembly in respect of matters brought to its attention under this Article will be subject to the provisions of Articles 11 and 12.

Article 36

1. The Security Council may, at any stage of a dispute of the nature referred to in Article 33 or of a situation of like nature, recommend appropriate procedures or methods of adjustment.

2. The Security Council should take into consideration any procedures for the settlement of the dispute which have already been adopted by the parties.

3. In making recommendations under this Article the Security Council should also take into consideration that legal disputes should as a general rule be referred by the parties to the International Court of Justice in accordance with the provisions of the Statute of the Court.

Article 37

1. Should the parties to a dispute of the nature referred to in Article 33 fail to settle it by the means indicated in that Article, they shall refer it to the Security Council.

2. If the Security Council deems that the continuance of the dispute is in fact likely to endanger the maintenance of international peace and security,

it shall decide whether to take action under Article 36 or to recommend such terms of settlement as it may consider appropriate.

Article 38

Without prejudice to the provisions of Articles 33 to 37, the Security Council may, if all the parties to any dispute so request, make recommendations to the parties with a view to a pacific settlement of the dispute.

Appendix 2 - UN Charter - Chapter VII: Action with respect to threats to the peace, breaches of the peace, and acts of aggression

Article 39

The Security Council shall determine the existence of any threat to the peace, breach of the peace, or act of aggression and shall make recommendations, or decide what measures shall be taken in accordance with Articles 41 and 42, to maintain or restore international peace and security.

Article 40

In order to prevent an aggravation of the situation, the Security Council may, before making the recommendations or deciding upon the measures provided for in Article 39, call upon the parties concerned to comply with such provisional measures as it deems necessary or desirable. Such provisional measures shall be without prejudice to the rights, claims, or position of the parties concerned. The Security Council shall duly take account of failure to comply with such provisional measures.

Article 41

The Security Council may decide what measures not involving the use of armed force are to be employed to give effect to its decisions, and it may call upon the Members of the United Nations to apply such measures. These may include complete or partial interruption of economic relations and of rail, sea, air, postal, telegraphic, radio, and other means of communication, and the severance of diplomatic relations.

Article 42

Should the Security Council consider that measures provided for in Article 41 would be inadequate or have proved to be inadequate, it may take such action by air, sea, or land forces as may be necessary to maintain or restore international peace and security. Such action may include demonstrations, blockade, and other operations by air, sea, or land forces of Members of the United Nations.

Article 43

1. All Members of the United Nations, in order to contribute to the maintenance of international peace and security, undertake to make available to the Security Council, on its call and in accordance with a special agreement or agreements, armed forces, assistance, and facilities, including rights of passage, necessary for the purpose of maintaining international peace and security.

2. Such agreement or agreements shall govern the numbers and types of forces, their degree of readiness and general location, and the nature of the facilities and assistance to be provided.

3. The agreement or agreements shall be negotiated as soon as possible on the initiative of the Security Council. They shall be concluded between the Security Council and Members or between the Security Council and groups of Members and shall be subject to ratification by the signatory states in accordance with their respective constitutional processes.

Article 44

When the Security Council has decided to use force it shall, before calling upon a Member not represented on it to provide armed forces in fulfilment of the obligations assumed under Article 43, invite that Member, if the Member so desires, to participate in the decisions of the Security Council concerning the employment of contingents of that Member's armed forces.

Article 45

In order to enable the United Nations to take urgent military measures Members shall hold immediately available national air-force contingents for combined international enforcement action. The strength and degree of readiness of these contingents and plans for their combined action shall be determined, within the limits laid down in the special agreement or agreements referred to in Article 43, by the Security Council with the assistance of the Military Staff Committee.

Article 46

Plans for the application of armed force shall be made by the Security Council with the assistance of the Military Staff Committee.

Article 47

1. There shall be established a Military Staff Committee to advise and assist the Security Council on all questions relating to the Security Council's military requirements for the maintenance of international peace and security, the employment and command of forces placed at its disposal, the regulation of armaments, and possible disarmament.

2. The Military Staff Committee shall consist of the Chiefs of Staff of the permanent members of the Security Council or their representatives. Any Member of the United Nations not permanently represented on the Committee shall be invited by the Committee to be associated with it when the efficient discharge of the Committee's responsibilities requires the participation of that Member in its work.

3. The Military Staff Committee shall be responsible under the Security Council for the strategic direction of any armed forces placed at the disposal of the Security Council. Questions relating to the command of such forces shall be worked out subsequently.

4. The Military Staff Committee, with the authorization of the Security Council and after consultation with appropriate regional agencies, may establish regional subcommittees.

Article 48

1. The action required to carry out the decisions of the Security Council for the maintenance of international peace and security shall be taken by all the Members of the United Nations or by some of them, as the Security Council may determine.

2. Such decisions shall be carried out by the Members of the United Nations directly and through their action in the appropriate international agencies of which they are members.

Article 49

The Members of the United Nations shall join in affording mutual assistance in carrying out the measures decided upon by the Security Council.

Article 50

If preventive or enforcement measures against any state are taken by the Security Council, any other state, whether a Member of the United Nations or not, which finds itself confronted with special economic problems arising from the carrying out of those measures shall have the right to consult the Security Council with regard to a solution of those problems.

Article 51

Nothing in the present Charter shall impair the inherent right of individual or collective self-defense if an armed attack occurs against a Member of the United Nations, until the Security Council has taken measures necessary to maintain international peace and security. Measures taken by Members in the exercise of this right of self-defense shall be immediately reported to the Security Council and shall not in any way affect the authority and responsibility of the Security Council under the present Charter to take at any time such action as it deems necessary in order to maintain or restore international peace and security.

Appendix 3 - UN Charter - Article 99

The Secretary General may bring to the attention of the Security Council any matter which in his opinion may threaten the maintenance of international peace and security.

Appendix 4 - Uniting for Peace Resolution

The General Assembly

Recognizing that the first two stated purposes of the United Nations are:

'To maintain international peace and security, and to that end; to take effective collective measures for the prevention and removal of threats to the peace, and for the suppression of acts of aggression or other breaches of the peace, and to bring about by peaceful means, and in conformity with the principles of justice and international law, adjustment or settlement of international disputes or situations which might lead to a breach of the peace', and

'To develop friendly relations among nations based on respect for the principle of equal rights and self determination of peoples, and to take other appropriate measures to strengthen universal peace',

Reaffirming that it remains the primary duty of all Members of the United Nations, when involved in an international dispute, to seek settlement of such a dispute by peaceful means through the procedures laid down in Chapter VI of the Charter, and recalling the successful achievements of the United Nations in this regard on a number of previous occasions,

Finding that international tension exists on a dangerous scale,

Recalling its resolution 290 (IV) entitled 'Essentials of peace', which states that disregard of the 'Principle of the Charter of the United Nations' is primarily responsible for the continuance of international tension, and desiring to contribute further to the objectives of that resolution,

Reaffirming the importance of the exercise by the Security Council of its primary responsibility for the maintenance of international peace and security, and the duty of the permanent members to seek unanimity and to exercise restraint in the use of the veto,

Reaffirming that the initiative in negotiating the agreements for armed forces provided for in Article 43 of the Charter belongs to the Security Council, and desiring to ensure that, pending the conclusion of such agreements, the United Nations has at its disposal means for maintaining international peace and security,

Conscious that failure of the Security Council to discharge its responsibilities on behalf of all the Member States, particularly those responsibilities referred to in the two preceding paragraphs, does not relieve Member States of their obligations or the United Nations of its responsibility under the Charter to maintain international peace and security,

Recognising in particular that such failure does not deprive the General Assembly of its rights or relieve it of its responsibilities under the Charter in regard to the maintenance of international peace and security,

Recognising that discharge by the General Assembly of its responsibilities in these respects calls for possibilities of observation which would ascertain the facts and expose aggressors; for the existence of armed forces which could be used collectively; and for the possibility of timely recommendation by the General Assembly to Members of the United Nations for collective action which, to be effective, should be prompt.

A

1. *Resolves* that if the Security Council, because of lack of unanimity of the permanent members, fails to exercise its primary responsibility for the maintenance of international peace and security in any case where there appears to be a threat to the peace, breach of the peace or act of aggression, the General Assembly shall consider the matter immediately with a view to making appropriate recommendations to Members for collective measures, including in the case of a breach of the peace or act of aggression the use of armed force when necessary, to maintain or restore international peace and security. If not in session at the time, the General Assembly may meet in emergency special session within twenty-four hours of the request therefor. Such emergency special session shall be called if requested by the Security Council on the vote of any seven members, or by a majority of the Members of the United Nations;

2. *Adopts* for this purpose the amendments to its rules of procedure set forth in the annex to the present resolution;

B

3. *Establishes* a Peace Observation Commission which, for the calendar years 1951 and 1952, shall be composed of fourteen Members, namely; China, Colombia, Czechoslovakia, France, India, Iraq, Israel, New Zealand, Pakistan, Sweden, The Union of Soviet Socialist Republics, the

United Kingdom of Great Britain and Northern Ireland, the United States of America and Uruguay, and which could observe and report on the situation in any area where there exists international tension the continuance of which is likely to endanger the maintenance of international peace and security. Upon the invitation or with the consent of the State into whose territory the Commission would go, the General Assembly, or the Interim Committee when the Assembly is not in session, may utilize the Commission if the Security Council is not exercising the functions assigned to it by the Charter with respect to the matter in question. Decisions to utilize the Commission shall be made on the affirmative vote of two-thirds of the members present and voting. The Security Council may also utilize the Commission in accordance with its authority under the Charter;

4. *Decides* that the Commission shall have authority in its discretion to appoint sub-commissions and to utilize the services of observers to assist it in the performance of its functions;

5. *Recommends* to all governments and authorities that they co-operate with the Commission and assist it in the performance of its functions;

6. *Requests* the Secretary General to provide the necessary staff and facilities, utilizing, where directed by the Commission, the United Nations Panel of Field Observers envisaged in General Assembly resolution 297 B (IV);

C

7. *Invites* each Member of the United Nations to survey its resources in order to determine the nature and scope of the assistance it may be in a position to render in support of any recommendations of the Security Council or of the General Assembly for the restoration of international peace and security;

8. *Recommends* to the Member States of the United Nations that each Member maintain within its national armed forces elements so trained, organized and equipped that they could promptly be made available, in accordance with its constitutional processes, for service as a United Nations unit or units, upon recommendation by the Security Council or the General Assembly, without prejudice to the use of such elements in exercise of the right of individual or collective self-defence recognized in Article 51 of the Charter;

9. *Invites* the Members of the United Nations to inform the Collective Measures Committee provided for in paragraph 11 as soon as possible of the measures taken in implementation of the preceding paragraph;

10. *Requests* the Secretary General to appoint, with the approval of the Committee provided for in paragraph 11, a panel of military experts who could be made available, on request, to Member States wishing to obtain technical advice regarding the organization, training and equipment for prompt service as United Nations units of the elements referred to in paragraph 5;

D

11. *Establishes* a Collective Measures Committee consisting of fourteen Members, namely Australia, Belgium, Brazil, Burma, Canada, Egypt, France, Mexico, Philippines, Turkey, the United Kingdom of Great Britain and Northern Ireland, the United States of America, Venezuela and Yugoslavia, and directs the Committee, in consultation with the Secretary General and with such Member States as the Committee finds appropriate, to study and make a report to the Security Council and General Assembly, not later than 1 September 1951, on methods, including those in section C of the present resolution, which might be used to maintain and strengthen international peace and security in accordance with the Purposes and Principles of the Charter, taking account of collective self defence and regional arrangements (Articles 51 and 52 of the Charter);

12. *Recommends* to all Member States that they co-operate with the Committee and assist it in the performance of its functions;

13. *Requests* the Secretary General to furnish the staff and facilities necessary for the effective accomplishment of the purposes set forth in sections C and D of the present resolution;

14. *Is fully conscious* that, in adopting the proposals set forth above, enduring peace will not be secured solely by collective security arrangements against breaches of international peace and acts of aggression, but that a genuine and lasting peace depends also upon the observance of all the Principles and Purposes established in the Charter of the United Nations, upon the implementation of the resolutions of the Security Council, the General Assembly and other principal organs of the United Nations intended to achieve the maintenance of international peace and security, and especially upon respect for and observance of human rights

and fundamental freedoms for all and on the establishment and maintenance of conditions of economic and social well-being in all countries; and accordingly;

15. *Urges* Member States to respect fully, and to intensify, joint action, in co-operation with the United Nations, to develop and stimulate universal respect for and observance of human rights and fundamental freedoms, and to intensify individual and collective efforts to achieve conditions of economic stability and social progress, particularly through the development of under-developed countries and areas.

Appendix 5 - Agenda for Peace - Preventive Diplomacy

United Nations operations in areas of crisis have generally been established after conflict has occurred. The time has come to plan for circumstances warranting preventive deployment, which could take place in a variety of instances and ways. For example, in conditions of national crisis there could be preventive deployment at the request of the Government or all parties concerned, or with their consent; in inter-State disputes such deployment could take place when two countries feel that a United Nations presence on both sides of their border can discourage hostilities; furthermore, preventive deployment could take place when a country feels threatened and requests the deployment of an appropriate United Nations presence along its side of the border alone. In each situation, the mandate and composition of the United Nations presence would need to be carefully devised and be clear to all.

In conditions of crisis within a country, when the Government requests or all parties consent, preventive deployment could help in a number of ways to alleviate suffering and to limit or control violence. Humanitarian assistance, impartially provided, could be of critical importance; assistance in maintaining security, whether through military, police or civilian personnel, could save lives and develop conditions of safety in which negotiations can be held; the United Nations could also help in conciliation efforts if this should be the wish of the parties. In certain circumstances, the United Nations may well need to draw upon the specialized skills and resources of various parts of the United Nations system; such operations may also on occasion require the participation of non-governmental organizations.

In these situations of crises the United Nations will need to respect the sovereignty of the State; to do otherwise would not be in accordance with the understanding of Member States in accepting the principles of the

Charter. The Organisation must remain mindful of the carefully negotiated balance of the guiding principles annexed to General Assembly Resolution 46/182 of 19 December 1991. Those guidelines stressed, *inter alia,* that humanitarian assistance must be provided in accordance with the principles of humanity, neutrality and impartiality; that the sovereignty, territorial integrity and national unity of States must be fully respected in accordance with the Charter of the United Nations; and that, in this context, humanitarian assistance should be provided with the consent of the affected country and, in principle, on the basis of an appeal by that country. The guidelines also stressed the responsibility of States to take care of the victims of emergencies occurring on their territory and the need for access to those requiring humanitarian assistance. In the light of these guidelines, a Government's request for United Nations involvement, or consent to it, would not be an infringement of that State's sovereignty or be contrary to Article 2, paragraph 7, of the Charter which refers to matters essentially within the domestic jurisdiction of any state.

In inter-State disputes, when both parties agree, I recommend that if the Security Council concludes that the likelihood of hostilities between neighbouring countries could be removed by the preventive deployment of a United Nations presence on the territory of each State, such action should be taken. The nature of the tasks to be performed would determine the composition of the United Nations presence.

In cases where one nation fears a cross-border attack, if the Security Council concludes that a United Nations presence on one side of the border, with the consent only of the requesting country, would serve to deter conflict, I recommend that preventive deployment take place. Here again, the specific nature of the situation would determine the mandate and the personnel required to fulfil it.

Appendix 6 - Agenda for Peace: Peace-Enforcement Units

The mission of forces under Article 43 would be to respond to outright aggression, imminent or actual. Such forces are not likely to be available for some time to come. Ceasefires have often been agreed to but not complied with, and the United Nations has sometimes been called upon to send forces to restore and maintain the ceasefire. This task can on occasion exceed the mission of peacekeeping forces and the expectations of peacekeeping force contributors. I recommend that the Council consider the utilization of peace-enforcement units in clearly defined circumstances and with their terms of reference specified in advance. Such units from Member States would be available on call and would consist of troops that have volunteered for such service. They would have to be more heavily armed than peacekeeping forces and would need to undergo extensive preparatory training within their national forces. Deployment and operation of such forces would be under the authorization of the Security Council and would, as in the case of peacekeeping forces, be under the command of the Secretary General. I consider such peace-enforcement units to be warranted as a provisional measure under Article 40 of the Charter. Such peace-enforcement units should not be confused with the forces which may eventually be constituted under Article 43 to deal with acts of aggression or with the military personnel which governments may agree to keep on standby for possible contribution to peacekeeping operations.

Just as diplomacy will continue across the span of all the activities dealt with in the present report, so there may not be a dividing line between peace-making and peacekeeping. Peace-making is often a prelude to peacekeeping - just as the deployment of a United Nations presence in the field may expand possibilities for the prevention of conflict, facilitate the work of peace-making and in many cases serve as a pre-requisite for peace-building.

Appendix 7 - Other UN Missions (this number does not include the following missions)

United Nations Mission in Haiti (UNMIH)

The first United Nations involvement in Haiti was to take place through the UN Observer Group for the Verification of the Elections in Haiti (ONUVEH), which were held in December 1990. However, the elected administration, led by President Jean-Bertrand Aristide, was deposed in a military *coup d'etat* on 29 September 1991. After international pressure (mainly through the imposition of a trade embargo) had forced the military regime to negotiate a transfer of power back to Aristide, a UN Mission in Haiti (UNMIH) was established by the Security Council in late September 1993 to oversee the transition. The military junta, however, prevented the deployment of the UN force in mid October, which led to the reimposition of sanctions by the international community. With sanctions having little effect on the intransigence of the junta, the Security Council adopted Resolution 940 on 19 July 1994 under Chapter VII of the Charter, mandating a multinational force (not under UN command), to use 'all necessary means to facilitate the departure from Haiti of the military leadership'.[1] The US led Multinational Force (MNF) was therefore deployed on 19 September 1994, after an agreement had been reached with the junta, to 'establish and maintain a secure and stable environment' in Haiti. Once such an environment was established Resolution 940 provided for a strengthened UNMIH to assume responsibility from the MNF and assist in the professionalisation of the Haitian armed forces and the creation of a separate police force. The approximately 6,000 strong UN force was also to help create conditions for, and monitor elections at the government's request. The transfer of responsibility took place pursuant to Security Council Resolution 975 of 30 January 1995. In his reports during 1995 the Secretary General expressed concern at the ability of UNMIH to maintain law and order without enforcement powers, but stated that the security situation in Haiti had continued to improve.[2]

United Nations Observer Mission in Tajikistan

Security Council Resolution 968 of 16 December 1994, established a forty strong United Nations Observer force in Tajikistan (UNMOT) which was mandated to assist in monitoring the implementation of the peace protocol (Tehran Agreement) signed by the Government of Tajikistan and its Islamic opposition on 17 September 1994. UNMOT was also to investigate reports of ceasefire violations; provide good offices; maintain close contacts with the parties to the conflict, the Organisation of Security and Co-operation in Europe mission in Tajikistan and the Collective Peacekeeping forces of the Confederation of Independent States; provide support for the efforts of the Secretary General's Special Envoy; and provide political liaison and co-ordination services for international humanitarian assistance operations.[3]

With the fourth round of talks between the parties, planned to be held in Moscow in December 1994, postponed due to disagreements which had emerged since the signing of the Tehran Agreement, the Secretary General recommended the extension of UNMOT's mandate until March 1995. He noted in his report of 4 February 1995 that although both parties had 'complied only partially with the requirements of SC Resolution 968' UNMOT continued to act as an 'important stabilising factor in the country'.[4]

United Nations Observer Mission in Liberia (UNOMIL)

With the collapse of the government of President Samuel Doe, civil war ensued in Liberia since 1990. The Economic Community of West African States sent a 12,000 multinational peacekeeping force (ECOMOG-ECOWAS Monitoring Group) to the country in September of the same year. By late 1992 the initial impartiality of the force had been lost, as ECOMOG attacked forces belonging to the army of Charles Taylor (the strongest of factions fighting for power) after the breakdown of the latest truce. Following negotiations between the parties, the Security Council, pursuant to Resolution 866, established UNOMIL in September 1993. As the first UN peacekeeping mission undetaken in co-operation with a peacekeeping operation already set up by another organisation UNOMIL's mandate was to monitor the agreed ceasefire; verify the disarmament of factions and prepare an election process. However, by September 1994 renewed fighting between the factions and continuing deadlock in the peace process had confined UNOMIL's activities to daily patrols, verification of disarmament (although the factions had not participated formally in the disarmament and demobilisation process, individual members continued to be disarmed. UNOMIL continued to play a role in verifying it and in registering demobilised combatants and providing them with some food and clothing) and the investigation of reported ceasefire violations. In his report of 24 February 1995, the Secretary General recommended that if the political stalemate was to continue the Security Council might consider withdrawing the force or converting it into a good offices mission. However, he also stated that if the parties made a clear demonstration that they wished to reactivate the peace process the Security Council could continue with the operation as it was, or establish a UN peacekeeping force.

United Nations Observer Mission in Georgia (UNOMIG)

Established pursuant to Resolution 858 of August 1993, UNOMIG consists of a small military observer force mandated to monitor the conflict which has arisen between Abkhazia separatists and the Georgian government. Efforts have been concentrated on finding a comprehensive political solution which would maintain some form of federal Georgian union whilst deferring sovereign rights upon Abkhazia. Without the necessary conditions to establish a UN military peacekeeping force, UNOMIG has been mandated to monitor the non-UN peacekeeping force deployed by the Confederation of Independent States. In May 1995 the Security Council, pursuant to Resolution 993, decided to extend its mandate until 12 January 1996.

Notes

1. *United Nations document, S/RES/940,* 31 July 1994.

2. *United Nations documents, S/1995/211,* 20 March 1995; *S/1995 614,* 24 July 1995; cited in Morris, J., 'Force and democracy: UN/US intervention in Haiti', *International Peacekeeping,* vol.2, no.3, Autumn 1995, pp.399-400.

3. 'Peacekeeping mission updates', *International Peacekeeping,* vol.2, no.1, 1995, Spring 1995, p.110.

4. *The UN and the situation in Tajikistan,* UN Department of Public Information, Reference Paper, March 1995.

Index

NB: Page references to tables are bold

Abdic, Fikret 189, 190
Abkhazia 231
Afghanistan 157
  Geneva Accords 62
  see also UNGOMAP
African Rights 138
Agenda for Peace 227-9
Agenda for Peace, An (B. Boutros-Ghali)
  92, 98, 101, 109, 123, 174, 184
aggression, dealing with threats and
  219-22
Ahtisaari, Marti 76
Aideed, Mohammed Farah 109, 135,
  136, 138, 139, 176-7
Ajello, Aldo 123, 130, 131, 133, 135-6,
  163, 169, 170, 171
Akashi, Yashushi 100, 132, 174, 175,
  188
Albright, Madaleine 117, 128, 130, 140,
  155, 156-7, 164, 193
Ali, Asif 161

ANC (African National Congress) 121
Angola 117, 118, 121, 156, 173
  see also UNAVEM I; UNAVEM II;
    UNAVEM III
Annan, Kofi 161, 173
Anstee, Margaret 102-3
Arab-Israeli conflicts 29-30
  1948 30
  1949 Armistice Agreements 30, 34
  1967 35, 47
  1973 47-8
  1978 49-50
  1982 50
  see also UNDOF; UNEF II
Aristide, Jean-Bertrand 229
Armistice Agreements 1949 30, 34
Arusha Accord 141-2, **158**, 192, 193

Bailey, Sydney 134
Balkans *see* UNSCOB
Bangladesh 32
Baril, Gen. Maurice 173
Barre, Siad 93

Belgium 38-9, 40, 192-3, 195
Berdal, M. 128, 139, 140, 175
Bernadotte, Count Folke 30
Beye, Alioune Blondin 159
Bihac 143, 180, 181, 182, 183, 186, 189, 190
Bir, Civik 139
Bolton, John 140
Bosnia-Herzegovina 97, 104, 105-7, 108, 126, 143, 144, 145, **158**, 171, 179-83, 185-7, 188, 189, 190, 191, 192
    London International meeting on 190
Boutros-Ghali, Boutros 91-2, 103, 118, 132, 157
    An Agenda for Peace 92, 98, 101, 109, 123, 174, 184
Briquemont, Lt.-Gen. 145
Britain 34
Bunche, Ralph 38, 43
Burundi 142, 157, 192
Bush, George 93, 99-100, 118, 127, 137, 139, 140, 174
Butmir 144

Cairo Agreement 1969 50
Cambodia (Kampuchea) 124-5, 132-3
    culture 134
    Jakarta talks on 74
    peace-enforcement 174-6
    State of (SoC) 129
    see also Khmer Rouge; UNAMIC; UNTAC
Camp David Agreement 48
Canada 145
Carrington, Lord 108
casualties, peacekeeping 14, 119, 176, 192
Central America *see* ONUCA
Cerska 143
Chapter VI Mandate; Chapter VII Mandate *see* UN Charter, mandates
Chapultepec Agreement 71, 72
Charter *see* UN Charter
Chebab, Fouad 36
Chiechanski, J. 18-19
China 176
Chissano, Joaquim 163
Chopra, J., et al. 175

Christopher, Warren 117-18
Churkin, Vitaly 186
CIAV (International Support and Verification Commission) 68, 77
CIVPOL (UN police monitors) 66, 81, 106, 129, 132, 163
Claes, Willy 193
Clinton, Bill 104, 117-18, 127, 138, 140, 155-6, 177, 183, 187
cooperation as key to peacekeeping success 83-4
Cold War period 1-2, 14-15, 25-57
    subdivisions 25, 26
Collective Measures Committee 226
Congo *see* ONUC
consent, loss of, in peacekeeping 184-5
'Contact Group' 186, 187, 190
'Contras' 67, 68, 84, 169
COPAZ (El Salvador peace commission) 71
Costa Rica 67
CPSC (Comprehensive Political Settlement of Cambodia) 74
crisis in peacekeeping, November 1992-1993 117-54
Cristiani, Alfredo 71
Croatia 97, 106-7, 142, 144-5, **158**, 181, 183, 185, 186-8, 189-92
Crocker, Chester A. 65, 76, 137, 140, 185
Cuba 63-4, 75-6
cultural diversity, intra-state peacekeeping and 133-6
Cyprus *see* UNFICYP

debts owing to UN 126-7, 164-5
decolonization 16, 37, 76
Dellaire, Romeo 193
de-militarized zones (DMZ) 120
Dhlakama, Alfonso 122, 135-6, 160, 163
Diehl, Paul 81
disputes, Charter on pacific settlement of 217-19
Doe, Samuel 230
dos Santos, José Eduardo 72, 121
DPKO (Department of Peacekeeping Operations) 102, 128, 171
Dumbarton Oaks 6, 10

Durch, William 16

ECOMOG-ECOWAS Monitoring Group
    230
Egypt 43
Egypt *see* Nasser; UNEF I
El Salvador 67, 120-1, 162-3, 165-8
    police force (PNC) 166
    soldiers: reintegration 166-7
    see also FMLN; MINUSAL;
        ONUSAL
Eliasson, Jan 138-9
Ellis, Richard 123
equipment, peacekeeping *see* personnel
    and equipment
Esquipulas II 67, 68, 77, 81-2
'Essentials of Peace' 223
Evans, Gareth 129-30

FADM (Mozambique national army)
    168, 169
FDR-FMLN (El Salvador liberation
    front) 70-1
Findlay, T. 102, 129, 130
FMLN (El Salvador liberation front) 71,
    96, 120-1, 162, 166, 170
force as peacekeeping tool 174-84, 213
    Peace-Enforcement Units 92, 228-9
France 34, 139, 193, 195, 196, 197
Franco, General 10
FRELIMO (Mozambique Liberation
    Front) 121-3
'frontier missions' 134
funding of peacekeeping 78-80
    crisis period 126-8, 144
    expansionary period 98-101
    retrenchment period 164-5
FYROM (Former Yugoslav Republic of
    Macedonia) 123-4, **158**, 182, 188

General Assembly 9, 33, 51, 223-7
    Resolution 46/182 228
    Resolution 47/217 127
    Resolution 290 (IV) 223
    Resolution 1000 34
Geneva Accords on Afghanistan 62
Geneva (Vance/Owen) Plan 143, 144
Georgia *see* UNOMIG
Giner, Ramon Gonzales 161

Golan Heights 48
Gorazde 143, 180, 181, 186, 187, 190
Gorbachev, Mikhail 59
Goulding, Marrack 26, 212
GPA (Rome General Peace Agreements)
    122
Granic, Pavel 190
Greece 28-9, 44
Greek Cypriots *see* UNFICYP
Grove, Eric 131
Guatemala 67
Gulf conflicts
    first *see* UNIIMOG
    second *see* UNIKOM

Habyarimana, President 192
Haiti *see* ONUVEH; UNMIH
Hammarskjöld, Dag 37-41
heads of state meeting 91
Herzegovina *see* Bosnia-Herzegovina
Holbrooke, Richard 190, 191
Honduras 67, 68, 77
Horst, Enrique Ter 161
Howe, Admiral Jonathan 139
Hrasnica 144
human rights 129
humanitarian relief 93, 105-9, 136-46
    crisis period 136-46
    Joint Declaration, November 1993
        145
    retrenchment period 185-97
Hun Sen 100, 101
Hurd, Douglas 178
Hutu tribe 142, 192, 193

impartiality, compromising of 177-8,
    213
    see also UNOSOM; Yugoslavia,
        former
India *see* UNMOGIP
Indonesia *see* UNTEA
Inspector General of UN 127
International Truth Commission 166,
    167
Iran-Iraq conflict *see* UNIIMOG
Iraq-Kuwait conflict *see* UNIKOM
Israeli-Arab conflicts *see* Arab-Israeli
    conflicts
Jakarta talks on Cambodia 74

James, Alan 15, 32, 212-13
Japan 98-9, 176
Juppe, Alain 189, 195

Kagame, Maj.-Gen Paul 193, 195
Kampuchea *see* Cambodia
Kanyarenwe, Alex 141
Karadzic, R. 187
Kashmir 31, 32, 46-7
Katanga 38, 40
Khieu Samphan 100
Khmer Rouge/PDK (Party of
    Democratic Kampuchea) 73, 94-5,
    97, 100-1, 103, 119-20, 124-5, 129,
    132, 175-6
Korea 10
Kozyrev, Andrei V. 183
Krajina 106, 107, 142, 181, 189-91
Kurds of Iraq 93
Kuwait-Iraq conflict *see* UNIKOM

League of Nations 5, 11, 13
Lebanon 177
Lebanon *see* UNIFIL; UNOGIL
Leotard, François 182
Liberia 156
    see also UNOMIL
Lizée, Pierre 134
Lon Nol 175
London Conference 1992 179
Loridon, Gen. 175
Lumumba, Patrice 38, 40
Lusaka Protocol **158**, 159-60

Macedonia, Former Yugoslav Republic
    of (FYROM) 123-4, **158**, 182, 188
Mackenzie, Gen. Lewis 171
Mackinlay, John 175
Makarios, Archbishop 44
Makinda, S.M. 137, 138
Mauritania 69-70
Mexico Accord 71
Milosevic, Slobodon 187
MINURSO (UN Mission for the
    Referendum in Western
    Sahara)(1991-present) **61**, 69-70,
    95, 96-7, 103, 124, 158-9
MINUSAL (UN Mission in El Salvador)
    161, 166-7

'mission creep' 105-6, 145, 191
Montenegro 107
Montgomery, Maj-Gen. Thomas 139
Morillon, Gen. 143
Morocco 69-70, 95, 103, 158-9
Mostar 186, 190
Mount Igman 144
Mozambique 130, 168-71
    see also ONUMOZ
MPLA (Angolan liberation movement)
    63-4, 72, 121
MSC (Military Staff Committee) 11, 221
Muslims *see under* Yugoslavia, former

NAC (North Atlantic Council) 186
Nagorno-Karabakh 157
Namibia 63, 76
    Accords 65
    see also UNTAG
Nasser, Gamal Abdel 16, 34, 35, 36
NATO (North Atlantic Treaty
    Organization) 179-84, 185, 186, 188,
    189, 190-1
Netherlands 41-2
'New World Order' 92-3, 98, 137, 174,
    197
NGOs (Non-Governmental
    Organizations) 137, 193
Nicaragua 67, 68, 77, 78, 84, 169, 170
'no-fly' zones 179-80
Nobel Peace Prize 60
Ntaryamira, Cyprien 192
Nye, Joseph S. 104

OAS (Organization of American States)
    67, 68
OAU (Organization of African Unity)
    159, 172
Ocampo, Augusto Ramirez 168
ONUC (UN Operation in the Congo)
    (1960-4) 10, 15, 17, **27**, 37-41, 211
ONUCA (UN Observation Mission in
    Central America) (1989-91) **61**, 67-8,
    77-8, 80-4, 96, 169
ONUMOZ (UN Operation in
    Mozambique) 93, 117, **119**, 121-3, 125,
    131, 133, 135-6, 156, 160, 168, 171,
    212
    success of 163-4

ONUSAL (UN Operation in El
Salvador) (1991-4) **61**, 70-2, 96, 120,
125, 161, 165-6, 167-8, 170, 212
success of 162-3
ONUVEH (UN Observer Group for the
Verification of the Elections in Haiti)
229
ONUVEN (UN Observer Mission to
Verify the Electoral Process in
Nicaragua) 96
'Operation Turquoise' 196
Owen/Vance (Geneva) Plan 143, 144

Pakistan 62, 176
see also UNMOGIP
Pale 183, 186, 187, 188
Palestine partition 9
Paris Peace Accords 74, 95, 101,
119-20, 125, 129, 174, 175
PDK (Party of Democratic
Kampuchea)/Khmer Rouge 73, 94-5,
97, 100, 101, 103, 119-20, 124-5,
129, 132, 175, 176
peace, UN on breaches of/threats to
219-22
Peace Observation Commission 224-5
Peace-Enforcement Units 92, 228-9
peacekeeping
1940s 25, 26
army doctrines of UK and USA 213
development phases 12
expansionary period 91-115
future 214
long-term aims 92
nature of 14-17
origins 14
over-ambitious 98
rebirth period 59-90
retrenchment period 155-210
second generation 213
UN definition 17
concluding remarks 211-15
peacekeeping operations
context of 15-16
established 1988-91 **61**
established 1992 **94**
established November 1992-3 **119**
established 1994 **158**
ongoing 94-6, 119-23, 158-61

peacekeeping periods
assertive (1956-74) 32-48, 51
early (1947-56) 27-32, 51, 213
evolutionary 25-57
quiescent (1974-87) 49-51
peacekeeping problems
crisis period 126-33
expansionary period 97-105
rebirth period 78-83
retrenchment period 164-73
peacekeeping successes
crisis period 124-6
expansionary period 96-7
rebirth period 75-8
retrenchment period 162-4
Pereira, Jose Manuel 173
Perelyakin, Gen. Alexander 133
Pérez de Cuellar, Javier 62
personnel and equipment, peacekeeping
crisis period 131-3
expansionary period 103-5
prosecution immunity 37
rebirth period 82-3
retrenchment period 171-3
planning of peacekeeping
crisis period 128-31
expansionary period 101-3
rebirth period 80-2
retrenchment period 1994-5 165-71
PLO (Palestine Liberation Organisation)
49, 50
Plunkett, Mark 129
POLISARIO (Western Sahara liberation
front) 69, 70, 159
Porcell, Girard 104
Portugal 121
Posovina corridor 187
preventive deployment of peacekeepers
123-4
Preventive Diplomacy, Agenda for
Peace 227-8
Principles of International Conduct **7-8**

Ramsbotham, Gen. Sir David 170
Reagan, Ronald 65, 71
RENAMO (Mozambique National
Resistance) 122, 130, 160, 163, 168,
169-70
resistance factions, internal, UN and 84

Resolutions *see* Security Council
  Resolutions
responsibility, primary 5-24
  conclusions 17-19
Rikhye, I.J. 16-17
Roberts, Adam 92, 118
Rome Accords 168, 169
Rome General Peace Agreements (GPA)
  122
Rose, Lt.-Gen. Sir Michael 186, 187
RPF (Rwandese Patriotic Front) 141, 196
RRF (Rapid Reaction Force) 189
Russian Federation 179, 182-3, 185,
  186, 188
  debt to UN 126-7
  see also USSR
Rwanda
  humanitarian aid 105, 141-2, 157-8,
    172-3
  see also UNAMIR; UNOMUR

'safe areas' 143-4, 181, 185, 188, 189,
  190, 191, 192
Sahnoun, Mohammed 109, 135
San Francisco conference 1945 6, 10,
  13
Sanderson, Lt.-Gen. 102, 130, 174, 175,
  176
Sarajevo 108, 143, 144, 180, 181, 182,
  183, 185, 186, 187, 188, 190
Saudi Arabia 43
Savimbi, Jonas 72, 99, 110, 121, 160
Schear, James 101
Secretary General of UN 13-14, 34, 39,
  42, 43, 51, 223
  see also Boutros-Ghali; Hammarskjöld;
    Pérez de Cuellar; Thant, U
Security Council 217-31
  and long-term issues 46
  members 11-12
  powers 9, 10, 11
  structure and functions 11-13
  voting and vetoes 12-13, 211
Security Council Resolutions
  143 38
  161 40
  169 40
  186 45
  211 46

425 49, 50
426 49
435 65, 79
566 65
598 62-3
626 64, 75
629 65
644 68
653 68
687 68
689 68
690 70
693 162
696 72
717 75
729 72, 96, 162
743 106
752 179
766 95
775 109
776 108
781 108, 179
787 179
794 137
795 123
797 122
802 142-3
806 120
812 141
814 138, 140
816 179
819 143, 180
824 143, 180, 185
832 120, 162
836 143, 180-1
837 139, 176
844 143-4
846 141
858 231
866 230
872 141
891 142
893 192
912 193
918 194, 195, 197
925 195, 196, 197
929 196
940 229-30
965 197

Security Council Resolutions cont
968 230
975 230
981 188
982 188
983 188
993 231
Segali, G. 175
Serbia and Serbs 97, 106-7, 123-4, 126,
142-3, 144-5, 179, 180-3, 185-91
taking of UN hostages 188-9
Shamun, Kamil 36
Shidane Abukar Arone 133
Sierra Leone 157
Sihanouk, Prince 73
Situation Room 128
Slavonia 106
Western 189
Slovenia 97
Smith, Lt.-Gen. 188
SoC *see under* Cambodia
Solarz, Stephen 125
Somalia 93
culture 134-5, 177
humanitarian aid 105-6, 136-41
peace-enforcement 176-8
US soldiers murdered in 118-19, 177
see also UNOSOM I; UNOSOM II
South Africa 10, 64, 65, 66, 79, 81,
121-2
Soviet Union *see* USSR
Spain 10
Srebrenica 143, 180, 186, 187, 189
Stahler-Sholk, Richard 166, 168
Stoltenberg, Thorvald 144, 145
Sudan 157
Suez *see* UNEF I
'sunset' clauses 156-7
SWAPO guerillas 66, 79-80, 81, 84,
134
SWAPOL (South West African Police)
65, 66, 81
Syria 48, 49

Tajikistan 157, 230
Tanzania 142
Taylor, Charles 230
Tehran conference 1943 5
Thant, U 40, 42

Tshombe, Moise 38, 40
Tudjman, President 187, 188
Turkey and Turkish Cypriots 44-5
Tutsi tribe 142, 192, 193
Tuzla 143, 144, 180, 186, 188, 190

UAR (United Arab Republic) 36
Uganda *see* UNOMUR
UN
coercive measures available to 9-11
establishment of 6
faltering public image 126
funding deficit 126-7, 164-5
impartiality threatened 191
indiscipline among personnel 132-3
insensitive dealings by 133-6
post-Cold War position 1
procurement 171-2
responsibilities, primary 5-24
UN Charter 6-11, **7**
UN Charter, Articles
2 **7-8**, 228
7 11
11 9
23 12
24 11
33-8 12, 217-19
33 8
39 9, 45
39-51 11, 12, 219-22
40 229
41 9-10
42 10
43 10, 223, 228, 229
47 11
51 225
97 13
99 13-14, 223
103 7
UN Charter, mandates
Chapter VI 8, 18, 40, 105, 184,
217-19, 223
Chapter VII 8-9, 13, 18, 40, 118,
126, 137, 174, 176, 185, 194-7,
213, 219-22, 229
*UN Peacekeeping in a New Era, A New
Chance for Peace* 118
UNAMIC (UN Transitional Authority in
Cambodia) (1991-2) **61**, 73-5, 94,

UNAMIC (UN Transitional Authority in Cambodia (1991-2) cont
96-7, 99, 102

UNAMIR (UN Assistance Mission in Rwanda) (1994-present) 141-2, **158**, 172, 192-3, 195, 196

UNAMIR II (UN Assistance Mission in Rwanda II) 194, 195, 196, 197

UNAVEM I (UN Angolan Verification Mission I) (1988-91) **61**, 63-4, 75-6

UNAVEM II (UN Angolan Verification Mission II) (1991-2) **61**, 72-3, 96-7, 99, 102-3, 131, 134, 169

UNAVEM III (UN Angolan Verification Mission III) (1995-present) **158**, 159-60, 171

UNCIP (UN Commission on India and Pakistan) 32

UNCRO (UN Confidence Restoration Operation) **158**, 188, 190

UNDOF (UN Disengagement Observer Force) (1974-present) **27**, 47, 48

UNEF I (UN Emergency Force I) (1956-67) 15, 16, **27**, 33-6, 39, 51
principles established by 35

UNEF II (UN Emergency Force II) (1974-9) **27**, 47-8

UNFICYP (UN Force in Cyprus) (1964-present) 15, **27**, 44-6, 157

UNGOMAP (UN Good Offices Mission in Afghanistan) (1988-90) 61-2, **61**, 75, 84

UNHCR (UN High Commission for Refugees) 108, 143, 145

UNIFIL (UN Interim Force in Lebanon) 26, **27**, 49-51

UNIIMOG (Iran-Iraq Military Observer Group) (1988-91) **61**, 62-3, 134

UNIKOM (UN Iraq-Kuwait Observer Mission) (1991-present) **61**, 68-9, 82-3, 96, 120, 134, 160

UNIPOM (UN India Pakistan Observer Mission) (1965-6) **27**, 32, 46-7

UNITA (Angolan independence movement) 64, 72, 84, 99, 121, 134

UNITAF (United Task Force) 126, 128, 137-8, 139
lessons to be learned from 140-1
'United Shield' 161

Uniting for Peace procedure 34
Uniting for Peace Resolution 9, 51-2, 223-7

UNMIH (UN Mission in Haiti) 229-30

UNMOGIP (UN Military Observer Group in India and Pakistan) (1949-present) **27**, 28, 31-2, 46, 47

UNMOT (UN Observer Mission in Tajikistan) 230

UNOGIL (UN Observation Group in Lebanon) (1958) **27**, 36-7, 51

UNOMIG (UN Observer Mission in Georgia) 231

UNOMIL (UN Observer Mission in Liberia) 230-1

UNOMUR (UN Observer Mission Uganda-Rwanda) **119**, 141, 142

UNOSOM I (UN Operation in Somalia I) (1992-3) **94**, 97, 109, 126, 128

UNOSOM II (UN Operation in Somalia II) (1993-4) **119**, 126, 135, 137-8, 156, 157, 160-1, 177, 178, 184, 213
end of 160-1
failure: reasons 138-9, 176
lessons to be learned from 140-1

UNPAs (UN Protected Areas) 97, 106-7, 145, 189, 192

UNPREDEP (UN Preventive Deployment Force) **158**, 188

UNPROFOR (UN Protection Force) (1992-5) **94**, 104, 106-8, 123, 126, 128, 131, 133, 143-5, **158**, 178, 180-1, 184, 185
lessons of Bosnia operation 191-2
restructuring 188

UNSAS (UN Standby Arrangements System) 172-3

UNSCOB (UN Special Commission on the Balkans) (1947-51) **27**, 28-9, 33

UNSCOP (UN Special Commission on Palestine) 29-30

UNSF (UN Security Force) 41, 42

UNTAC (UN Transitional Authority in Cambodia) (1992-3) **61**, 73-5, 94, 95, 96-7, 99, 100-1, 102, 103-4, 119-20, 124, 128-30, 131, 169, 171, 175-6, 212

UNTAG (UN Transitional Assistance Group) (1989-90) **61**, 65-6, 76-7,

UNTAG (UN Transitional Assistance
 Group) (1989-90) cont
 79-80, 81, 83, 84, 103, 134, 212
UNTEA (UN Temporary Executive
 Authority) (1962-3) 16, **27**, 41-2, 51
UNTSO (UN Truce Supervision
 Organization) (1948-present) **27**, 28,
 29-30
UNYOM (UN Yemen Observation
 Mission) (1963-4) 16, 17, **27**, 42-4
Urquart, Brian 174
USA 118-19
 Assistant Secretary for Peacekeeping
  117
 debt to UN 126-7
 policy towards UN 155-6
 Presidential Decision Directive 25
  (PD25) 155-6, 164
 and Rwanda 197
 and Serbs 180
 see also Bush; Clinton; Reagan;
  UNOSOM I; UNOSOM II
USSR 43, 62
Uwilingiyimana, Agathe 192

'Vance Plan' 106
Vance/Owen (Geneva) Plan 143, 144

voting and vetoes 12-13, 211

Warner, N. 130
West Irian *see* UNTEA
Western Sahara *see* MINURSO

Yalta Conference 6
Yeltsin, Boris 179, 183
Yemen *see* UNYOM
Yugoslavia
 federation 93, 107
 National Army (JNA) 107, 179
Yugoslavia, former 97, 126
 humanitarian aid provision, 1994-5
  105-8, 142-6, 185-92, 192-7
 Muslims 108, 123, 143, 179, 186-7,
  188, 189, 190, 191
 Split Declaration 186-7, 189, 190
 see also Bosnia-Herzegovina;
  Croatia; Krajina; Macedonia;
  Montenegro; Serbia and Serbs;
  Slavonia; Slovenia; UNPROFOR

Zaire 142, 172
Zepa 143, 144, 180, 186, 187, 189, 190
Zetra 181
Zimbabwe (Rhodesia) 121